ISLAM UNVEILED

Eric!
Thank you very
much, so to speak —

Robert Spencer

ISLAM UNVEILED

DISTURBING QUESTIONS ABOUT
THE WORLD'S FASTEST-GROWING FAITH

R O B E R T   S P E N C E R
FOREWORD BY DAVID PRYCE-JONES

ENCOUNTER BOOKS
SAN FRANCISCO

First edition published in 2002 by Encounter Books, an activity of Encounter for Culture and Education, Inc., a nonprofit tax exempt corporation.

Encounter Books website address: www.encounterbooks.com

Manufactured in the United States and printed on acid-free paper.

The paper used in this publication meets the minimum requirements of ANSI/NISO Z39.48-1992 (R 1997) *(Permanence of Paper)*.

FIRST EDITION

Library of Congress Cataloging-in-Publication Data

Spencer, Robert, 1962–
    Islam unveiled : disturbing questions about the world's fastest-growing faith / Robert Spencer.
    p. cm.
    Includes bibliographical references (p.) and index.
    ISBN 1-893554-58-9 (alk. paper)
    1. Islam—Controversial literature. 2. Apologetics. 3. Islam—Relations—Christianity. 4. Christianity and other religions—Islam. I. Title.
BT1170 .S65 2002
297—dc21   2002073545

10 9 8 7 6 5 4 3 2 1

For S.

Contents

Foreword

MOST PEOPLE IN THE WEST KNOW VIRTUALLY nothing about Islam. A few may visit one or another Muslim country as tourists or perhaps on business, and find that the inhabitants, hospitable and vivacious, seem to be getting on with their lives like everybody else. The events of September 11 therefore appeared to come from nowhere. What was this holy war against the United States and the West, this jihad, declared by Osama bin Laden, and how was it possible that to the Arab and wider Muslim world he became an instant popular hero because he had organized the murder of several thousand innocent people in New York and Washington? Westerners in general, and perhaps Americans in particular, had little or no idea that there were Muslims out there who so hated them, and little or no idea either of the causes of that hate.

In a series of interviews and statements, bin Laden made it clear that in attacking the United States he saw himself as a Muslim doing God's work. And that is the reason why so many Muslims from Beirut and Baghdad to Indonesia cheered and danced in the streets at the news of September 11. Leaders and opinion makers including President George W. Bush, however, were quick to assert that bin Laden was a terrorist pure and simple, whose actions were a violation of Islam rather than a natural expression of it. Islam, these leaders maintained, is essentially a peaceful religion.

Apologetics of this kind served a useful purpose. At a time of tension and potential backlash, it was right to ensure that innocent Muslims were not held guilty by association. But in *Islam Unveiled,* Robert Spencer now argues that indeed bin Laden sincerely meant what he said, and that he and the millions of Muslims who admire him find sanction

in Islam. Far from being extremists or perverters of the faith, they interpret its tenets correctly.

From its inception, Islam has been a revealed religion with a text,
the Qur'an, which is considered the Word of God and therefore sacro-
sanct. The Prophet Muhammad, founder of Islam, and then the caliphs
who immediately succeeded him at a time of war and imperial expansion, were simultaneously head of state and religious leader. Down the
centuries, and still today, in spite of exposure to nationalism and the for-
mation of a variety of nation states, that combination has remained an
ideal form of governance for many Muslims. Islam has never known the
separation of church and state which has determined the political and
social evolution of the West, leading as it does from absolutism to democracy, from obedience to civil rights and from blind faith to reason. Judaism
and Christianity were also originally revealed religions. The Reformation and the Enlightenment set in motion a process of rational inquiry
that gradually altered the nature of their dogmas, developing the con-
cessions and compromises towards those of other faiths upon which a
civil society rests.

For many centuries, absolutism served Islam well enough, and there
are great achievements to show for it, such as the science and architecture of the Muslim Middle Ages. Certain of their superiority, Muslims
felt they had nothing to learn from the despised and barbarian West. By
the time they realized that this was a mistake of historic proportions, it
was too late to do anything about it. Stultified in their absolutism, altogether backward, Muslims and their lands were almost entirely overrun
by one or another Western empire. This prolonged contact with the West
has changed the landscape with such physical features as oil wells and
airports and skyscrapers, but only a minority of individuals have adopted
Western values and ways of thinking.

Through the twentieth century, Muslims struggled to regain control of their history from the Western empires. In the outcome they won
their independence, but not their freedom. Absolutism remains the rule.
Some Muslim countries have religious rulers, others have nationalist and
secular rulers, but all (with the doubtful exception of Turkey) are despo-
tisms, in which the rule of law is a matter to be negotiated. Everywhere
the secret police and the military are an ominous presence. This is what
inhibits the creative energies of Muslims and prevents them doing justice to themselves. Anyone who knows Muslim countries, however, will

also be aware that the rigidity of Islamic doctrine conflicts with the actual daily conduct of Muslims. The imam or mullah who comes beseeching for a bottle of whisky or a bribe is a familiar figure, and so is the rabid anti-Western Islamic extremist who asks how to get his son into an Ivy League university. Hypocrisy smoothes the rough surfaces of every society, and perhaps there is more to rejoice in that than to blame.

Ernest Renan, who founded the study of comparative religion more than a century ago, thought that Islam was the engine of this spiritual and temporal despotism, describing it as "the heaviest chains that ever shackled humanity." Robert Spencer follows in that tradition. To him, the concept that the Qur'an is a perfect book leads to anti-intellectualism. Certainly there have been no Islamic Renans; and exegesis of the sacred text as practiced by Christians and Jews would be blasphemous. The result, as Spencer puts it, is that "bigotry, fanaticism and plain ignorance are rooted in some of the central tenets of Islam." There is no scope for questioning the absolutism inherent in the faith and its accompanying Islamic society, or for reforming the injustices deriving from it.

One unequal relationship postulated by Islam is that between men and women, and another is between master and slave. Robert Spencer may sound polemical on these topics, but he is only reporting the reality. Women in Islam are victimized by the Sharia, or Islamic law, which privileges men in numerous social and legal instances, and in some countries they are further victimized by customs such as polygamy and female circumcision. As for slavery, it still survives in a few Arab countries including Sudan, Saudi Arabia and Mauritania.

A third unequal relationship goes back to the origins of Islam, when Muslims conquered other peoples, then put them to the sword, converted them or offered them the choice of becoming *dhimmi,* that is, second-class citizens suffering social and financial impositions that did not affect Muslims, but protected by the state in return. The assumption of Muslim superiority and *dhimmi* inferiority underlay the rightful ordering of the Islamic world. In the modern age, however, such an assumption evidently became absurd. Twin reactions have followed in the House of Islam: self-pity at finding itself in such backwardness, and hatred of those thought to be responsible for it. Inflamed by this mindset, Muslims all around the perimeter of the Islamic world are fighting their neighbors of other religions—Hindus in India, Communist and Buddhist

Chinese, Jews, Christians in a score of countries, and pagan animists in Africa. In this light, it is wishful thinking to bracket Islam and peace.

It is, or ought to be, an unarguable and universal truth that Muslims and their neighbors should meet on equal terms. Should Muslims instead follow the likes of bin Laden and other extremists, insisting on inequality and the enforcement of absolutism, they will have to be resisted, if need be militarily. Muslims themselves will have to find the way out of this dilemma of their own making. Elsewhere I have called for the Muslim equivalent of an Andrei Sakharov and a Solzhenitsyn, brave and challenging thinkers who showed their fellow Russians how to escape from the dead end of absolutism, to democratize and modernize.

Robert Spencer doesn't see much prospect of such an eventuality. He tends to believe that the West has so lost confidence in itself and its spiritual, cultural and political values that it is defenseless before violence—in which case absolutism will triumph and the Muslim fantasy of superiority will come true. In its own lively style, this book puts down a strong and significant marker to what lies ahead, as Islam and the rest of the world strive to come to terms.

—David Pryce-Jones

Author's Note

NO SYSTEM OF TRANSLITERATION FOR ARABIC names is entirely satisfactory. English simply is not equipped to render the subtleties of the Arabic alphabet. I have chosen "Muhammad" and "Qur'an" over "Mohammed" and "Koran" more or less arbitrarily, following the more common usage of the present day. My other choices are no more systematic, but they generally have the advantage of being common. The sources I quote often use quite divergent spellings, which I hope will not try the reader's patience too much. Most often the differences are no more serious than the employment or omission of a terminal "h." Also, the verse numbers in the Qur'an, and its various English translations, are not standard. But the passages quoted can usually be found within a verse or two of the number given.

PROLOGUE

What Does Islam Really Stand For?

BY NOW EVERYONE HAS HEARD THAT "Islam means peace." Everyone up to and including the President of the United States and the Prime Minister of Great Britain has been saying so ever since the terrorist attacks of September 11, 2001. Yet open the pages of Islam's holy book, the Qur'an, and you find statements like this: *Slay the pagans wherever you find them.* Such commands inspire people like Amir Maawia Siddiqi, the Pakistani son of a small businessman, to take oaths like this: "I, Amir Maawia Siddiqi, son of Abdul Rahman Siddiqi, state in the presence of God that I will slaughter infidels my entire life.... May God give me strength in fulfilling this oath."[1]

The dissonance between the prevailing conventional wisdom and the Qur'anic injunction to slay "pagans" calls for a deeper investigation into Islam's commitment to peace, and it encapsulates a set of larger problems with the West's perceptions of Islam.

Most Americans got their first taste of contemporary Islamic terrorism at the Munich Olympics of 1972, when Muslim terrorists murdered Israeli athletes. But at that time observers, both Western and Middle Eastern, assured us that this attack had nothing to do with true Islam, that it was simply another skirmish in the protracted war between Israel and Palestine. We have heard this line again since then. In 1979, Muslims stormed the U.S. embassy in Iran and took fifty-two hostages. Once more we were advised that this had nothing to do with Islam, but instead was an expression of the rage that Iranian citizens felt toward the American government for its support of the hated shah. When a Muslim suicide bomber blew up a U.S. Marine barracks in Beirut in 1983 and killed 241 Americans, news analysts again explained that this had nothing to do with Islam per se; it was another purely political matter.

1

Over and over, the counterpoint between violence and exculpation has been repeated: when Muslim terrorists threw the elderly, wheelchair-bound Leon Klinghoffer to his death off the hijacked cruise ship *Achille Lauro* in 1985; when militant Muslims first bombed the World Trade Center in 1993; when they killed nineteen American soldiers in the bombing of the Khobar Towers in Saudi Arabia in 1996; when they bombed the U.S. embassies in Kenya and Tanzania in 1998; when they bombed the USS *Cole* in 2000. Each time that Muslim terrorists struck, Americans hastened to assure themselves and the world: We know this is not real Islam; we know these terrorists are hijacking the religion of peace.

This chorus swelled after September 11. George W. Bush, Tony Blair and virtually every other Western leader insisted that their shadowy foe in this strange new war was not Islam, but terrorism, and that the relationship between the two was only coincidental.

Among the Western heads of state, only Italy's Silvio Berlusconi was out of step: "We must be aware of the superiority of our civilisation, a system that has guaranteed well-being, respect for human rights and—in contrast with Islamic countries—respect for religious and political rights, a system that has as its value understanding of diversity and tolerance."[2] But the West, apparently, was aware of no such thing, for Berlusconi's pronouncement set off an international furor. Guy Verhofstadt, Prime Minister of Belgium and president of the European Union, lit into Berlusconi for inciting reprisals from Muslims: "These remarks could, in a dangerous way, have consequences. I can hardly believe that the Italian prime minister made such statements. . . . Rather than bringing civilisations together, they could feed a feeling of humiliation."[3] Berlusconi then backed away from his remarks with the all-purpose dodge that they were "taken out of context."

Silvio Berlusconi gained an unlikely ally several months later in American evangelist and sometime presidential candidate Pat Robertson. On CNN's *Late Edition* Robertson said, "I have taken issue with our esteemed president in regard to his stand in saying Islam is a peaceful religion. It's just not. And the Koran makes it very clear, if you see an infidel, you are to kill him. That's what it says. Now that doesn't sound very peaceful to me."

This, too, elicited outrage. For example, the *Washington Post* wondered: "Is Mr. Robertson trying to start a pogrom? If so, he's headed in the right direction." A pogrom! There was exquisite irony in the choice of terms. But the *Post* was more worried about violence from anti-Muslim Americans than from Muslims:

> These sorts of words aren't innocent talk—particularly not when broadcast into millions of homes by a religious leader to whom many look for moral guidance. This country has seen several serious attacks against innocent Muslims, and those taken for Muslims, in recent months. That there have not been more is a testament both to the seriousness of law enforcement in responding to attacks and, more important, to the insistence of leaders across the political spectrum—starting with President Bush—that this country is at war neither with Islam nor with its Muslim citizens. Against that backdrop, the Robertson statement is astonishingly irresponsible.[4]

The responses to Berlusconi and Robertson both stressed the potency of ideas as inducements to action—in this case, Western action harmful to Muslims. But ideas have consequences within the Muslim world as well. What ideas in Islam lead so easily to terrorism? Why is the Islamic religion such a fertile breeding ground for violence?

The politically correct answer is that all religions, or at least the three great monotheistic faiths, have a murderous edge, perhaps tamed or muted for a time, but always there on the fringes. "There are Jews and Christians who justify violence with reference to their religion," noted the *Post*.

That is historically true; but what the *Post* neglected to mention is that in this day, neither Judaism nor Christianity has any violent organization equaling the al-Qaeda network, or Hezbollah, or Islamic Jihad, or Hamas, or any of the myriad other Muslim terrorist groups. The occasional abortion clinic bomber or the Jewish Defense League is hauled out when needed to illustrate Christian and Jewish violence, but they are nothing compared with Osama bin Laden's organization.

Is the connection between these groups and Islam merely accidental? Does it result from political pressures in the Muslim world? If political conditions were different, might the world be afflicted with hundreds of thousands of Christian terrorists, instead of Muslim ones? Or is there something about Islam itself that gives rise to this sort of thing?

Few have cared, or dared, to deal with this question openly and honestly. The reasons for this curious silence are manifold and revealing. One Middle Eastern scholar was recently quoted in the *New York Times* as observing that: "Between fear and political correctness, it's not possible to say anything other than sugary nonsense about Islam."[5] Political correctness is one thing, but fear? What are people like this professor—who declined to be identified—afraid of? Professional censure? Disapproval? Firing? No—these anxieties are the luxuries of academics in other fields. Scholars who dare to depart from "sugary nonsense" about Islam have more basic fears.

The experience of scholar Christoph Luxenberg indicates that such fears are not groundless. Luxenberg wrote a scholarly book suggesting that the Qur'an, the sacred book of Islam, has been mistranslated and misinterpreted by Muslims themselves. His work may be likened to that of the Christian deconstructionists of the Jesus Seminar, who challenge and occasionally attack traditional dogmas in trying to determine whether Jesus actually said and did what the New Testament reports. But there's a crucial difference. According to the *New York Times,* "Christoph Luxenberg is a pseudonym, and his scholarly tome 'The Syro-Aramaic Reading of the Koran' had trouble finding a publisher, although it is considered a major new work by several leading scholars in the field." No scholar of the Jesus Seminar has ever felt a need to hide behind a pseudonym, or even had trouble getting his work published. In fact, in the publish-or-perish world of modern academia, it's virtually inconceivable that any professor would even consider using a pseudonym.

Luxenberg may have been trying to avoid suffering the fate of another scholar, Suliman Bashear, who "argued that Islam developed as a religion gradually rather than emerging fully formed from the mouth of the Prophet." For this his Muslim students in the University of Nablus in the West Bank threw him out of a second-story window.[6] Most notoriously, novelist Salman Rushdie was sentenced to death by Iran's Ayatollah Khomeini for portraying Muhammad and the early days of Islam in an unflattering light.

By contrast, Bertrand Russell did not have a bounty on his head after writing *Why I Am Not a Christian.* Episcopalian bishop John Shelby Spong gained notoriety for challenging virtually every traditional belief of Christianity, but has not been punished with defenestration. The famous atheist Madalyn Murray O'Hair was murdered, it is true, but this was for her money, not for her blasphemy. In fact, these people and others like them have won respect in some circles, being hailed for their intellectual courage and honesty. Some have even enjoyed a certain vogue.

Certainly they have sparked controversy, sometimes quite heated. But they haven't lived in fear for their lives.

Speaking freely about Islam clearly is more risky. But difficult questions must be asked—and answered—if the West is going to face the terrorist threat adequately. For if there are elements of Islam itself that engender violence, it is neither irresponsible nor hateful to say so. This is not in order to incite thugs to attack Muslims on the street, but to look squarely at what the West is really up against.

In that connection, the following chapters also look closely into the Islamic world's human rights record, its treatment of women, and some noteworthy elements of the moral code that Muslims take from the Qur'an and the example of Muhammad. I explore the question of why Islam was once a fertile soil for the flourishing of science and culture, but is no longer—and what this change entails for present-day relations between Islam and the West. Another historical question with important implications for our own age concerns the vaunted Islamic tolerance of religious minorities, which virtually all observers agree was considerably greater than that shown by the Christian societies of premodern Europe. Likewise, I look into the Crusades, that perennial focus of shame for the West, to evaluate whether the role they have been assigned in the contemporary debate—as evidence of the (once and future) rapacity and imperialism of the West—is actually justified.

In so doing, I do not mean to exonerate the modern, secular West any more than to indict Muslims in general or Islam as a whole. Indeed, there is a great deal to love in Islamic culture, literature and music. Islam is not a monolith, and the culture it has inspired has bestowed great beauty upon the world. But these facts should not preempt further analysis on a question of tremendous importance to the future of the West: whether Islam can be secularized, purged of its martial elements, and brought into a framework of cultural and religious pluralism.

I must emphasize here at the outset that my intention is in no way to focus hate upon Muslims. At a personal level, I have known quite a few Muslims whose personal charity puts me to shame. Any reasonable person understands that a criticism of Islam is not an attack on all those who adhere to that faith. If the seeds of terrorism are found to lie at the heart of Islam, that does not make every Muslim a terrorist, nor does it excuse any injustice toward Muslims. Today, Palestinians and other Muslims in fact suffer wrongs that cannot be justified. But in the chapters to come—a step beyond wishful thinking—we will consider whether Islam itself in some way exacerbates the conflicts in which these wrongs occur.

ONE

Is Islam a Religion of Peace?

"ISLAM IS PEACE."

George W. Bush went to a mosque to say it late in 2001. The September 11 terrorist attacks, he averred, "violate the fundamental tenets of the Islamic faith." In his September 20 address to Congress, he elaborated: "The terrorists practice a fringe form of Islamic extremism that has been rejected by Muslim scholars and the vast majority of Muslim clerics—a fringe movement that perverts the peaceful teachings of Islam."[1]

The President's counterpart in London, Prime Minister Tony Blair, concurred: September 11, he said flatly, "has nothing to do with Islam."

In 1998, President Bill Clinton had made a similar pronouncement in a speech before the United Nations:

> Many believe there is an inevitable clash between Western civilization and Western values, and Islamic civilizations and values. I believe this view is terribly wrong. False prophets may use and abuse any religion to justify whatever political objectives they have—even cold-blooded murder. Some may have the world believe that almighty God himself, the merciful, grants a license to kill. But that is not our understanding of Islam. . . . Americans respect and honor Islam.[2]

Of course Americans should respect and honor Muslims, like all people. But does Islam teach Muslims to return the courtesy? Is George Bush right in saying that the terror of September 11 represented only a "fringe form of Islamic extremism"?

Certain assumptions are so ingrained that it is difficult even to notice their presence. In the contemporary Western world, one such assumption is that all religions are fundamentally benign—in other words, essentially like Christianity. Westerners are fond of assuming that because

Islam is (like Christianity) a religion, it must be (like Christianity) peaceful at its heart. And just as Christianity has its belligerent fundamentalists who misunderstand and distort its message of peace, so does Islam.[3]

Western commentators these days are fond of pointing out that Muslims, like Christians, worship one God only, respect Jesus and Mary, and base their faith on a book considered to be the revealed Word of God, which contains stories of Adam and Abraham and Moses and David. One prominent scholar of Islam, Karen Armstrong, notes: "Constantly the Quran points out that Muhammad had not come to cancel the older religions, to contradict their prophets or to start a new faith. His message is the same as that of Abraham, Moses, David, Solomon, or Jesus."[4] Armstrong, indeed, even blames Christians for the misapprehension that Islam is not a peaceful religion:

> Ever since the Crusades, the people of Western Christendom developed a stereotypical and distorted vision of Islam, which they regarded as the enemy of decent civilization. . . . It was, for example, during the Crusades, when it was Christians who had instigated a series of brutal holy wars against the Muslim world, that Islam was described by the learned scholar-monks of Europe as an inherently violent and intolerant faith, which had only been able to establish itself by the sword. The myth of the supposed fanatical intolerance of Islam has become one of the received ideas of the West.[5]

If Islam truly is peaceful, then of course President Bush is right: the terrorists who attacked America must be acting against the principles of their own religion. That was the assumption at CNN when, in the aftermath of the terrorist attacks on the World Trade Center and the Pentagon, the network posted this poll question on its website: "Should a religion be judged by the acts of its followers?"[6] For Westerners with Christian backgrounds—that is, most Westerners—it was a loaded question. With public opinion running high against Islam, the media was keeping up steady pressure on what it saw as unenlightened religious bigotry. If Christianity shouldn't be judged by the sins of particular Christians, then Islam shouldn't be judged by the sins of those Muslims who hijacked planes and rammed them into buildings full of innocent people.

It seems a reasonable enough caveat. But the reality is more complicated. Islam is indeed like Christianity in many ways, but in others it is as different as the sun is from the moon.

Who Speaks for Islam?

It all depends on whom you ask.

To some Muslims, the terrorist attacks on America violated the fundamental tenets of Islam and the plain words of the Qur'an. To some, they didn't. This is not a matter of learned Muslims looking askance while the uneducated, inflamed by the self-serving propaganda of extremist leaders, cheer for the cameras in Palestine as they watch replays of the planes hitting their targets. In fact, it's the learned Muslims who are split on the issue of terrorism.

This, in large part, results from the nature of authority in Islam. The religion has no central authority beyond the Qur'an, the holy book that Muslims believe was given by the one almighty God, Allah, to the Prophet Muhammad in the seventh century. There is no supreme Islamic teacher who can tell Muslims—and the world—what Islam is and what it isn't. This makes for a multiplicity of voices in Islam, all appealing to Qur'anic authority and claiming to speak for true Islam.

This multiplicity is not the same as the Protestant idea that the believer can read the Bible and work out the truth on his own. Just as Protestant groups in practice developed their own traditions for interpreting the Bible and applying its message to their lives, so individual Muslims are guided in their communities to a right understanding of their sacred book. In Sunni Islam, which comprises over 85 percent of Muslim believers worldwide, a certain teaching authority is invested in the *ulama:* the (often national) community of muftis, the teachers and scholars of the Qur'an and Sunnah, or Muslim traditions, whose *fatwas,* or legal rulings on matters open to question or dispute, are generally accepted by believers.[7]

But the muftis don't all agree about terrorism.

Some Muslim leaders have indeed condemned bin Laden's attacks outright. Saudi Arabia's Sheikh Saalih al-Lehaydaan, the head of the Islamic judiciary in a country that knows no law outside of Islam, declared: "Killing a person who has not committed a crime is one of the major sins and terrible crimes.... What happened in America is ... undoubtedly a grave criminal act which Islam does not approve of and no one should applaud."[8]

Another prominent Saudi teacher of the faith, Sheikh Saalih as-Suhaymee, agreed. He observed in his fatwa that Muslims are forbidden from "killing women, children, the elderly." He addressed a popular Muslim claim when he went on to say that this prohibition still holds "despite the fact that the associates of these categories of people may be involved in fighting with the Muslims." He thus concluded that the terrorist attacks on the World Trade Center, because they killed "none but innocent non-Muslims and Muslims, from all the various parts of the world, of different races," were "not permissible." In fact, "Islam does not allow [this kind of attack] in any form whatsoever." He even claimed that "none of the scholars" who hold "the correct form of Islam, affirm the likes of these actions."[9]

But this sheikh could establish no unanimity for his "correct form of Islam." Some other Muslim leaders did agree with him—to a point. One was Sheikh Omar bin Bakri bin Muhammad, the judge of Great Britain's Sharia, or Islamic law court, secretary general of the Islamic World League, and spokesman for the International Islamic Front for Europe, as well as founder of the radical international Muslim group al-Muhajiroun. On its website al-Muhajiroun posted a fatwa by Sheikh Omar, saying that, yes, the terrorist attacks on the World Trade Center and the Pentagon were "a crime and violation for the sanctity of Human beings [sic] which is prohibited in Islam." They were a crime even though the "US Government and its Military forces are a legitimate target as far as Islam is concerned." Muslims can legitimately attack American troops, Sheikh Omar explained, because the United States is "engaging in aggression and atrocities" against Muslims in Iraq, Palestine, Afghanistan and Sudan—and because of American support for "the Pirate State of Israel and the dictator Leaders in the Muslim world." Nevertheless, he tended to agree with the Saudi sheikh on the matter of noncombatants: "it is not a justification to attack American People because Islam forbid us to fight people because of their Nationality, Color, etc.... rather because of their aggression or occupation [sic]."

Yet this same imam, when asked what lessons Muslims could draw from the attacks on the United States, passed up the opportunity to instruct his coreligionists in how they could have responded to this "American aggression" without committing a crime in the eyes of Allah. Instead, all the lessons he drew were directed squarely at the Great Satan itself. The attacks, explained Sheikh Omar, were a consequence of "atrocities and the aggression committed by the US Government and its forces against the third World in general and the Muslim World." Going beyond even Osama bin Laden, this influential divine enumerated atrocities including not only American support of Israel, the occupation of Somalia and the bombing of Iraq and Sudan, but also the occupation of "Muslim land in Saudi Arabia, Kuwait, Egypt and Turkey."

He further condemned Western governments and media as "people who victimize Muslims and Islam." The Western powers, explained the sheikh, are indifferent to "Muslim lives and blood." He pointed out that the attacks showed that Muslims had the "determination to die for a just cause." They "shake the arrogance of the Western Government and undermine their claims to be invulnerable country in the World [*sic*]."

The success of the attacks, Sheikh Omar concluded, showed that "there is no defense system could stand in the way of the determination of a person who wants to become a Martyr."[10] His conception of a martyr, it should be noted, differs from the common Western idea, derived from Christianity. A Christian martyr is someone who is killed for his faith, without bringing his own death upon himself. The notion of a "martyr" as someone who kills others viewed as enemies of the faith, and in the process gets himself killed, is a distinctly Islamic construct.

Sheikh Omar's pronouncements about the reasons for the attack aren't too far removed from those voiced by icons of the left such as Noam Chomsky and Susan Sontag; though presumably they didn't intend to inspire young men to dedicate themselves to destroying the Great Satan.

Meanwhile, Osama bin Laden's favorite imams went even further. In the celebrated video in which bin Laden, for all intents and purposes, admitted complicity in the September 11 terrorism, he asked his guest: "What is the stand of the Mosques there [in Saudi Arabia]?" The sheikh who had come to pay homage to the terrorist mastermind replied, "Honestly, they are very positive." One prominent Saudi sheikh, he said, "gave a good sermon in his class after the sunset prayers.... His position is really very encouraging." Another, said the sheikh, "gave a beautiful fatwa, may Allah bless him."[11]

On the thorniest question arising from the terrorist attacks, this second sheikh disagreed absolutely with those who condemned the attacks because they killed innocents: "This was jihad and those people were not innocent people [World Trade Center and Pentagon victims]. He swore to Allah."[12]

The Wahhabis

Those who defend Islam say that these pro–bin Laden Saudis are Wahhabis, and that this explains their hard line.

The Wahhabis are the notoriously strict Muslim sect that holds sway in Saudi Arabia and maintains a haughty sense of superiority over the rest of the Muslim world. Founded by the Sunni reformist Sheikh Muhammad ibn Abdul al-Wahhab (ca. 1700–1792), the Wahhabis purport to restore the purity of Islam by rejecting all innovations that occurred after the third Islamic century—that is, around the year 950. (Presumably Islamic practice before that date could be directly traced to the words and actions of the Prophet, but after that the connection to Muhammad becomes more tenuous.)

The most visible consequence of this reform is that Wahhabi mosques lack minarets, but the Wahhabis cut far deeper into the Islamic consciousness than that. Al-Wahhab rejected the widespread Sunni practice of venerating Muslim saints, calling it a species of *shirk,* the cardinal Muslim sin of worshiping created beings along with Allah. Based largely on this perception, he declared all non-Wahhabi Muslims to be unbelievers, and waged *jihad,* or holy war, against them. Wahhabi fortunes waxed and waned throughout the nineteenth century, but in 1932 the Wahhabi Sheikh Ibn Saud captured Riyadh and established the Kingdom of Saudi Arabia on Wahhabi principles.

Other Muslim groups, in turn, despise the Wahhabis and deny their claim to represent anything like true or pure Islam. One Muslim characterized the Wahhabis venomously as unprincipled opportunists:

> While claiming to be adherents to "authentic" Sunnah [Muslim tradition], these deviants are quick to label anyone who opposes their beliefs ... as "sufi," [that is, akin to adherents of the mystical Sufi sect, elements of which Wahhabis and other Muslims consider heretical] while exploiting the Muslims' love for Islam by overexaggerating the phrase "Qur'an and Sunnah" in their senseless rhetoric.[13]

Many Western scholars blame the Wahhabis almost exclusively for terrorism, while maintaining a sharp distinction between Islam in its Wahhabi form and the genuine article. Journalist Stephen Schwartz, for instance, calls Wahhabism "the main form of Islamic fundamentalism." He asserts that "fundamentalism was always a tendency in Islam, as in every other religion, but did not gain permanent influence until the 18th century and the rise of Wahhabism." The Wahhabis, he says, prosper on Saudi oil money and an American military presence. If their funding were cut off, they would "dwindle to a feeble remnant," and presumably terrorism would decline as well.[14]

Certainly Wahhabis have generously supported terrorists. The Saudi government's affection for the Taliban is well documented. But the problem of Islamic terror is not simply the problem of the Wahhabis. There are disquieting signs that Muslim terror is much more broadly based. It is precisely the Wahhabis' claim to represent pure Islam that has inspired Muslim groups from North Africa to Indonesia—and gives the Wahhabis and their spiritual kin resilience and staying power. As former education secretary William J. Bennett has said, Islam itself "is not without its deeply problematic aspects, particularly when it comes to relations with non-Muslims. The superiority of Islam to other religions, the idea that force is justified in defending and spreading the faith—these teachings have been given high visibility in Wahhabism, but they are authentic teachings."[15]

Wahhabi Opponents, Terror Allies

Ten days after the attacks, al-Muhajiroun held a press conference in Lahore, Pakistan. This group was founded by Britain's Sheikh Omar bin Bakri bin Muhammad as an "Islamic Intellectual and a Political organization" that is "working to establish Islam in its totality wherever we are, through an Intellectual and a Political struggle."[16] Sheikh Omar is no Wahhabi; in fact, he calls the Wahhabi king of Saudi Arabia "the pirate ruler of the pirate state of so-called Saudi-Arabia."[17] Nevertheless, his organization had no trouble declaring its sympathies for bin Laden.

At the Lahore press conference, al-Muhajiroun issued a declaration that said nothing at all about whether the September 11 terrorist attacks were legal or not. Instead, it simply took them as an occasion to declare world war:

1. The Shariah [Islamic law] verdict dictates that the life and wealth of anyone who attacks Muslims has no sanctity. [That is, those who are considered to have attacked Muslims can be killed at any time, with the murderer incurring no legal or moral penalty.]

2. We call upon the Muslims to side with their Muslim brothers in Afghanistan and engage in Jihad against USA and target their government and military installations.
3. We warn the West to be ready for a World War against Islam in which they will suffer not only militarily but also economically.

Although it distinguishes between soldiers and civilians (without reference to or apology for the killing of noncombatants on September 11), the document warns that Muslim warriors will make no distinction between "soldiers fighting against the Taliban or soldiers relaxing in the US," for "this war is not a war against Terrorism but rather this is a war against Islam." Accordingly, "This war will not be restricted to this region but rather this war will, unless the aggressors withdraw from the Muslim lands, encapsulate the entire world. No country will escape the effects of this war."[18]

Likewise, Hassan Butt, a leader of al-Muhajiroun, told the BBC early in 2002 that British Muslims trained by the Taliban who had survived the American bombings would soon return to the sceptered isle—chastened not a whit. There they would "take military action" against "British military and government institutes, as well as British military and government individuals."[19]

Ominous as all this is, even more so is the silence of so-called "moderate" Muslim clerics—that is, clerics who are about as far from Wahhabism as an imam can get. An alarming number of imams in the Western world simply said nothing about the September 11 attacks, or sent out a vague statement that could be interpreted favorably by both sides. Few have stood up and said in so many words that they condoned the terrorist acts, but few have condemned them either.

There have been, of course, notable exceptions. Sheikh Abdul Hadi Palazzi, the secretary general of the Italian Muslim Association, led the Italian Muslim leadership to condemn Palestinian suicide bombings in no uncertain terms: "In defense of a wicked regime [Yasir Arafat's Palestinian Authority], innocent ignorant children are sent to be killed in criminal actions. . . . This regime even dares to declare that Islam approves of these criminal acts."[20]

Yet a chorus of imams did not join Palazzi. The strange silence was noted within the Muslim community. For instance, the Egyptian Muslim journalist Mona Eltahawy declared in early 2002, "Moderate and progressive Muslims must speak out.... It is no longer enough for the clerics to issue tired platitudes on how Islam means peace.... Where were they when Osama bin Laden and his coalition of terrorists vowed to target every American man, woman and child? We have to look inward and ask ourselves: What in Islam, what in the way it is practiced today, allowed bin Laden to promote his murderous message?"[21]

Even some of those clerics who appeared with President Bush in the wake of the attacks had skeletons in their closets. The president of the American Muslim Council, Abdurahman Alamoudi, joined Bush at a prayer service for the victims; but not quite a year before September 11, 2001, he had said to a Muslim group, "Hear that, Bill Clinton! We are all supporters of Hamas. I wish they add that I am also a supporter of Hizballah [sic]."[22] According to news reports, Alamoudi wasn't the only one who took that position:

> Also invited to the prayer service attended by Alamoudi after the attacks was Muzzammil Siddiqi, the spiritual leader of the Islamic Society of Orange County. At that service, Siddiqi prayed: "keep our country strong for the sake of the good." Only a year earlier, Siddiqi was an organizer of the rally where Alamoudi expressed support for HAMAS and Hezbollah. Then, Siddiqi said, "The United States of America is directly and indirectly responsible for the plight of the Palestinian people. If you remain on the side of injustice the wrath of God will come."

Confronted with this, Siddiqi pleaded ignorance. Even though he had been one of the rally's organizers, Siddiqi claimed that he "was not aware of all the speakers at the rally and doesn't support the extremist viewpoints some expressed." Evidently it isn't extremist to invoke the wrath of God; it's only extremist to be the agent of this wrath. Said Siddiqi, "I don't support Hezbollah and HAMAS. I don't support any terrorist groups. Terrorism is not what Islam teaches."[23] Yet apparently what the terrorists teach is not so foreign to Islam as to bring Siddiqi or anyone else to want to keep these groups from appearing at the rally.

Another Muslim who prayed with Bush was Hamza Yusuf, a California-based imam:

> On Sept. 20, FBI agents showed up at the house of Hamza Yusuf, a Muslim teacher and speaker in Northern California. They wanted to question him about a speech he had given two days before the Sept. 11 attacks,

in which he said that the U.S. "stands condemned" and that "this country has a great, great tribulation coming to it."

"He's not home," his wife said. "He's with the president."

The agents thought she was joking, Yusuf said. But she wasn't. That day Yusuf was at the White House, the only Muslim in a group of religious leaders invited to pray with President Bush, sing "God Bless America," and endorse the president's plans for military action.

To his credit, Hamza Yusuf says the attacks were sobering: "This has been a wake-up call for me as well, in that I feel in some ways there is a complicity, that we have allowed a discourse centered in anger."[24]

Meanwhile, Muslim crowds worldwide were hardly condemning the attacks. Besides the now-infamous Palestinians dancing in the streets for CNN's cameramen at the news that the World Trade Center towers had collapsed, demonstrators around the world chanted their approval. These people were not all Wahhabis or uneducated mobs. "Reporters from Arab shores," according to Johns Hopkins University professor Fouad Ajami, "tell us of affluent men and women, some with years of education in American universities behind them, celebrating the cruel deed of Muhammad Atta and his hijackers." A Libyan told the *New York Times:* "September 11 was the happiest day of my life."[25]

As crowds chanted their approval of bin Laden's terrorism, even imams who condemned the terrorist attacks declined opportunities to condemn also the imams who approved of the attacks—a fact with enormous significance for the Bush/Blair attempts to portray the terrorists as a fringe group within Islam. Soon after September 11, for example, Jake Tapper of the Internet magazine *Salon* tried to get the communications director of the Council on American-Islamic Relations (CAIR), an American Muslim named Ibrahim Hooper, to speak out against Osama bin Laden. Hooper ducked:

> "We condemn terrorism, we condemn the attack on the buildings," Hooper said. But why not condemn bin Laden by name, especially after President Bush has now stated that he was clearly responsible for the Sept. 11 attacks? "If Osama bin Laden was behind it, we condemn him by name," Hooper said. But why the "if"—why qualify the response? Hooper said he resented the question. And what about prior acts of terror linked to bin Laden? Or that bin Laden has urged Muslims to kill Americans? Again,

Hooper demurred, saying only that he condemns acts of terror. Both groups [CAIR and the American Muslim Council] also refuse to outright condemn Islamic terrorist groups Hamas and Hezbollah.[26]

Why?

Perhaps a clue lies in the nature of the book that all Muslims regard as their supreme authority: the Qur'an.

The Centrality of the Qur'an

When Nobel Prize winner V. S. Naipaul traveled into the lands of Islam in 1979, on a seven-month expedition he recorded in his book *Among the Believers: An Islamic Journey,* he had an encounter in Pakistan that concisely illustrated Muslim attitudes toward the Qur'an. When a Pakistani government official told a colleague that Naipaul wanted to see "Islam in action," the colleague responded, "He should read the Koran."[27]

The Qur'an is the highest authority in Islam, believed by Muslims to have been dictated by Allah and delivered to the Prophet Muhammad by the Angel Gabriel. The Islamic scholar Seyyed Hossein Nasr of George Washington University explains: "The Quran constitutes the alpha and omega of the Islamic religion in the sense that all that is Islamic, whether it be its laws, its thought, its spiritual and ethical teachings and even its artistic manifestations, have their roots in the explicit or implicit teachings of the Sacred Text."[28]

The Qur'an's authority in the Muslim world far surpasses the authority the Bible has held in the West. An Islamic introduction to the study of the Qur'an calls the book a "protective haven and lasting gift of bliss, excellent argument and conclusive proof." Moreover, "it cures the heart's fear, and makes just determinations whenever there is doubt. It is lucid speech, and final word, not facetiousness; a lamp whose light never extinguishes ... an ocean whose depths will never be fathomed. Its oratory stuns reason ... it combines concise succinctness and inimitable expression."[29] Because it contains laws as well as dogmas, the Qur'an is the Muslim's fundamental guide to living. "More than representing the supreme embodiment of the sacred beliefs of Islam, its bible and its guiding light," says another Muslim scholar, "the Qur'an constitutes the Muslim's main reference not only for matters spiritual but also for the mundane requirements of day to day living."[30]

Muslims have a tremendous affection and reverence for the Qur'an as the speech of almighty God. In the words of the English Muslim convert Mohammed Marmaduke Pickthall, it is an "inimitable symphony, the very sounds of which move men to tears and ecstacy."[31] Its poetic character is legendary. Some of the suras that Muhammad gave to his followers at Mecca early in his prophetic career are hypnotically powerful even in translation:

> When the sun ceases to shine;
> when the stars fall down and the mountains are blown away;
> when camels big with young are left untended,
>   and the wild beasts are brought together;
> when the seas are set alight and men's souls are reunited;
> when the infant girl, buried alive, is asked for what crime she was
>   slain;[32]
> when the records of men's deeds are laid open, and heaven is stripped
>   bare;
> when Hell burns fiercely and Paradise is brought near:
> then each soul shall know what it has done. (Sura 81:1–14)

Qur'anic rhythms are captivating even to the listener who does not understand Arabic; many a non-Muslim through the centuries has remarked on the singular appeal of the Qur'an chanted.

Muslims speak of the Qur'an's mesmerizing quality as proof of its divine origin, and they commit large portions of it to heart before they are able to understand what it says. According to the scholar John Esposito:

> Today, crowds fill stadiums and auditoriums throughout the Islamic world for public Quran recitation contests. Chanting of the Quran is an art form. Reciters or chanters are held in an esteem comparable with that of opera stars in the West. Memorization of the entire Quran brings great prestige as well as merit. Recordings of the Quran are enjoyed for their aesthetic as well as their religious value.[33]

A Muslim will look to muftis and imams for guidance, but will also read the Qur'an on his own. Concerning the topic of how to treat non-Muslims, the sacred book will tell him: "Prophet, make war on the unbelievers and the hypocrites and deal rigorously with them. Hell shall be their home: an evil fate" (Sura 9:73).[34] Inside the House of Islam there may be peace, or at least the absence of war, but Islam declares perpet-

ual war between believers and unbelievers. "The true believers fight for
the cause of God, but the infidels fight for the devil. Fight then against
the friends of Satan" (Sura 4:76). The Muslim who doesn't fight is hardly
worthy of the name:

> Those that stayed at home were glad that they were left behind by God's
> apostle [Muhammad], for they had no wish to fight for the cause of God
> with their wealth and with their persons. They said to each other: "Do
> not go to war, the heat is fierce." Say to them: "More fierce is the heat of
> Hell-fire!" Would that they understood! (Sura 9:81)

Muslims often maintain that Western commentators have distorted
the concept of war in the Qur'an—the jihad. We'll delve into this issue
more deeply later, but it warrants some attention here. One Muslim commentator complains, "A great misconception prevails, particularly among
the Christians, propagated by their zealous missionaries, with regard to
the duty of jihad in Islam." It doesn't refer solely to the taking up of arms
against the enemies of Islam, he says, defining it as "The use of or exert-
ing of one's utmost powers, efforts, endeavours or ability in contending
with an object of disapprobation, and this is of three kinds, namely, a visible enemy, the devil and against one's own self."[35] Other Muslim divines
distinguish the "greater jihad," which involves the individual's spiritual
struggle, from the "lesser jihad," which takes the struggle outward against
enemies of the faith. Most Muslims will be concerned in their daily lives
with the greater jihad—their own efforts to live out their faith. The term
can also be applied to any action taken to defend or propagate the faith.

As for the "lesser jihad," one manual of Islamic law defines it simply as "war against non-Muslims."[36] It can be waged with the weapons
of apologetics and debate, but an uncomfortable fact for Islamic moderates is that nothing says it cannot involve the force of arms. Though
considered lower than the spiritual struggle, armed force is an integral
element of jihad. When Sheikh Omar Bakri (whose muted applause for
bin Laden's terrorism we quoted above) called jihad "a sacred duty imposed
by Allah on all young males in good health," he did not mean simply
that Allah wants all young males to study the Qur'an and struggle against
sin: "The Koran," Sheikh Omar explained, "lays down that the Muslim
must be capable of bearing arms and should be ready for the Jihad."[37]

There has always been a martial element in jihad. Toward the end
of the seventh century, Hajjaj, the governor of Iraq, wrote after a battle:

"The Great God says in the Koran: 'O true believers, when you encounter the unbelievers, strike off their heads.' The above command of the Great God is a great command and must be respected and followed."[38] Indeed, the military aspect of jihad is firmly rooted in the Qur'an itself. The verse that Hajjaj invoked, and others like it, leave little room for doubt:

> When you meet the unbelievers in the battlefield, strike off their heads and, when you have laid them low, bind your captives firmly. (Sura 47:4)

> Fight for the sake of God those that fight against you, but do not attack them first. God does not love the aggressors. Slay them wherever you find them. Drive them out of the places from which they drove you. Idolatry is worse than carnage. (Sura 2:190–191)*

> When the sacred months are over slay the idolaters wherever you find them. Arrest them, besiege them, and lie in ambush everywhere for them. If they repent and take to prayer and render the alms levy [i.e., the *jizya*, the special tax on non-Muslims], allow them to go their way. God is forgiving and merciful. (Sura 9:5)

The word translated as "idolaters" in the last passage, *al-Mushrikun*, is sometimes rendered as "pagans" or "polytheists." Although some Muslims refrain from using *al-Mushrikun* to refer to those whom the Qur'an denotes as "People of the Book"—chiefly Jews and Christians (as well as Zoroastrians)—this word and this verse are commonly used in Muslim literature as a guide for dealing with any other group that supposedly worships created beings along with God. Strictly speaking this would not include Jews, yet the Qur'an seems to place them within it by asserting that "the Jews say Ezra is the son of God" (Sura 9:30)—a claim that corresponds to no known Jewish tradition. Christians, of course, are considered guilty of *shirk*—worshiping created beings—because of the doctrine of the Trinity. While Muslims insist that they respect Jesus, and indeed they do within the bounds of what the Qur'an says about him, the twelfth-century Persian poet Farid ud-Din Attar sums up a prevalent Muslim view of Christianity when he calls it "a blasphemous disgrace."[39]

The command to make war against Jews and Christians is clearer in other portions of the Qur'an, which tie this obligation to their supposed disbelief in what was revealed to them. "Fight against such of those

---

*The first part of this passage is the foundation for the general Muslim view that jihad must be a defensive operation only, an idea we shall examine in detail in chapter ten.

to whom the Scriptures were given as believe neither in God nor the Last Day, who do not forbid what God and His Apostle have forbidden, and do not embrace the true Faith, until they pay tribute out of hand and are utterly subdued" (Sura 9:29). And similarly: "Muhammad is God's Apostle. Those who follow him are ruthless to the unbelievers but merciful to one another" (Sura 48:29).

There are no mitigating verses prescribing mercy toward unbelievers. Therefore, when former pop star Cat Stevens—a convert to Islam who now goes by the name Yusuf Islam—appealed to terrorists for the release of American journalist Daniel Pearl, his words may not have resonated well with their intended audience. "Now the time has come to show the world the Mercy of Islam," said the author of "Peace Train."[40] But where is there any explicit Qur'anic warrant for extending mercy to unbelievers? Boxing legend Muhammad Ali's appeal for Pearl's release displayed a similar assumption: "I have not lost [Allah's] hope in us to show compassion where none exists and to extend mercy in the most difficult of circumstances. We as Muslims must lead by example."[41] Since Pearl wasn't a fellow believer, however, his captors could have replied to these famous converts from Christianity simply by invoking Sura 48:29, according to which he was entitled to no compassion.[42]

Still, maybe all this isn't as bad as it looks. Maybe Muslims, or at least a sizable number of them, read the Qur'an's verses about killing unbelievers in some allegorical fashion. Perhaps something has happened in Islam analogous to the slow development within Christendom that brought us from the days when a figure no less august than St. Thomas Aquinas advocated the execution of heretics, to our present-day state of enlightened toleration. Perhaps Osama is out of the mainstream.

Secular commentators are confident that this is, or will be, the case. Islam, they explain, is "still in the Middle Ages." After all, it has now been only 1400 years since the time of Muhammad, and 1400 years after Christ, goes the analogy, Christians were killing infidels (often fellow Christians of different sects) themselves. Islam is simply a religion that will eventually mature, as did Christianity, into a more tolerant, more expansive faith. Moreover, such observers say, it already has to some degree, and the moderates now show the true face of Islam. The benighted young men training in al-Qaeda camps to kill themselves and other people are simply clinging, out of fears and resentments of various kinds, to a more primitive and violent form of their religion.

Maybe. But this scenario has serious problems.

In the first place, why should the development of Islam mirror that of Christianity? Not only George Bush and Tony Blair, but Westerners in general misunderstand Islam on a massive scale because they persist, probably without realizing it, in viewing the religion of Muhammad in light of Christian categories and experience. The most prominent indication of this is the constant reference to Islamic "fundamentalists." This has become the common label for those who take the above-quoted verses of the Qur'an literally enough to strap bombs to themselves and become human missiles.

The word, of course, has been imported from Christianity. In Christian parlance, a fundamentalist is someone who adheres to the core beliefs—the fundamentals—of the faith. A fundamentalist Christian holds to the traditional, literal understanding of elements of the faith such as the Virgin Birth and bodily Resurrection of Christ. Liberal Christians read the life of Jesus as metaphor and fable; fundamentalists read it as historical fact.

But if a Christian fundamentalist is someone who strictly maintains the traditional core teachings of the faith, by analogy a Muslim fundamentalist would simply be someone who upholds the Five Pillars of Islam. Inside and outside the *umma* (the worldwide community of Muslim believers), Muslims agree that these Pillars are the heart of their religion: the confession of faith, daily prayer, almsgiving, fasting during Ramadan, and the pilgrimage to Mecca. In this sense, virtually all Muslims are fundamentalists.

To isolate Islamic terrorists as "Muslim fundamentalists" is absurd, then, because it suggests something that those who use the term would deny: that violence and terror are fundamentals of Islam.

The Living Qur'an?

Muslims everywhere almost all view the Qur'an as literally and eternally true, including its exhortations to violence. There are liberal Muslims who read the Qur'an's exhortations to battle as a call to wage spiritual warfare against sin and error, but they are difficult to find. Liberalism and modernism have not invaded the House of Islam in any significant measure or had any general influence on the way the average Muslim reads the Qur'an. At this time, the novelist Salman Rushdie is one of the very few Muslims in the world who are trying to bring Islam into the modern world, calling his coreligionists to see the tenets of their faith as metaphor and parable rather than as simple, unalloyed, all-encompassing fact.

In addition to allegorical interpretation, the idea of progressive revelation is generally absent from Islam, whereas in Judaism and Christianity, it is commonly accepted. The Old Testament has numerous passages that no Jew or Christian would take as marching orders for today. No Christian or Jew is likely to sell his daughter into slavery (Exodus 21:7), for example, or put to death someone who works on the Sabbath (Exodus 35:2). But for the Muslim, all of the Qur'an's commands are valid for all time.

This fact is often overlooked when religionists of all persuasions start waging scripture wars. For instance, a Muslim spokesman who expressed outrage at Pat Robertson's remarks about Islam, Hussein Ibish of the American-Arab Anti-Discrimination Committee, asserted: "I could come here ... with quotes from the Talmud and quotes from the Bible and try to paint Judaism and Christianity, or any other religion, in this negative light too. I think that is ... a really despicable and sick game."[43] It is true that Ibish wouldn't have difficulty finding violent statements in the Bible, such as to cause modern Jews and Christians to cringe. There is Psalm 137:9, speaking to the Babylonians who have subjugated the Israelites: "Happy shall be he who takes your little ones and dashes them against the rocks!" Another Psalm vows: "Morning by morning I will destroy all the wicked in the land, cutting off all evildoers from the city of the LORD" (Psalm 101:8). After David performs heroically in battle, the Israelite women sing, "Saul has slain his thousands, and David his ten thousands" (I Samuel 18:7). The Book of Joshua is full of bloody, merciless battles waged at the command of God.

Even so, these are not really equivalents of the violent passages in the Qur'an, for no modern Jew or Christian reads the stories and celebrations of Hebrew warriors as a guide for behavior in the present. *Newsweek* religion expert Kenneth Woodward explains the difference:

> The Qur'an does contain sporadic calls to violence, sprinkled throughout the text.... The Bible, too, has its stories of violence in the name of the Lord. The God of the early biblical books is fierce indeed in his support of the Israelite warriors.... But these stories do not have the support of divine commands. Nor are they considered God's own eternal words, as Muslims believe Qur'anic verses to be.[44]

Jews and Christians do consider the violent passages in the Psalms, the
Book of Joshua and elsewhere to be part of God's Word, but not in the
same sense that Muslims regard all of the Qur'an. Rather than a strict
moral code for all time, these passages are a portion of the historical
record of how God brought his people out of sin and gradually into the
light. Virtually all Christians, including fundamentalists, would agree
that they pertained to a particular time and set of circumstances, and
reflected an incomplete stage of the divine revelation, which would eventually be fulfilled—and superseded—by the New Testament gospel of
love and reconciliation. Jews as well as Christians have developed highly
refined methods of allegorical interpretation through which they view
bellicose scriptural passages.

Islam, by contrast, generally rejects any idea of a historical progres-
sion in revelation, and allows little latitude for allegorical interpretation
of the martial verses in the Qur'an. This is partly because Muslim beliefs
about the authorship of the Qur'an differ from Christian beliefs about
how the Bible came to be. As Woodward explains,

> Like the Bible, the Qur'an asserts its own divine authority. But whereas
> Jews and Christians regard the biblical text as the words of divinely inspired
> human authors, Muslims regard the Qur'an, which means "The Recita-
> tion," as the eternal words of Allah himself. Thus, Muhammad is the con-
> duit for God's words, not their composer.[45]

The Muslim scholar Ahmad Von Denffer summarizes the Muslim understanding of the holy book thus: "The Qur'an can be defined as follows:
The speech of Allah, sent down upon the last Prophet Muhammad,
through the Angel Gabriel, in its precise meaning and precise wording
... inimitable and unique, protected by God from corruption."[46] Everywhere around the globe, all sects of Islam teach that the Qur'an is the
perfect word of Allah, valid for all peoples and all times.

In fact, Muslim tradition goes even further, holding that the Qur'an
is eternal and uncreated, and that it resided in heaven with Allah before
he began to reveal it to Muhammad. Because it is considered to be Allah's
actual speech in its "precise wording," traditionally minded Muslims even
frown on translations of the Qur'an (although such translations nonetheless proliferate). Allah revealed the Qur'an in Arabic, and its Arabic language is part of its perfection: "We have revealed the Koran in the Arabic
tongue so that you may grow in understanding" (Sura 12:2).

A book with this kind of pedigree and claim to literal perfection tends to resist any interpretation that diminishes the literal truthfulness of any of its statements.[47] Only a minority of Muslims favor such interpretations: "Modern deconstructionists, mainly European scholars, have boldly stated that the Qur'an should be treated as a historical document subject to modern notions of critical analysis as has the Bible in recent times."[48] It doesn't take much analytical acumen, however, to figure out that the opinions of "deconstructionists" and "European scholars" carry little weight for most Muslims. After all, that is the kind of thinking that got Suliman Bashear thrown out of a second-story window.

Canadian Muslim journalist Irshad Manji draws the logical conclusion of mainstream Muslim reasoning:

> It's time to question publicly whether Islam lends itself to fundamentalism [i.e., a literal reading of Qur'anic exhortations to violence] more easily than other world religions. Here's my case for why it might: We Muslims are routinely told that The Holy Koran is a book about which there is no doubt. By building upon the Torah and the Christian Bible, the Koran perfects their teachings. No need to interpret the final draft of G-d's manifesto. It is what it is, and that is that.[49]

For orthodox Muslims, everything in the Qur'an is valid unless it has been abrogated by another part of the same book. There are such passages, but the violent ones I have quoted are not among them.

There have been attempts throughout the history of Islam to temper the aggressive understanding of the Qur'an, often with hermeneutical ideas imported from Christianity and from classical Greek philosophy. The most notable of these efforts was the Mu'tazilite movement, which originated in the theological and philosophical ideas of Wasil bin ʿAta (699–749) and swept furiously through the House of Islam, becoming the state religion of the Abbasid Caliphate in the ninth century.[50]

Having imbibed pagan Greek philosophy, the Mu'tazilites (a name that means "Separated Ones" or "Those Who Have Withdrawn") held that reason must play a role in the Muslim's encounter with God. Accordingly, Mu'tazilite divines were uncomfortable with literal readings of the Qur'an's anthropomorphisms. They even went so far as to declare that the book itself was *created,* a notion contrary to the orthodox Muslim idea of a miraculous book that resided eternally with Allah in heaven.

The debate over whether the sacred book was created or existed eternally had great practical implications. It allowed the Mu'tazilites to develop a method of Qur'anic interpretation that diverged further from the literal meaning of the text than most Muslim divines dared to venture. For instance, in reading Sura 14:27, "He leads the wrongdoers astray," Mu'tazilite theologians contradicted the literal meaning with its predestinarian implications, maintaining that it was not reasonable that Allah would lead people astray and condemn them to hell.

Notwithstanding their respect for reason, however, the Mu'tazilites were no prototypes of modern, Western rationalists, and in power they were just as absolutist as many other Muslim regimes. Under the Abbasid caliph Abdullah al-Mamun (813–833) and his successors Muhammad al-Mu'tasim (833–842) and Harun al-Watiq (842–847), they initiated a full-fledged inquisition, the Mihna. During this fifteen-year period, the *qadis,* or judges of religious questions, throughout the caliphate were forced to swear that the Qur'an was created, not eternal. This oath was fiercely resisted by the common folk, who had never warmed to the intellectualism and apparent skepticism of Mu'tazilism, and by some scholars as well. No less a personage than Ahmad ibn Muhammad ibn Hanbal (780–855), one of Sunni Islam's "Four Great Imams," was imprisoned and scourged for refusing to affirm the Mu'tazilite doctrine.

Harun al-Watiq's successor, Ja'far al-Mutawakkil (847–861), ended the Mihna and turned the tables on the Mu'tazilites: the assertion that the Qur'an was created became a crime punishable by death. Although the Shi'ite Muslims of Iran adopted certain Mu'tazilite perspectives, with the end of the Mihna the movement largely lost its dynamism within the House of Islam in general. Over time, the less rationalistic views of anti-Mu'tazilites such as Ibn Hanbal and other revered Muslim scholars became entrenched within Sunni orthodoxy. Their chief concern was to uphold the literal and absolute truth of the words of the Qur'an.

The marginalizing and discrediting of the Mu'tazilites has cast a long shadow over "moderate Islam," for it stands as a historical precedent that literalists can use to dismiss any interpretation of the Qur'an that doesn't take all its words at face value. If today's moderates stray too far from a literal reading of the sacred book (including its ferocity toward unbelievers), they risk being accused of trying to revive a long-discredited way of thinking.

Some Muslims have tried in other ways to soften the harshness of certain Qur'anic verses. The Turkish Muslim apologist Adnan Oktar, who writes under the biblically inspired nom de plume Harun Yahya (Aaron John), doesn't take the bellicose pronouncements as a direct call to arms for today. Working within the bounds of a literal reading of the Qur'an, he has tried to construct an Islamic answer to violence and terrorism on the basis of this verse:

> That was why We laid it down for the Israelites that whoever killed a human being, except as a punishment for murder or other villainy in the land, shall be looked upon as though he had killed all mankind; and that whoever saved a human life shall be regarded as though he had saved all mankind. (Sura 5:32)

Harun Yahya concludes, "This being the case, it is obvious what great sins are the murders, massacres and attacks, popularly known as 'suicide attacks,' committed by terrorists."[51]

A Religious Duty to Wage War

Alas, it isn't obvious to all. For one thing, Harun Yahya does not address the martial verses quoted earlier. (After all, what can he say about them?) And the verse he does quote includes a large exception: "punishment for murder or other villainy [or, corruption] in the land." Bin Laden and his ilk charge America with these very crimes. Denouncing the infidel presence in the Islamic holy land and declaring that America has sown corruption in Palestine, Saudi Arabia, Iraq and elsewhere, they lay claim to Qur'anic carte blanche for their terrorist acts.

There is no Muslim version of "love your enemies, and pray for those who persecute you" (Matthew 5:44) or "if anyone strikes you on the right cheek, turn to him the other also" (Matthew 5:39). Instead, there is something more like the ethos that Jesus exhorts his followers to rise above, that of "love your neighbor and hate your enemy" (Matthew 5:43). The Qur'an instructs:

> God does not forbid you to be kind and equitable to those who have neither made war on your religion nor driven you from your homes. But He forbids you to make friends with those who have fought against you on account of your religion and driven you from your homes or abetted

others so to do. Those that make friends with them are wrongdoers. (Sura 60:9)

From the militant Muslim perspective, Americans have done just what the Qur'an specifies as ruling out the need for kindness. The Americans, bin Laden might say, have indeed made war on our religion and driven us from our homes. Therefore, as he has declared, he owes us no mercy, but actually has a religious duty to make war against us. Indeed, he would be a wrongdoer if he overlooked our alleged offenses.

And so, rather than join Harun Yahya in condemning suicide attacks, some Muslims celebrate them. In June 2001, Sheikh Ibrahim Mahdi exclaimed on Palestine's official TV station, "Blessings on whoever has put a belt of explosives on his body and plunged into the midst of the Jews."[52] On its website, al-Muhajiroun posted this perspective:

> The name "suicide-operations" used by some is inaccurate, and in fact this name was chosen by the Jews to discourage people from such endeavours. How great is the difference between one who commits suicide ... because of his unhappiness, lack of patience and [the] weakness or absence of [an imam—] and [who] has been threatened with Hell-Fire—and between the self-sacrificer who embarks on the operation out of strength of faith and conviction, and to bring victory to Islam, by sacrificing his life for the upliftment [sic] of Allah's word![53]

According to the Qur'an, the "self-sacrificer" has much to look forward to: "He that leaves his dwelling to fight for God and His apostle and is then overtaken by death, shall be rewarded by God" (Sura 4:100). These rewards are well known: a heaven filled with the delights of the flesh, vividly described in many verses of the Qur'an: dark-eyed maidens, nonintoxicating liquors and so forth. The blessed

> shall recline on jeweled couches face to face, and there shall wait on them immortal youths with bowls and ewers and a cup of purest wine (that will neither pain their heads nor take away their reason); with fruits of their own choice and flesh of fowls that they relish. And theirs shall be the dark-eyed houris, chaste as hidden pearls: a guerdon for their deeds. (Sura 56:15–24)

That these promises are real incentives for many Muslims today was underscored by a jarring incident witnessed by Jack Kelley of *USA*

Today. At a school run by Hamas, he saw a youth of eleven years give a report to his class:

> "I will make my body a bomb," said the boy, "that will blast the flesh of Zionists, the sons of pigs and monkeys.... I will tear their bodies into little pieces and will cause them more pain than they will ever know." His classmates shouted in response, "Allah Akhbar," [God is great] and his teacher shouted, "May the virgins give you pleasure."[54]

The Parameters of Islamic Belief

Are these Muslims not deriving their conclusions straight from the Qur'an? Thus how can Harun Yahya insist that "Islam is by no means the source of this violence and that violence has no place in Islam"?[55]

In fact, it isn't all that easy to say that something—even terrorism—has no place in Islam, unless it's explicitly condemned in the Qur'an. The American Taliban soldier John Walker Lindh (no authority, to be sure, but certainly a zealous student, or *talib,* of the religion) put it this way to an Internet newsgroup in 1997: "If a person or a group of people believe in the unity of Allah and the day of judgement, believe in the prophethood of Muhammad, believe in the angels, if they keep up Salat [Friday prayers], pay Zakat [alms], fast in Ramadan, and perform the Hajj [the pilgrimage to the Muslim holy city of Mecca] if they're able to, they are Muslims." That's it, according to this budding Taliban fighter: "They can believe things completely contradictory to the Qur'an, or the words of any of the prophets and still be Muslim. They can commit any imaginable sin and still be Muslim, so long as they still fulfill the aforementioned items."[56]

This is overstated, but it expresses the common view in Islam that the elements enumerated by Lindh—the Five Pillars—are indeed the essentials. If someone observes those, it would be very difficult to read him out of Islam. "No group may be excluded from the community unless it itself formally renounces Islam," says a Muslim writing team, Mohamed Azad and Bibi Amina, coauthors of the incomparably titled *Islam Will Conquer All Other Religions and American Power Will Diminish.*[57] No group—not even a terrorist group. An important manual of Islamic law declares that to classify a Muslim as an unbeliever is itself an act of apostasy.[58] Although this law is often honored in the breach, it does indicate that unless they deny that Allah is God and Muhammad is his prophet, Muslim terrorists cannot easily be read out of Islam by anyone—not even by the President of the United States.

This law is recorded in *Reliance of the Traveller,* compiled by the fourteenth-century Muslim scholar Ahmad ibn Naqib al-Misri from numerous ancient and respected sources. It is no mere museum piece. Based largely on the legal rulings of some of the most highly regarded imams in Islamic history, it is updated in a new edition to deal with modern questions.

Reliance of the Traveller is a product of the Shafi'i school of Sunni Islam. Comprising roughly 85 percent of all Muslims, Sunni Islam is divided into four "rites" (*madhhabs*), or schools of Islamic law and practice: Shafi'i, Maliki, Hanafi and Hanbali. Sunni Muslims understand their religious duties according to the guidance of the imams of their school. A Sunni may switch from one *madhhab* to another without jeopardizing his orthodoxy. Moreover, the four schools agree on about three-fourths of their rulings.[59] Noted Shafi'is in Muslim history include all the compilers of the six collections of traditions about Muhammad generally recognized as authentic: Bukhari, Muslim, Tirmidhi, Ibn Majah, Abu Dawud and an-Nasai. These collections are second only to the Qur'an in importance for Muslims.

Thus, not without reason does Al-Azhar, the thousand-year-old Islamic university in Egypt, state that even today *Reliance of the Traveller* "conforms to the practice and faith of the orthodox Sunni Community."[60] I will return to it repeatedly for examples of Islamic law, not because it is the sole or even the principal Islamic legal manual, but because it is in many ways typical of such manuals and representative of widespread and long-established currents of thought in the *umma.*

What Would Muhammad Do?

The example of the Prophet Muhammad is a supreme paradigm for Muslims. And as we shall later see more fully, Muhammad was a man of war. He led armies. He ordered his enemies killed. He never shrank from bloodshed. Notes Kenneth Woodward, "Israeli commandos do not cite the Hebrew prophet Joshua as they go into battle, but Muslim insurgents can readily invoke the example of their Prophet, Muhammad, who was a military commander himself."[61]

In one celebrated incident among the many in which Muhammad lashed out violently against his opponents, he took his revenge on two poets: Abu ʿAfak, a man who was reputed to be over one hundred years old, and ʿAsma bint Marwan, a woman. These poets were not just entertainers. Their verses ridiculing Muhammad and his new religion were, in his eyes, costing him prestige and followers. When Muhammad had had enough, he cried out, "Will no one rid me of this daughter of Marwan?"[62] One of his followers, ʿUmayr ibn ʿAdi, went to her house that night and found her sleeping next to her children. The youngest, a nursing babe, was in her arms. But that didn't stop ʿUmayr from murdering her, a deed for which the Prophet commended him: "You have done a great service to Allah and His Messenger, ʿUmayr!" Abu ʿAfak was also killed in his sleep, in response to the Prophet's question, "Who will avenge me on this scoundrel?"[63]

Muhammad's example of intolerance has been often imitated. Most students of history know that Christendom's treatment of religious minorities was far from spotless, but fewer know that the celebrated Islamic tolerance of Christianity and Judaism was not as enlightened and expansive as it may seem. Modern-day terrorists are the sons and heirs of the Islamic warriors who overwhelmed the ancient Christian lands of the Middle East and North Africa by the force of arms, and who made it so humiliating and difficult for the Christians who survived the conquests to continue to live in their homelands that many gave up the struggle: they converted to Islam just to survive.

Christian and post-Christian citizens of Western republics, surrounded by material comforts and hearing constantly the mantra of "tolerance," may blanch to read about what life was like for their forefathers in the Faith who had the misfortune of falling under the heel of Islam. First, there was the onerous poll-tax levied on non-Muslims unless they converted to Islam.[64] In Muslim Spain, innumerable Christians and Jews converted in order to escape this crushing burden; but this meant a loss of revenue to the treasury. So Muslim officials sometimes closed off this escape route from a miserable existence by forbidding Christians and Jews to convert to Islam. Too many converts would destroy the tax base. Besides having to pay prohibitive taxes, Christians in the lands of St. Augustine, St. Athanasius and St. Ignatius of Antioch were forbidden to build new churches or repair old ones, forbidden to try to prevent the conversion of a child to Islam, forbidden to hold authority over a

Muslim, forbidden to ring bells or perform other acts of worship that offended Muslim sensibilities, and made to wear distinctive clothing. The spiritual children of St. John Chrysostom and St. Basil the Great became a despised, inferior caste.

Most humiliating and outrageous of all was the Ottoman Empire's practice of *devshirme:* the Muslims' drawing of their most formidable warriors against Christianity from among Christians themselves.[65] Christian fathers were forced to appear in the town squares with their sons, the strongest and brightest of whom would be seized from their parents, converted to Islam and trained up to be part of the empire's crack fighting force, the janissaries. In some areas this became an annual event.

Granted, in the days of the *devshirme,* most cultures condoned slavery, and most behaved in war the way Muslims did. The difference is the presence of the Qur'an, whose injunctions validate such behavior for all time. And the oppressed and enslaved peoples had no recourse; for according to a preeminent historian of the experience of religious minorities under Islam, "all litigation between a Muslim and a *dhimmi* [a non-Muslim, chiefly a Jew or a Christian] was under the jurisdiction of Islamic legislation, which did not recognize the validity of the oath of a *dhimmi* against that of a Muslim."[66] *Reliance of the Traveller* stipulates that "legal testimony is only acceptable from a witness who ... is religious"—that is, Muslim—for, it further explains, "unbelief is the vilest form of corruption, as goes without saying."[67] By this a Christian's or Jew's testimony was, at the least, devalued.

Even in our own day, Christians in Sudan, Pakistan and other Muslim lands have lost their lives for blaspheming the prophet Muhammad, on the basis of accusations which they could not defend against. For instance, Pakistan's blasphemy law is, in effect, a declaration of open season against Christians: "Whoever by words, either spoken or written, or by visible representation, or by imputation, innuendo, or insinuation, directly or indirectly defiles the sacred name of the Holy Prophet Muhammad ... shall be punished with death and shall be liable to a fine."[68] Ayub Masih, a Pakistani Christian, was arrested under this law in 1996 for allegedly making a reference to Salman Rushdie's book *The Satanic Verses*—a charge he denied. He has been sentenced to death and repeatedly tortured.

Theological Equivalence

When confronted with this kind of evidence, many Western commentators practice a theological version of "moral equivalence," analogous to the geopolitical form which held that the Soviet Union and the United States were essentially equally free and equally oppressive. "Christians," these commentators say, "have behaved the same way, and have used the Bible to justify violence. Islam is no different: people can use it to wage war or to wage peace."

This is a book about Islam, not about Christianity. Nevertheless, since proponents of certain policies toward the Muslim world use this argument to support their case, it bears examining.

The main features of the case that Christian violence equals Muslim violence are well known. After Pat Robertson's statement about violence in Islam hit the headlines, the *National Catholic Reporter* ran a cartoon of a haloed Robertson clasping his palms together in the posture of prayer and piously asking, "Whoever heard of violence in the name of Christ?" Behind him loom the menacing figures of a Crusader brandishing a sword, the Grand Inquisitor, a Puritan holding a torch ready to burn a wretched accused witch at the stake, and a Ku Klux Klansman holding a noose and standing beside a burning cross.[69]

The humanist Samuel Bradley relates one notorious blot on Christian history:

> It was for this country's God that Central America was savaged. In *Guns, Germs, and Steel,* the Pulitzer-prize winning history of human societies, Jared Diamond recounts the tale of Spanish conquistador Pizarro defeating an army of 80,000 belonging to Atahuallpa with his 168 soldiers. I quote from a journal written that day: "If night had not come on, few out of the more than 40,000 (sic) Indian troops would have been left alive. Six or seven thousand Indians lay dead, and many more had their arms cut off or other wounds." I now quote from the same man's journal. "Truly, it was not accomplished by our own forces, for there were so few of us. It was by the grace of God, which is great."[70]

Bradley does not mention the appalling cruelty of the Inca practice of human sacrifice, which Pizarro's conquest halted. But our concern is that the conquistador justified his own brutality, according to Bradley, as being accomplished "by the grace of God."

This is fundamentally different from terrorists' use of the Qur'an for several key reasons. As we have seen, the Bible does contain martial verses—although in this account Pizarro quoted none of them. More important, his claim that he massacred by God's grace violates clear Christian principles that are held by Catholics, Protestants and Orthodox alike. His bloodlust does not accord with the teachings of Jesus in the Sermon on the Mount, or with the Just War principles of his own Roman Catholic Church. As Kenneth Woodward says in a different context, "While the Crusaders may have fought with the cross on their shields, they did not—could not—cite words from Jesus to justify their slaughters."[71]

Pizarro, like the rest of mankind according to Christian doctrine, was a sinner. His sinful status is obvious with reference to the clear teachings of Jesus Christ, whom he professed to follow, and who said, "Love your enemies and pray for those who persecute you" (Matthew 5:44). This attitude is not ruled out in the Christian understanding of a just war. It is easy to see how Pizarro and the other conquistadors violated central tenets of Christianity.

Mutatis mutandis, did the Muslims who practiced the *devshirme* or turned the great Christian populations of the Middle East into despised *dhimmis* pervert the true principles of Islam? Is Osama bin Laden a sinner and thus no fit representative of Islam? Which teachings of Islam has he violated?

William J. Bennett sums up the difference: "To put the issue at its starkest, there is simply no equivalent in the Koran to the New Testament's admonition to 'turn the other cheek'; conversely, there is no equivalent in the New Testament to the Koranic injunction to 'kill the disbelievers wherever [you] find them.'"[72] For Christians, the New Testament supersedes the Old and corrects its violent tendencies, as in Jesus' celebrated admonition, "You have heard that it was said, 'An eye for an eye and a tooth for a tooth' [Leviticus 24:20]. But I say to you, Do not resist one who is evil" (Matthew 5:38–39). Judaism itself, of course, cultivated a rich tradition in which the violence of the Old Testament was regarded as anything but a guide for believers' daily behavior. But Muslims have no such tradition, and nothing akin to the New Testament corrective of the gospel of mercy.

Those who say that Islam is peace constantly invoke Qur'anic injunctions against killing innocents. But Osama insists that his victims were not innocents. The terrorists kill unbelievers in keeping with the commands of Allah's book and the example of his Prophet. They plot to strike as hard as they can at the nation that, in their view, has humiliated and oppressed the House of Islam—and they do this because the Qur'an tells them to.

A Muslim's Duty

In slaying infidels, are the terrorists not acting as pious Muslims? They believe they are, and the letter of the Qur'an seems to back them up. The challenge, therefore, that confronts those Muslims who say they are discredited fundamentalist fringe groups is to formulate a refutation of the terrorists' own justifications for their actions. To be effective, such a refutation would have to be an Islamic argument, based on clear Muslim principles.

But the bellicosity of the Qur'an and Muslim tradition makes this virtually impossible. As Iran's Ayatollah Khomeini put it:

> Islam makes it incumbent on all adult males, provided they are not disabled or incapacitated, to prepare themselves for the conquest of [other] countries so that the writ of Islam is obeyed in every country in the world.... But those who study Islamic Holy War will understand why Islam wants to conquer the whole world.... Those who know nothing of Islam pretend that Islam counsels against war. Those [who say this] are witless. Islam says: Kill all the unbelievers just as they would kill you all! Does this mean that Muslims should sit back until they are devoured by [the unbelievers]? Islam says: Kill them [the non-Muslims], put them to the sword and scatter [their armies]. Does this mean sitting back until [non-Muslims] overcome us? Islam says: Kill in the service of Allah those who may want to kill you! Does this mean that we should surrender [to the enemy]? Islam says: Whatever good there is exists thanks to the sword and in the shadow of the sword! People cannot be made obedient except with the sword! The sword is the key to Paradise, which can be opened only for the Holy Warriors! There are hundreds of other [Qur'anic] psalms and Hadiths [sayings of the Prophet] urging Muslims to value war and to fight. Does all this mean that Islam is a religion that prevents men from waging war? I spit upon those foolish souls who make such a claim.[73]

Going even further are the terrorists of bin Laden's al-Qaeda. A terrorist manual found in a safe house in Manchester, England, declared that "Islamic governments have never and will never be established through peaceful solutions and cooperative councils. They are established as they [always] have been by pen and gun, by word and bullet, by tongue and teeth."[74] The manual doesn't explain at what point the pen, word and tongue give way to the gun, bullet and teeth; but if Islamic governments have "never been established through peaceful solutions," one may assume that the peaceful instruments give way fairly early in the struggle for Islam.

The Iranian writer Amir Taheri, author of *Holy Terror,* the landmark study of Islamic terrorism, remarks that "Khomeini's teachings are Islamic, but Islam is not limited to what Khomeini teaches."[75] Quite so. But what kind of firewall exists between Khomeiniism and "moderate" Islam? Imams who issue fatwas have followers. Those who have issued fatwas condoning or even praising the terrorist attacks are not preaching to empty mosques, for individual Muslims can easily see how their teachings reflect the Qur'an and the life of Muhammad. Thus, the Western view of peaceful Islam as having been "hijacked" by terrorists is simplistic and superficial—and the West's current sanguinity toward Islam could turn out to be fatally unwise.

The fastest-growing religion in the world today, Islam now counts among its adherents one out of every five people on earth. President Bush thus has very good reasons to try to encourage a belief that the terrorists are but a tiny minority among these hundreds of millions of Muslims. He is prudent to emphasize the existence of moderate elements in Islam, and to play up the extent of their influence in the Muslim world. No European or American in his right mind wants Osama bin Laden's vision of a war between the West and the entirety of Islam to become a reality.

But the number of terrorist sympathizers in Muslim countries is considerable. Middle East analyst Daniel Pipes estimates it as between 100 million and 150 million people.[76] This doesn't mean that the remaining 850 to 900 million Muslims around the world are all peace-loving. Granted, people find it wearying to live in a state of constant conflict, and so they settle down to lead ordinary lives. But in Islam, ordinary life can always be disrupted by the call of religion. Radical Muslims have at times treated nonradicals as one large sleeper cell that can be activated by a summons to the full practice of their religion. This is illustrated by a chilling story from the Ottoman Empire of the late nineteenth century:

Then one night, my husband came home and told me that the padisha had sent word that we were to kill all the Christians in our village, and that we would have to kill our neighbours. I was very angry, and told him that I did not care who gave such orders, they were wrong. These neighbours had always been kind to us, and if he dared to kill them Allah would pay us out. I tried all I could to stop him, but he killed them—killed them with his own hand.[77]

In this light, the number of terrorists and their sympathizers is likely to grow beyond Pipes' 100 to 150 million. In a very real sense this group is what the less militant majority considers to be the conscience of the *umma*. They are the people who actually dare to do what Allah said to do, whatever the cost. The average Muslim can easily find enough in the Qur'an at least to discourage him from condemning them. He can read that the holy book instructs him to kill unbelievers, and conclude that Khomeini, bin Laden and the like are the true Muslims, just as they claim to be.

For all too many, being a serious Muslim means doing Allah's work by any means necessary. Of course, most Muslims will never be terrorists. The problem is that for all its schisms, sects and multiplicity of voices, Islam's violent elements are rooted in its central texts. It is unlikely that the voices of moderation will ultimately silence the militants, because the militants will always be able to make the case that they are standing for the true expression of the faith. Liberal Muslims have not established a viable alternative interpretation of the relevant verses in the Qur'an. "When liberal Muslims declare that Sept. 11 was an atrocity contrary to the Koran," observes Farrukh Dhondy, "the majority of Muslims around the world don't believe them. They accept the interpretation of fundamentalists, whom liberal Muslims have allowed to remain unchallenged."[78]

This is why the Bush/Blair cure for terrorism may end up being worse than ineffectual. The Islam that the West embraces in order to co-opt bin Laden today may be the Islam that assaults the West tomorrow. This is not idle fear-mongering. Taheri points out that "the Muslim world today is full of bigotry, fanaticism, hypocrisy and plain ignorance—all of which create a breeding ground for criminals like bin Laden."[79] Violent Islam has the enemy (us) and the scriptural justification (in the Qur'an) to keep pushing until they win—that is, until the West is Islamicized. And moderate Islam is essentially powerless to stop it.

Please put me on your mailing list

for future announcements.

Name
_____

Company
_____

Address
_____

City, State, Zip
_____

E-mail
_____

ENCOUNTER BOOKS
665 Third Street
Suite 330
San Francisco, CA 94107-1951

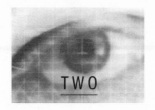

TWO

Does Islam Promote and Safeguard Sound Moral Values?

MUSLIMS STILL BRISTLE AT THE OLD European Christian term for their religion: "Muhammadan." This was one of the first things my earliest Muslim acquaintances hastened to assure me: "We do not worship Muhammad. It is an insult to call us Muhammadans." Referring to Muslims by this hated name is to fall once again into the Christian error, as they see it, of deifying one of God's prophets and taking his name for the name of God's cause.

Yet even without being deified, Muhammad wields enormous influence down through the history of Islam. Muslims revere him above all other men. Throughout the world, Muslims show tremendous respect and genuine affection for the Prophet. By all accounts, he was an exceptionally charismatic and appealing man who won the hearts of the men and women who followed him. He was charming, delightfully down-to-earth, and full of vigor and zest for life. His courage and cunning made him one of the most successful generals in history.

But for Muslims, he is even more than all this: he is the supreme model for human behavior. As Seyyed Hossein Nasr remarks:

> It may be said that the Prophet is the perfection of both the norm of the human collectivity and the human individual, the norm for the perfect social life and the prototype and guide for the individual's spiritual life.... He is both the Universal Man and the Primordial Man (*al-insan al-qadim*). As the Universal Man he is the totality of which we are a part and in which we participate; as the Primordial Man he is that original perfection with respect to which we are a decadence and a falling away.[1]

The great Persian poet and revered Muslim saint Sheikh Moslehedin Saadi Shirazi summed it up succinctly, addressing Muhammad: "In short,

after God you are the greatest."[2] Professor Akbar S. Ahmed of Cambridge
concurs:

> As the Prophet is the messenger, the Quran is the message of God. Together
> they provide the basis for the ideal type of Muslim behaviour and
> thought.... The Prophet himself had said in his last sermon: "I leave
> behind me two things, the Quran and my example the *sunnah* [traditions
> about the words and deeds of the Prophet], and if you follow these you
> will never go astray."[3]

So it is essential for anyone trying to understand Islam to look
closely at the figure of Muhammad. From Tehran to Toronto, from Dar
es Salaam to Des Moines, Muslims emulate him today. As the Universal and Primordial Man, he offers a unique view of Islamic morality incar-
nated in its purest form.

But this undertaking may be more challenging than it initially
seems. Nasr says, "it is in a sense easier for a non-Muslim to see the spiritual radiance of Christ or even medieval saints, Christian or Muslim,
than that of the Prophet, although the Prophet is the supreme saint in
Islam without whom there would have been no sanctity whatsoever."[4]
It's hard to see Muhammad's sanctity, Nasr explains, because he is fundamentally different from the central figures of other religions:

> If the contour of the personality of the Prophet is to be understood, he
> should not be compared to Christ or the Buddha whose messages were
> meant primarily for saintly men and who founded communities based
> on monastic life which later became the norm of entire societies. Rather,
> because of his dual function as "king" and "prophet," as the guide of men
> in this world and the hereafter, the Prophet should be compared to the
> prophet-kings of the Old Testament, to David and Solomon, and espe-
> cially to Abraham himself.[5]

Nasr's assessment of Christ's mission is, of course, highly debatable, but
his point about Muhammad is clear: the prophet of Islam cannot be
regarded as an ascetic holy man who renounced this world in search of
a better one, but as a man very much *of* this world, a leader of men in
the great cause of Allah.

Fair enough. Certainly Muhammad was no ascetic. Even in the
heaven that he imagined, as we've seen, the pleasures of the flesh were
paramount. The righteous "shall recline on couches lined with thick

brocade.... Therein are bashful virgins whom neither man nor jinnee [spirit beings] will have touched before.... Virgins as fair as coral and rubies" (Sura 55:54, 56, 58). (No mention is made in the Qur'an of what heaven will be like for women.)

How Allah Cared for His Prophet

At a point in Muhammad's life when he already had nine wives and numerous concubines, Allah gave him special permission to collect as many women as he wished:

> Prophet, We have made lawful to you the wives to whom you have granted dowries and the slave-girls whom God has given you as booty; the daughters of your paternal and maternal uncles and of your paternal and maternal aunts who fled with you; and any believing woman who gives herself to the Prophet and whom the Prophet wishes to take in marriage. This privilege is yours alone, being granted to no other believer. (Sura 33:50)

The circumstances of this revelation show a great deal about Muhammad. The Prophet had adopted a former Christian slave, Zayd ibn Haritha, as his son, and married him to a woman named Zaynab bint Jahsh. This marriage was unhappy. According to early Muslim sources (as retold by historian Maxime Rodinson):

> One day Muhammad knocked on the door, looking for Zayd. He was not at home; but Zaynab met him in a state of undress and asked him in. After all, he was as father and mother to her. Muhammad declined but the wind lifted the curtain, evidently while she was hurriedly dressing. He fled in some confusion, muttering something which she did not quite catch. All she heard was: "Praise be to Allah the Most High! Praise be to Allah who changes men's hearts!"[6]

Zaynab was, by all accounts, spectacularly beautiful, and obviously Muhammad noticed.

As for Zayd, he took this with equanimity. "Messenger of Allah," he said to Muhammad, "it has come to my ears that you went to my house. Why did you not go in? Are you not father and mother to me, O Messenger of Allah? Can it be that Zaynab found favour with you? If that is so, I will part from her!"

Muhammad responded, "Keep your wife for yourself."

But that was not the end of the matter. Soon Allah himself, ever attentive to the needs of his Prophet, intervened:

> You [Muhammad] said to the man [Zayd] whom God and yourself have favoured: "Keep your wife and have fear of God." You sought to hide in your heart what God was to reveal [i.e., your attraction to Zaynab]. You were afraid of man, although it would have been more proper to fear God. And when Zayd divorced his wife, We gave her to you in marriage, so that it should become legitimate for true believers to wed the wives of their adopted sons if they divorced them. God's will must needs be done. (Sura 33:37)

And so Muhammad married Zaynab. To forestall, or answer, any criticism from the community, the Qur'an then enjoins: "No blame shall be attached to the Prophet for doing what is sanctioned for him by God" (Sura 33:38). The Muslim scholar Caesar Farah explains:

> A study of Muhammad's marital inclinations reveals that . . . pity and elementary concern prompted him in later years to take on wives who were neither beautiful nor rich, but mostly old widows. . . . His marriage to Zaynab, wife of his adopted son, was the result of her unhappy marital relationship with Zayd. Both she and her family, the noble of Hashim and Quraysh, frowned upon a marriage to a freed slave. Muhammad, however, was determined to establish the legitimacy and right to equal treatment of the adopted in Islam.[7]

He was determined, that is, until the revelation came from Allah indicating that he should marry Zaynab. Then what could he do but obey?

But this was not a marriage to someone who was "neither beautiful nor rich." Zaynab, as Farah acknowledges, was nobly born, and despite later Muslim commentators' attempts to downplay her looks on account of her "advanced" age of thirty-five, all the early accounts say she was beautiful. According to Rodinson, "the Arabic histories and traditional texts . . . stress Muhammad's disturbed state of mind after his glimpse of Zaynab in a state of undress; it is they that describe her remarkable beauty."[8] One of Muhammad's other wives, Aisha, bears witness as well, saying, "Zainab was competing with me (in her beauty and the Prophet's love)."[9]

It is easy to conclude from these incidents (and others that we'll recount shortly) that prophethood was exceedingly comfortable for

Muhammad. He could indulge himself in any way he wished, and Allah would supply divine sanction for his behavior, no matter how egregious.

Defenders of Christianity as far back as al-Kindi, who wrote an apology for the Christian faith against Islam in the ninth century, have compared the libertine Muhammad unfavorably with Jesus and Christian ascetics.[10] At this, Muslims cry foul. Nasr explains that Muhammad's marriages "are not at all signs of his lenience vis-à-vis the flesh. During the period of youth, when the passions are strongest, the Prophet lived with only one wife who was much older than he and also underwent long periods of sexual abstinence. And as a prophet many of his marriages were political ones which, in the prevalent social structure of Arabia, guaranteed the consolidation of the newly founded Muslim community."[11]

Yet Muhammad's self-control in his youth says nothing about his behavior as an older man. After all, Henry VIII had no trouble becoming an elderly libertine. Moreover, it's hard to see how Muhammad's divinely certified sexual access to the daughters of his uncles and aunts, as well as to "any believing woman who gives herself to the Prophet and whom the Prophet wishes to take in marriage," would guarantee "the consolidation of the newly founded Muslim community," as Nasr claims.

Political stratagems are hard to find also in the celebrated incident that forms the background of Sura 66 in the Qur'an. Muhammad's wife Hafsa found him in bed with yet another woman, Mary the Copt (a Christian girl), on the day allotted to Hafsa. Furious, she enlisted the help of another of Muhammad's wives, Aisha, and confronted the Prophet. Muhammad sheepishly promised to avoid Mary.[12] But again Allah intervened:

> Prophet, why do you prohibit that which God has made lawful to you, in seeking to please your wives? God is forgiving and merciful. God has given you absolution from such oaths.... If you two [Hafsa and Aisha] turn to God in repentance (for your hearts have sinned) you shall be pardoned; but if you conspire against him, know that God is his protector, and Gabriel, and the righteous among the faithful. The angels too are his helpers. It may well be that, if he divorce you, his Lord will give him in your place better wives than yourselves, submissive to God and full of faith, devout, penitent, obedient, and given to fasting; both formerly-wedded and virgins. (Sura 66:1–5)[13]

Of course, it may be that Muhammad sincerely believed Almighty God was granting him special privileges as his chosen prophet. But in any case, the effect on Islam has been deleterious. Men who look to Muhammad as an example, whether they marry many wives or not, find nothing in him of the mutuality, self-giving and self-sacrifice that most Westerners assume should be part of marriage. Certainly Muhammad was kind to his wives, but they were in effect little more than his servants, on hand to cook his food and meet his sexual demands. Most in the modern West would disapprove, for here, Christian ideals of marriage are still pervasive, even among non-Christians and post-Christian secularists.

The Importance of the Sunnah

The Sunnah of the Prophet—early Muslim traditions about the sayings and doings of Muhammad—raise even more serious questions about his status as a moral example for all Muslims. In Islam, these texts have a status just below the Qur'an, and because they are much more voluminous and detailed than the Qur'an, they are the main source for the Sharia, or Islamic law, and much of Islamic practice. The Islamic scholar Mohammed Nasir-ul-Deen al-Albani states the traditional Muslim position when he says, "There is no way to understand the Qur'an correctly except in association with the interpretation of the Sunnah."[14] According to another scholar, Wael B. Hallaq, that "the Sunna is binding on Muslims has ... been demonstrated by Shafi'i (as well as by later jurists) on the basis of the Quran which enjoins Muslims to obey the Prophet and not to swerve from his ranks."[15]

Western academics have elaborated numerous theories about the provenance and importance of the Sunnah, but these have not had much impact in the House of Islam itself. Some rigorist movements within Islam have discounted the Sunnah in their zeal to emphasize the uniqueness and centrality of the Qur'an, but this view has not displaced the Sunnah from its traditional standing in Islamic theology. A Muslim scholar, Abu Abdir Rahmaan, says it is Satan who has suggested "to the hearts of some of the Muslims that the Qur'an, as Glorious as it is, is sufficient enough alone as guidance for Mankind. Meaning that the Sunnah, or way of the Messenger of Allah ... is something that can be left off, or abandoned. Without a doubt this is a growing disease that has no place in this wonderful way of life of ours."[16] In his guide to the study of the Qur'an, Ahmad Von Denffer sums up the prevailing view: "There is agreement among Muslim scholars that the contents of the *sunna* are also from Allah. Hence they have described it as also [after the Qur'an, that is] being the result of some form of inspiration."[17]

There's a tremendous proliferation of these traditions, including numerous forgeries. Western scholars such as Ignaz Goldhizer have demonstrated that there is an astonishingly high number of these inauthentic tales about Muhammad. Goldhizer speculates about the motives behind them:

> It is a matter for psychologists to find and analyze the motives of the soul which made such forgeries acceptable to pious minds as morally justified means of furthering a cause. . . . The most favourable explanation which one can give of these phenomena is presumably to assume that the support of a new doctrine . . . with the authority of Muhammad was the form in which it was thought good to express the high religious justification of that doctrine. The end sanctified the means.[18]

Faced with a situation that was rapidly spinning out of control, several Muslims relatively early in the history of Islam assembled collections of accounts *(hadiths)* of the Prophet's words and deeds that were considered more or less definitive and authentic.[19] Six collections were almost universally recognized early on, and continue to be regarded today, as the most reliable, generally free of forgeries and inaccuracies. These were given the collective name of *Sahih Sittah*, the six authentic and trustworthy collections. (*Sahih* means "sound" or "reliable.") These are *Sahih Bukhari*, that is, the collection of hadiths made by the imam Muhammad ibn Ismail al-Bukhari (810–870); *Sahih Muslim*, a similar collection compiled by Muslim ibn al-Hajjaj al-Qushayri (821–875); the *Sunan* of Abu Dawud as-Sijistani (d. 888); and works by Muhammad ibn Majah (d. 896), Abi ʿEesaa Muhammad at-Tirmidhi (824–893), and Ahmad ibn Shuʾayb an-Nasai (d. 915).

The appearance of a hadith in one of these respected sources, however, isn't enough by itself to guarantee its authenticity. Muslims classify hadiths variously as "sound" *(sahih),* "good" or "approved" *(hasan),* "weak" *(daʾif),* and "forged" *(maudu').* These categories are based on how many times a hadith is repeated in the traditions, how many different sources report it, its agreement (or disagreement) with the teachings of the Qur'an, the strength of the chain of reporters that link it to the Prophet, and other factors.

The fact that the entire collections by Bukhari and Muslim bear the name *Sahih* is one indication of their prestige among Muslims. These collections "have enjoyed an especially high status as authoritative sources," says Muslim scholar John Esposito.[20] The English translator of *Sahih Muslim,* Abdul Hamid Siddiqi, agrees: "The collections by Bukhari and Muslim are particularly held in high esteem." He explains that the hadiths "which are recognized as absolutely authentic are included in these two excellent compilations," and that "even of these two, Bukhari's occupies a higher position in comparison to Muslim's."[21]

Indeed, Dr. Muhammad Muhsin Khan of the Islamic University in Medina declares that "many religious scholars of Islam tried to find fault in the great remarkable collection *Sahih Al-Bukhari,* but without success. It is for this reason, they unanimously agreed that the most authentic book after the Book of Allah [the Qur'an] is *Sahih Al-Bukhari.*" He explains that the imam Bukhari dreamt that he was "standing in front of Prophet Muhammad having a fan in his hand and driving away the flies from the Prophet," and after this dream was interpreted as meaning that he would "drive away the falsehood asserted against the Prophet," he spent his life distinguishing authentic hadiths from forgeries. Bukhari ultimately winnowed down the 300,000 he collected to the slightly over 2,000 that he includes (some several times) in *Sahih Bukhari.*[22]

Even if a hadith is included in Bukhari or Muslim, some Muslim scholar somewhere may classify it as "weak" or "forged." Still, these collections carry such weight in Islam that virtually everything in them bears a presumption of reliability and authenticity. Thus, whether the stories to follow are classified as weak or strong or somewhere in between, their place in Bukhari and/or Muslim gives them an immediate claim to reliability and an undeniable influence—an influence that is highly damaging.

Child Brides

Given the stature that the traditions of the *Sahih Bukhari* and the *Sahih Muslim* have in Islam, it is worth noting what they say about Muhammad and his child bride Aisha.

Bukhari lets Aisha recount in her own words how she came to be the bride of the Prophet:

Narrated Aisha: My marriage (wedding) contract with the Prophet was written when I was a girl of six (years). [Apparently three years then elapsed.] . . . My mother, Umm Ruman, came to me while I was playing in a swing with some of my girl friends. She called me, and I went to her, not knowing what she wanted to do to me. She caught me by the hand and made me stand at the door of the house. I was breathless then, and when my breathing became normal, she took some water and rubbed my face and head with it. Then she took me into the house. There in the house I saw some Ansari [recent Muslim converts] women who said, "Best wishes and Allah's Blessing and a good luck." Then she entrusted me to them and they prepared me (for the marriage). Unexpectedly Allah's Messenger came to me in the forenoon and my mother handed me over to him, and at that time I was a girl of nine years of age.[23]

At this point, according to the best Muslim sources, the Prophet was a little over fifty.[24]

This marriage at least could have been politically motivated, as Nasr maintains. Muhammad may have married Aisha to cement the loyalty of her father, who was his principal disciple and who had earlier agreed to give Aisha's hand in marriage to a pagan. Even if that were his only reason to take his child bride, however, surely he could have waited until Aisha was older to consummate the marriage. But Bukhari reports: "Narrated ʿUrwa: 'The Prophet wrote the (marriage contract) with Aisha while she was six years old and consummated his marriage with her while she was nine years old and she remained with him for nine years (i.e. till his death).' "[25]

Of course, this was not unusual by the prevailing standards. Muslims in Muhammad's day thought nothing of marrying girls who had just begun menstruating—and even girls who had not yet reached that point. Indeed, this practice was common enough that, after the Qur'an instructs that a man must wait three months before divorcing a wife who has ceased menstruating (in order to make sure she isn't pregnant), there is this additional command: "The same shall apply to those who have not yet menstruated" (Sura 65:4). Those who have not yet menstruated! One may imagine that the prospects of a prepubescent divorcee would have been rather dim.

Problems arise when behavior like this is abstracted from its historical context and proposed as a paradigm for human behavior in all times and places. The results can be seen all over the *umma*. In imitation of the Prophet, many Muslims have taken child brides. The Ayatollah Khomeini himself, at age twenty-eight, married a ten-year-old girl.[26] She became pregnant at eleven, but miscarried. Khomeini called marriage to a girl before her first menstrual period "a divine blessing," and he advised the faithful: "Do your best to ensure that your daughters do not see their first blood in your house."[27]

This practice continues to this day, despite the severe injuries girls often incur from early intercourse and childbirth. One example of its prevalence came from an anguished young Muslim who wrote in to a fatwa website, asking if he could legitimately marry a girl even though he lusted after her mother. "I have looked at my mother-in-law (Auntie) with lust at her breasts, thinking that her daughter when she will grow up will have breasts like that etc."[28] Note that he is imagining what his fiancée will look like when she reaches sexual maturity! The fact that he is about to marry a child doesn't trouble either him or the imam he is consulting.

The United Nations Children's Fund (UNICEF) reports that child marriage is by no means a minor problem today; in fact, over half of the girls in the Muslim strongholds of Afghanistan and Bangladesh are married before they reach the age of eighteen.[29] In early 2002, researchers in refugee camps in Afghanistan and Pakistan found half the girls married by age thirteen. In an Afghan refugee camp, more than two out of three second-grade girls were either married or betrothed, and virtually all the older girls were already married. One ten-year-old was engaged to a man of sixty.[30] Likewise, *Time* magazine reports:

> In Iran the legal age for marriage is nine for girls, 14 for boys. The law has occasionally been exploited by pedophiles, who marry poor young girls from the provinces, use and then abandon them. In 2000 the Iranian Parliament voted to raise the minimum age for girls to 14, but this year, a legislative oversight body dominated by traditional clerics vetoed the move. An attempt by conservatives to abolish Yemen's legal minimum age of 15 for girls failed, but local experts say it is rarely enforced anyway. (The onset of puberty is considered an appropriate time for a marriage to be consummated.)[31]

Apparently these child brides need a considerable amount of discipline to keep them in line. According to one researcher, "in Egypt 29 percent of married adolescents have been beaten by their husbands; of those, 41 percent were beaten during pregnancy. A study in Jordan indicated that 26 percent of reported cases of domestic violence were committed against wives under 18."[32]

Temporary Marriage

The Prophet also brought to life a notion that American high school boys have only been able to fantasize about: temporary marriage (*mut'a*). According to Bukhari: "Narrated Jabir bin ʿAbdullah and Salama bin Al-Akwa': While we were in an army, Allah's Messenger came to us and said, 'You have been allowed to do the *Mut'a* (marriage), so do it.'"[33] The parenthesis is in the original, and a footnote further explains that this Arabic word means "temporary marriage for a limited period of time." (It also means simply "pleasure.")

Another hadith explains that "their marriage should last for three nights, and if they like to continue, they can do so, and if they want to separate, they can do so."[34] The editors of *Sahih Bukhari* also note that "this type of marriage was allowed in the early days of Islam in cases of necessity, but the Prophet finally prohibited it forever."[35] However, Shi'a Muslims in Iran dispute with Sunnis on this, and it is a relatively conventional practice in the Islamic Republic. Its defenders point to Sura 4:24, translated thus: "To women whom you choose in temporary and conditional *(muwaqat* and *muta'a)* marriage, give their dowry, as a duty."[36] (The Arabic words are supplied in the translation as quoted.)

Shi'ite apologists argue that the *mut'a* is an acceptable Islamic method of avoiding fornication, a wise provision by the Prophet of a sexual outlet that is morally superior to masturbation. The fifth imam of Shi'a Islam is said to have remarked: "If the second Caliph had not prohibited temporary marriages, no Muslim, save perchance a few utterly degraded lewd fellows of the baser sort, would have ever committed fornication."[37]

Perhaps. But what is the essential difference between fornication and temporary marriage? The giving of the dowry? If that's it, how then is this practice to be distinguished from prostitution—especially given that in Iran, contracts for temporary marriage can be for as short a duration as one hour?

"Temporary wives" congregate in seminary towns (such as the holy city of Qom), which are full of restless theological students away from their wives for extended periods. These students know what temporary marriage is for. At the dawn of the twentieth century, the seminarian Aqa Najafi Quchani wrote a vivid account of a temporary marriage:

> ... Fortunately, the woman was at home and I married her for a while. When I had quietened my desire and enjoyed the pleasure of the flesh from my lawful income, I gave the woman the *qeran* [an old Iranian monetary unit].... It is reported that the Imams have said that whoever makes love legitimately has in effect killed an infidel.[38] That means killing the lascivious spirit.[39] It is obvious that when a *talabeh* [student] has no problem with the lower half of his body he is happier than a king.[40]

Most "temporary wives" in Iran, according to Amir Taheri, were "young widows, who used the opportunity for making ends meet." But if they became pregnant in a temporary marriage, they would be worse off than before, for the contract gave them no claim on their "temporary husband" for child support.[41]

The issue of temporary marriage is complicated, but the potential for abuse is obvious. It is difficult to see how women would be safeguarded from being essentially used and abandoned. One defender of temporary marriage points out:

> There exists no law anywhere in the world which is not twisted by the wicked to their own ends and against its original purpose. This is true of laws which are of the greatest benefit to society. The law of "temporary marriage" is one such. It should be backed with the full authority of the state. Those who misuse it should be punished. Those who use it right should be supported and aided in their righteous living.[42]

It is true that any good law can be abused; but some are more susceptible to abuse than others. Muhammad's "wise" provision for temporary marriage is susceptible to abuse to an extent that's truly outstanding.

Take Any Slave Girl

If the potential for abuse in temporary marriage is great enough, even worse is the license that Muhammad allowed for rape—at least in certain circumstances. I have already noted that the Qur'an permits Muslim men to have intercourse with their slave girls as well as their wives. The holy book, moreover, rules out any exception for slave girls who happen to be married: "Forbidden to you are your mothers, your daughters, your sisters, your paternal and maternal aunts.... Also married women, except those whom you own as slaves. Such is the decree of God" (Sura 4:23–24).

Numerous hadiths make it clear that these slave girls were usually the captives of war. Muhammad himself did not disdain to find wives and consorts this way. After one successful battle, he told one of his fellows, "Go and take any slave girl." But someone else informed the Prophet that the slave girl thus selected was "the chief mistress of (the ladies) of the tribes of Quraiza and An-Nadir"—therefore "she befits none but you."[43] The Prophet then changed his mind and took the girl for himself. His followers wondered if she would become his wife or his slave: "The Muslims said amongst themselves, 'Will she (i.e. Safiya) be one of the mothers of the believers, (i.e. one of the wives of the Prophet) or just (a lady captive) of what his right-hand possesses?' "[44] In this case, he made the lady one of his wives.

After one battle, some of Muhammad's men presented him with an ethical question, as Bukhari reports:

> Narrated Abu Said Al-Khudri that during the battle with Bani Al-Mustaliq they (Muslims) captured some females and intended to have sexual relations with them without impregnating them. So they asked the Prophet about *coitus interruptus.* The Prophet said, "It is better that you should not do it, for Allah has written whom He is going to create till the Day of Resurrection." Qaza'a said, "I heard Abu Sa'id saying that the Prophet said, 'No soul is ordained to be created but Allah will create it.' "[45]

When Muhammad said "It is better that you should not do it," he was referring to *coitus interruptus,* not to raping their captives. He took that for granted. These men were concerned with one moral question, yet neither they nor the Prophet seemed at all troubled about the more important question concerning what was, essentially, rape. These women had just suffered the trauma of seeing their fathers and brothers murdered, their homes vandalized and perhaps burned to the ground, their possessions seized or destroyed. Then they themselves were taken captive. It just doesn't seem to be the right setting for a "consensual relationship," as they say these days.

In any case, the Qur'an is silent about the preferences of the girls. As we'll see more fully later on, neither the Qur'an nor the traditions of the Prophet have provided adequately for protecting women from rape. There is no clear definition of the crime in the Sharia, and the rules of evidence dictate that the testimony of the victim has no weight because she is female; rape can be proven only by the testimony of four male eye-witnesses to the act itself.[46]

In other words, rape can almost never be proven. Not surprisingly, women have been prosecuted under Sharia adultery laws when they have actually been the *victims* of rape.

Here Muhammad's lack of respect for women takes its toll in human lives: his own example, as well as the rules of evidence that he established for Islam, leave them at the mercy of anyone who chooses to take advantage of them.

No Mercy to the Unbelievers

Related to the jeopardy of women is the problem of Muhammad's brutality in warfare and in his general dealings with his enemies. Here again he presents a figure of a prophet quite different from the Western model. The ultimate Western prototype of the prophet/king, of course, is still Jesus. Some apologists for Islam promoted the idea of Muhammad as a sort of Arabian Jesus—more robust, as required by the harsh climate of the desert, than the Europeanized figure of the One that Julian the Apostate called the "Pale Galilean," but like him, essentially a prince of peace.

Because of the role this analogy plays in modern Western assessments of Muhammad, it is useful to look at Muhammad's actual behavior in comparison with that of Jesus, which is relatively familiar even to post-Christian Westerners.

Muslims themselves acknowledge that the hallmark of Jesus' teaching is mercy. The Qur'an says so: "We sent other apostles, and after those Jesus the Son of Mary. We gave him the Gospel, and put compassion and mercy in the hearts of his followers" (Sura 57:27). It is difficult to picture Jesus saying these words from the Qur'an: "When you meet the unbelievers in the battlefield, strike off their heads and, when you have laid them low, bind your captives firmly" (Sura 47:4).

Indeed, the contrasts between Jesus and Muhammad are many and obvious. For example, here is how Jesus dealt with rejection and unbelief in one case:

When the days drew near for him to be received up, he set his face to go to Jerusalem. And he sent messengers ahead of him, who went and entered a village of the Samaritans, to make ready for him; but the people would not receive him, for his face was set toward Jerusalem. And when his disciples James and John saw it, they said, "Lord, do you want us to bid fire to come down from Heaven and consume them?" But he turned and rebuked them. (Luke 9:51–55)

The example that the Prophet of Islam gave of how to react to opposition is quite different. At one point, two young men murdered one of Muhammad's fiercest opponents, Abu Jahl, in cold blood as he was "walking amongst the people." Abu Jahl's crime? One of the murderers explained: "I have been informed that he abuses Allah's Apostle."

Just as in the *coitus interruptus* case, when his focus was on the completion of the sexual act rather than on the moral implications of rape, here Muhammad was concerned not with the murder, but merely with the proper distribution of the spoils: "Allah's Apostle asked, 'Which of you has killed him?' Each of them said, 'I have killed him.' Allah's Apostle asked, 'Have you cleaned your swords?' They said, 'No.' He then looked at their swords and said, 'No doubt, you both have killed him and the spoils of the deceased will be given to Mu'adh bin ʿAmr bin Al-Jamuh,'" one of the murderers.[47]

Another enemy of the Prophet, named Umaiya, provoked a hadith that establishes, in a chilling fashion, Muhammad's unimpeachable veracity. In the course of a dispute with Umaiya, the Muslim Saʿd bin Muʿadh cried: "Be away from me, for I have heard Muhammad saying that he will kill you."

Umaiya responded, "Will he kill me?"

When Saʿd answered that he would indeed, Umaiya showed that even though he opposed Muhammad, he knew his character: "Umaiya said, 'By Allah! When Muhammad says a thing, he never tells a lie.'"

Umaiya recounted the incident to his wife, who agreed: "She said, By Allah! Muhammad never tells a lie." Sure enough, at the Battle of Badr, Umaiya was done in, although the hadith is silent about whether or not Muhammad himself did the deed. All it says is that "Allah got him killed."[48]

Muhammad's truth-telling is a preoccupation of many hadiths. In another, the Prophet climbed a mountain and began calling the various tribes of the Quraysh, a people who opposed him. When they assembled, he asked them, "Suppose I told you that there is an (enemy) cavalry in the valley intending to attack you, would you believe me?"

They knew they were standing before an honest man, and so responded, "Yes, for we have not found you telling anything other than the truth."

Muhammad replied, "I am a warner to you in face of a terrific punishment."

This pious warning annoyed one man of the Quraysh, Abu Lahab, who doubted Muhammad's prophethood. Abu Lahab was Muhammad's uncle, but after all, no prophet is honored in his own country. He called out to Muhammad, "May your hands perish all this day. Is it for this purpose you have gathered us?"[49]

Whereupon the Prophet received a new revelation from Allah: "May the hands of Abu Lahab perish! May he himself perish! Nothing shall his wealth and gains avail him. He shall be burnt in a flaming fire, and his wife, laden with faggots, shall have a rope of fibre around her neck!" (Sura III:1–5) A hadith adds, "and he indeed perished,"[50] but doesn't specify how.

Although he never told a lie, Muhammad didn't hesitate to grant those close to him permission to do so for a good cause—in this case, another murder: "Allah's Apostle said, 'Who is willing to kill Ka'b bin al-Ashraf who has hurt Allah and His Apostle?'"

Ka'b bin al-Ashraf was a poet from a Jewish tribe in the area. He seems to have "hurt" Allah and his Prophet with his words only. *Sahih Muslim* specifies the offense this way: "He has maligned Allah, the Exalted, and His Messenger."[51]

The story continues: "Thereupon Muhammad bin Maslama [one of the followers of the Prophet] got up saying, 'O Allah's Apostle! Would you like that I kill him?'

"The Prophet said, 'Yes.'

"Muhammad bin Maslama said, 'Then allow me to say a (false) thing (i.e. to deceive Ka'b).'

"The Prophet said, 'You may say it.'"

The hadith goes on to recount how Ka'b was deceived and murdered by Muhammad bin Maslama.[52] But after all, according to the Prophet, "war is deceit."[53]

On another occasion the Prophet was at prayer when his enemies committed a particularly vile deed, evocative of the barbarism of the

place: "Narrated ᶜAbdullah: While the Prophet was in the state of pros-
tration, surrounded by a group of people from [the] *Mushrikun*
[unbelievers] of the Quraish, ᶜUqba bin Abi Mu'ait came and brought
the intestines of a camel and threw them on the back of the Prophet."
The great man found in this undeniable humiliation no occasion for
mercy:

> The Prophet did not raise his head from prostration till Fatima (i.e. his
> daughter) came and removed those intestines from his back, and invoked
> evil on whoever had done (that evil deed). The Prophet said, "O Allah!
> Destroy the chiefs of Quraish, O Allah! Destroy Abu Jahl bin Hisham,
> ᶜUtba bin Rabi'a, Shaiba bin Rabi'a, ᶜUqba bin Abi Mu'ait, ᶜUmaiya bin
> Khalaf (or Ubai bin Kalaf)." Later on I saw all of them killed during the
> battle of Badr and their bodies were thrown into a well except the body
> of Umaiya or Ubai, because he was a fat man, and when he was pulled,
> the parts of his body got separated before he was thrown into the well.[54]

A shorter version of what seems to be the same incident is even
more unsettling, as Muhammad goes one better than Jesus' cursing of
the fig tree in demonstrating his awesome power: "Narrated ᶜAbdullah
bin Mas'ud: The Prophet faced the Ka'ba and invoked evil on some people of Quraish, on Shaiba bin Rabi'a, ᶜUtba bin Rabi'a, Al-Walid bin
ᶜUtba and Abu Jahl bin Hisham. I bear witness, by Allah, that I saw them
all dead, putrefied by the sun as that day was a very hot day."[55]

Muhammad vs. the Qur'an?

Are these stories from the hadiths in harmony with the Qur'an? Actually, they fit in quite well with the book that commands the Prophet to
"deal rigorously" with unbelievers (Sura 9:73). This he did. When the
Muslims defeated the Jewish tribe of Bani Qurayzah, he ordered that
trenches be dug in what had been the marketplace of their town. Then
the men of the tribe, seven hundred in all, were made to sit alongside
the trenches, where the Muslims beheaded them. The women and children, in accord with what Muhammad called "the judgment of God from
above the seven heavens," were enslaved.[56]

The forthright bloodlust and barbarism of stories like these—and
there are many others like them—is not exclusive to the Muslims of
Muhammad's day. Christian armies of that era behaved much the same

way, particularly the Crusaders whose memory inflames Osama bin Laden and other terrorists to this day. But here again, Christians have no justification in their Scriptures or anywhere else to behave this way. Jesus did say, "I have not come to bring peace, but a sword" (Matthew 10:34), yet he was speaking in metaphor, and he forbade his followers to fight when he was arrested (Luke 22:51).

Muslims, on the other hand, have no verses to mitigate the violent passages from the Qur'an and the Sunnah. To minimize these stories of Muhammad's bloody escapades by referring to the historical context in which they occurred is not compelling, because as we have seen, Muslims themselves do not do this. The Qur'an and its Prophet are guides valid for all time. To admit any shame at the bloody exploits of Muhammad or those who emulate him today would be to judge Muhammad. But in Muslim tradition, Muhammad cannot be judged; rather, he is the standard by which all others are judged.

THREE

Does Islam Respect
Human Rights?

LIKE CHRISTIANITY, ISLAM TEACHES THAT ONE God created the heavens and the earth, and all things visible and invisible. Like Christianity, Islam calls out to all people on earth, offering them what it proclaims as the only way to salvation. But while these elements of their faith led Christians—with the help of John Locke and other founding fathers of the Enlightenment—to articulate what the world knows today as fundamental human rights, the same rights which triumphed dramatically in the West have not taken hold in Islam.

Hard-line Muslims have openly admitted this fact. In 1985, Sa'id Raja'i-Khorassani, the permanent delegate to the United Nations from the Islamic Republic of Iran, declared, according to Amir Taheri, that "the very concept of human rights was 'a Judeo-Christian invention' and inadmissible in Islam. . . . According to Ayatollah Khomeini, one of the Shah's 'most despicable sins' was the fact that Iran was one of the original group of nations that drafted and approved the Universal Declaration of Human Rights."[1]

Does God Desire the Death of the Sinner?

Islam's quite different understanding of human rights is manifested in microcosm in the way the Qur'an regards unbelievers. Here Islam sharply divides the world in half, with harsh consequences for non-Muslims. Taheri explains that besides maintaining strict distinctions between men and women, "Islam further divides human beings into two groups: the Muslims and the non-Muslims. All male Muslims are equal and enjoy the same individual and collective rights and privileges. Non-Muslims living in a society where Muslims form the majority and control the state,

57

however, are treated separately."[2] We'll examine the details of this sepa-rate treatment later on; at this point it suffices to note that Muslim soci-ety is divided in such a manner, and this division makes it tough for the concept of universal human rights to gain much of a foothold.

The reasons why are rooted in the Qur'an, which proclaims that "Muhammad is God's Apostle. Those who follow him are ruthless to the unbelievers but merciful to one another" (Sura 48:29). Far from being endowed with unalienable rights according to the Western idea, unbe-lievers in the realm of Islam do not seem to be entitled to anything but hatred and contempt, and ultimately great suffering. A huge portion of the Qur'an is taken up with hellfire-and-brimstone warnings of terrible intensity.

Hell exists in the Christian scheme of things, of course, and is often harrowingly portrayed. Yet Christianity, in contradistinction to Islam, declares unequivocally that God "has no pleasure in the death of any one, says the LORD God; so turn, and live" (Ezekiel 18:32). Moreover, Christian thinkers in most churches and denominations throughout his-tory have regarded hell as a consequence of the sinner's free choice.*

The Qur'an, on the other hand, repeatedly announces that Allah "leads the wrongdoers astray" (Sura 14:28) and "had He pleased, He would have given you guidance all" (Sura 16:9). Evidently he does not so please: the judgment and torture of the wicked is a great preoccupation of the Muslim holy book, dwelt upon with unmistakable relish. The vision of horror is repeated many times. For instance:

> For the wrongdoers We have prepared a fire which will encompass them like the walls of a pavilion. When they cry out for help they shall be show-ered with water as hot as molten brass, which will scald their faces. Evil shall be their drink, dismal their resting-place. (Sura 18:29)[3]

> Those who have denied the Book and the message We sent through Our apostles shall realize the truth hereafter: when, with chains and shackles

---

*The concept of God's leading a wrongdoer astray originally appears in the Old Testament (Exo-dus 9:12 and other passages), but there it refers only to Pharaoh, not to all mankind. St. Paul refers to it in setting forth his doctrine of justification (Romans 9:18), and a recurring strain of Christian thought, running chiefly through St. Augustine of Hippo and John Calvin, has hinted or held outright that God predestines people to Hell. Still, the idea stated so boldly in the Qur'an—that God actually leads people astray—has never been generally accepted in Christianity.

around their necks, they shall be dragged through scalding water and burnt in the fire of Hell. (Sura 40:71)

They that deny Our revelations We will burn in fire. No sooner will their skins be consumed than We shall give them other skins, so that they may truly taste the scourge. God is mighty and wise. (Sura 4:56)

Christianity too has had a full share of fire-and-brimstone preachers, but neither the Bible nor Christian tradition depicts hell with such lurid delight. The paintings of Hieronymous Bosch and the *Divine Comedy* of Dante Alighieri contain some analogous imagery, but neither has ever enjoyed the canonical status of the Qur'an. Indeed, Dante's splendid poem, which no one has ever mistaken for divine revelation, falls within a long tradition of allegory. The Bible itself does contain warnings of hellfire, but these are in no way as graphically detailed as those in the Qur'an, and do not appear in the context of a Divine Will so zealous to punish unbelief as to lead sinners purposely astray.

It is no surprise that this dogma should have implications in the behavior of individual believers. A man who imbibes the words of the Qur'an from his earliest days, memorizing long passages even before he has any idea what it means, singing it, chanting it, repeating it, proclaiming it every day of his life, will unavoidably be influenced by the spirit of the pages. The Muslim world not only welcomes that influence, but even celebrates and glories in it.

The spirit of the Qur'an is one of judgment, not mercy. About the only place where the Qur'an mentions Allah's mercy is the heading of each Sura: "In the Name of Allah, the compassionate, the merciful." Beyond that and scattered passages, the reader will have a hard time finding evidence of his compassion and mercy—at least for non-Muslims.

The pious Muslim is the executor of the divine judgment, at least toward those who war against Muslim armies.

Those that make war against God and His apostle and spread disorder in the land shall be put to death or crucified or have their hands and feet cut off on alternate sides, or be banished from the country. They shall be held up to shame in this world and sternly punished in the hereafter: except those that repent before you reduce them. For you must know that God is forgiving and merciful. (Sura 5:33)

Is this the content of Islamic mercy: accept Islam or suffer banishment, amputation or death by crucifixion?

The Qur'an further enjoins: "Believers, make war on the infidels who dwell around you. Deal firmly with them. Know that God is with the righteous." (Sura 9:123)

And also: "Prophet, make war on the unbelievers and the hypocrites and deal rigorously with them. Hell shall be their home: an evil fate." (Sura 9:73)

Those who reject the message of the Qur'an but live in Muslim societies are entitled to a small number of narrowly delineated rights, as we shall see in more detail later on. Those who resist incorporation into those societies are entitled only to the judgment executed by the good Muslims here on earth and by Allah Himself in the hereafter. Muslim sinners, according to the letter of the Sharia (although, to be sure, this has been interpreted variously in different times and places), deserve not mercy but the harshest of punishments.

The world recoiled when the Taliban began to use a soccer stadium that Western relief agencies had built in Kabul for executions of those who violated Islamic law. When questioned about this horrifying development, a Taliban official simply requested that a Western agency build them a suitable stadium for public executions, so that they could go back to playing soccer in the stadium! He felt no need to apologize for the executions themselves. They were simply the Taliban's Islamic duty.

When Amnesty International lodged a protest, Taliban leader Mullah Muhammad Omar protested in turn. The Pakistani News Network International reported:

> Threatening Amnesty International with grave consequences for criticism of Taliban's human rights, its supreme leader Mullah Omar, has said the student [that is, the Taliban] is simply implementing and observing Islamic injunctions. In an interview with Voice of America, Mullah Omar said Taliban would react sharply if AI continued the criticism. He rejected the AI report as mere allegations. "We are just implementing the divine injunctions," he maintained.[4]

Is it unfair to use the Taliban as exemplar when discussing the fate of human rights under Islam? Maybe it would be if their behavior were unusual, or against the words of the Qur'an. But throughout Islamic history, Muslims have used the plain words of the Qur'an that we have already quoted in order to justify the idea that it isn't a sin to kill non-Muslims.

Opium and the Kafirs

On the issue of drugs, too, the Taliban divides the world into Muslims and non-Muslims. In his seminal study of the Taliban, journalist Ahmed Rashid reports:

> Abdul Rashid, the head of the Taliban's anti-drugs control force in Kandahar, spelt out the nature of his unique job. He is authorized to impose a strict ban on the growing of hashish, "because it is consumed by Afghans and Muslims." But, Rashid tells me without a hint of sarcasm, "Opium is permissible because it is consumed by kafirs [unbelievers] in the West and not by Muslims or Afghans."[5]

This seems to have been a common view among the Taliban. Another Talib named Khaled asked, "Who cares if heroin is wreaking havoc in the West? It doesn't matter; they aren't Muslims."[6]

Meanwhile, a Malaysian Muslim told V. S. Naipaul that believers should not use tobacco, for essentially the same reason that the Taliban encouraged non-Muslims to use opium: "Most of the tobacco manufacturers are Jewish, and in order to destroy the Jews we must not consume their products.... The Jews are the enemies of God."[7]

Many mullahs would be quick to reply that Islam prohibits all drug trafficking, whether to believers or to enemies of God. Yet although what the Taliban did was extreme, it wasn't without support in Islamic thought. After all, what respect do Muslims owe unbelievers? The Qur'an says to fight them and subdue them everywhere. If selling them drugs will do the job, why not? For fourteen hundred years, Muslims have regarded infidels as not entitled to the basic rights and respect owed to Muslims. Why then should the Taliban be expected to subscribe to the Western notion of universal human rights?

The Cost of Conversion

A Muslim convert to Christianity (or to anything else) in a Muslim land forfeits his life. By classical Muslim understanding, the apostate "deserves to die."[8] The full story comes later on, but a few representative details have a place here. In Saudi Arabia and other Muslim countries that follow the strict letter of Islamic law, the Sharia, conversion from Islam is a capital offense. A fine Catholic priest of my acquaintance had to flee Egypt in the 1990s or face almost certain death. His crime? Making converts from Islam.

Even in a relatively open Muslim society like Egypt, Christians live under constant threat. According to Amnesty International, in July 2000 "the Sohag Criminal Court sentenced Sourial Gayed Ishaq, a 37-year-old Coptic Christian, to three years' imprisonment for publicly insulting Islam."[9] This parallels the case of Ayub Masih, who faces execution in Pakistan for allegedly suggesting that a Muslim read Salman Rushdie. Because the testimony of Christians weighs less than that of Muslims, Masih's denials have been discounted.

Nor are Christians the only targets for such punishment; Muslims in minority sects receive hardly more tolerance. On August 10, 1998, Mullah Manon Niazi, the Taliban governor of the Afghan city of Mazar-e Sharif, had this to say about Afghanistan's minority Hazara people, who are not Sunni Muslims like the Taliban, but Shi'ites like the Ayatollah Khomeini: "Hazaras are not Muslim. You can kill them. It is not a sin." This idea is based on the Qur'anic injunction to "slay [unbelievers] wherever you find them" (Sura 2:191; also 4:89). Niazi added the invitation: "Oh Hazaras! Become Muslims and pray God as us."[10] The Taliban massacred large numbers of Hazaras—enough to get the Hazaras listed as victims of genocide by international human rights groups.[11]

Shi'ite Muslims, the largest minority Muslim sect worldwide, are also in danger in Saudi Arabia, the Muslim holy land controlled by Wahhabi Muslims. Amnesty International reports this incident from Saudi Arabia: "ʿAbd al-Karim Mal al Allah, a Shia Muslim, was found guilty of apostasy and executed in 1992. It has been reported that he was told by the judge 'abandon your rejectionist beliefs or I will kill you.'"[12] The situation has not improved since then. Sheikh Ali Khursan, an official of al-Dawa, a Saudi government organization dedicated to promoting Wahhabism, said this of the Shi'ites: "These people are infidels because they do not follow the Sunna [the traditions about Muhammad].... They don't believe that the Quran is complete and they hate the Sunnis."[13] To classify them as infidels is to expose them to a variety of harsh punishments. According to news reports, "Four Shiite high school students in Najran [a Shi'ite city in Saudi Arabia], aged 16 and 17, were arrested after a fight with a Wahhabi instructor who insulted their faith. They received two to four years in jail and 500 to 800 lashes each."[14] Two teachers suspected of fomenting riots among the Shi'ite minority in Saudi Arabia were each sentenced to be given 1,500 lashes, "to be carried out in front of their families, students and other teachers."[15]

Other countries are little better. In the Comoro Islands off Madagascar (home of the "living fossil" fish, the coelacanth), there are no particular incidents of repression against religious minorities to rival those recounted above, for such minorities do not exist: all religious observance outside of Islam is prohibited. Members of other religions aren't even allowed to meet together.

Slavery in the Qur'an

Non-Muslims in at least two Muslim countries, Sudan and Mauritania, also face the threat of slavery. This is an especially touchy issue for Islam, because its apologists often refer to past slavery in the West to compare Islam favorably with Christianity. Yet slaveholding, a topic of perennial reproach in the history of the United States, is today practiced not within the former bounds of Christendom, but *only* in Muslim lands.

Once again, chief responsibility for this must be placed upon the Qur'an. Slavery, especially of war prisoners, is taken for granted throughout the Muslim holy book. The Qur'an casually assumes that a believer will be a slaveowner: "The penalty for a broken oath is the feeding of ten needy men with such food as you normally offer to your own people; or the clothing of ten needy men; or the freeing of one slave" (Sura 5:89). The Qur'an also includes directions about marriage with slaves: "Take in marriage those among you who are single and those of your male and female slaves who are honest" (Sura 24:32). Taking slaves as concubines (in addition to one's wives) is expressly allowed as well: "Blessed are the believers, who are humble in their prayers; who avoid profane talk, and give alms to the destitute; who restrain their carnal desires (except with their wives and slave-girls, for these are lawful to them)" (Sura 23:1).

Slavery is, admittedly, also taken for granted in the Bible. But here again the radically different ways that Christians and Muslims understand their scriptures, and the different contents of the *rest* of each book, are decisive. The abolitionist movement grew in the United States because of Christians who reasoned from the Bible's declarations of universal salvation and the Christian understanding of the dignity of mankind as created by God. Confederate Protestants pointed to passages of the New Testament in support of the "peculiar institution," but Christians were not restricted to this single interpretation.

Despite the words of the Qur'an, many Muslims have attempted to construct arguments against slavery on Islamic principles. Shehzad Saleem, director of the Institute of Islamic Studies in Lahore, Pakistan, states flatly: "Among many other misconceptions about Islam is the notion that it gives sanction to slavery and permits its followers to enslave prisoners of war, particularly women and establish extra-marital relations with them. We strongly affirm that Islam has not the slightest link with slavery and concubinage. On the contrary, it completely forbids these practices." This is a noble assertion, but wholly at odds with the Qur'anic passages quoted above, which Saleem doesn't refer to in his article, "The Condemnation of Slavery in Islam." Instead, he ascribes Muslim acceptance of slavery to prevailing social conditions, saying, "Islam had adopted a gradual process to abolish the institution of slavery because of the social conditions prevalent in Arabia at that time. It must be kept in mind that slavery was an integral part of the pre-Islamic Arab society."[16]

Christians often make a similar argument: the Church didn't move against slavery in apostolic times because of prevailing social conditions. This may be true in the histories of both religions, but here again the established understanding of the Qur'an handicaps the Muslim. The verses above make reformists like Saleem vulnerable to charges that they are disobedient to Allah. Since Muslims almost universally hold the Qur'an to be the perfect Word of Allah, valid for all time, those who join Saleem in suggesting that it doesn't enunciate a universal moral principle because of variable "social conditions" are inviting suspicion of their Islamic loyalty. The continuing existence of slavery in pockets of the Islamic world indicates that some Muslims still take the Qur'an at face value on this matter.

Slavery, moreover, has been taken for granted throughout Islamic history—as it was in the West until recently. The impetus to end it moved from Christendom into Islam. When the British government in the nineteenth century began pressuring pro-slavery regimes to curtail or end the practice, the reaction from at least one Muslim leader was incredulity. The Sultan of Morocco wrote that "the traffic in slaves is a matter on which all sects and nations have agreed from the time of the sons of Adam

... up to this day." He said that he was "not aware of its being prohibited by the laws of any sect" and that the very idea that anyone would question its morality was absurd: "no one need ask this question, the same being manifest to both high and low and requires no more demonstration than the light of day."[17]

Most slaves in the Islamic world were captured during jihad. This developed into an organized system:

> The *jihad* slave system included contingents of both sexes delivered annually in conformity with the treaties of submission by sovereigns who were tributaries of the caliph. When Amr conquered Tripoli (Libya) in 643, he forced the Jewish and Christian Berbers to give their wives and children as slaves to the Arab army as part of their *jizya* [tax on non-Muslims]. From 652 until its conquest in 1276, Nubia was forced to send an annual contingent of slaves to Cairo. Treaties concluded with the towns of Transoxiana, Sijistan, Armenia, and Fezzan (Maghreb) under the Umayyads and Abbasids stipulated an annual dispatch of slaves from both sexes. However, the main sources for the supply of slaves remained the regular raids on villages within the *dar-al-harb* [non-Islamic regions; see chapter nine] and the military expeditions which swept more deeply into the infidel lands, emptying towns and provinces of their inhabitants.[18]

Still Slaveholding Today

In Sudan and Mauritania, the Muslim record on slavery is not a matter of history but of current events.

The primary reason someone will be enslaved in Sudan is because he or she is a Christian. In this colonial fiction of a country, the Arab Muslims in the north are in the process of stamping out black Christianity in the south by imposing the Sharia over the entire country. The Coalition Against Slavery in Mauritania and Sudan (CASMAS), a human rights, abolitionist movement founded in 1995, says:

> The current Khartoum government wants to bring the non-Muslim Black South in line with Sharia law, laid down and interpreted by conservative Muslim clergy. The Black animist and Christian South remembers many years of slave raids by Arabs from the north and east and resists Muslim religious rule and the perceived economic, cultural, and religious expansion behind it.[19]

Critics worldwide have denied that slavery exists in Sudan, but there is no doubt for anyone willing to face the hard facts. "In 1996," according to the American Anti-Slavery Group, "after Minister Louis Farrakhan, leader of the Nation of Islam, challenged the press to find slavery in Sudan, two reporters from the *Baltimore Sun,* Gilbert Lewthwaite and Gregory Kane, risked their lives to fly into Southern Sudan to do just that."[20] They returned with an abundance of evidence, having themselves bought the freedom of a group of young slaves.

Slave raids are particularly inhuman. The American Anti-Slavery Group also reports:

> Women and children abducted in slave raids are roped by the neck or strapped to animals and then marched north. Along the way, many women and girls are repeatedly gang-raped. Children who will not be silent are shot on the spot. In the north, slaves are either kept by individual militia soldiers or sold in markets. Boys work as livestock herders, forced to sleep with the animals they care for. Some who try to escape have their Achilles tendons cut to hamper their ability to run. Masters typically use women and girls as domestics and concubines, cleaning by day and serving the master sexually by night. Survivors report being called "abeed" ("black slave"), enduring daily beatings, and receiving awful food. Masters also strip slaves of their religious and cultural identities, giving them Arabic names and forcing them to pray as Muslims.[21]

One Sudanese Christian slave was James Pareng Alier, who was kidnapped and forced into slavery at the age of twelve. Reports Alier: "I was forced to learn the Koran and re-baptised Ahmed. They told me that Christianity was a bad religion. After a time we were given military training and they told us we would be sent to fight." Alier has no idea of his family's whereabouts.[22]

Another slave was Francis Bok, a Christian who was abducted in the late 1980s from his home village and sold into slavery. He was seven years old at the time. "It was terrible," he recounted. "Men were killed, the women were raped. Everything happened in front of us. It was terrible." He was tied to the side of a donkey to be transported to the place of sale; two girls were tied to the other side. "The girls couldn't stop crying, so the men shot them. After that, I learned to be quiet." He was, as the American Anti-Slavery Group report indicates, beaten every day and called "abeed"—until, after ten years of this, he finally escaped.[23]

Muslims who grant that Islam's slaveholding record isn't pure have tried to mitigate their religion's bad name in this area by claiming that at least slavery in Islam has never been race-based: no Muslim slaveholder ever taught the execrable doctrine (once common in the West) that blacks were less than human, and therefore born to be slaves.

Although slavery there was never restricted only to blacks, the Muslim world for centuries imported, captured and purchased black African slaves.[24] In Islam, this racial element has not disappeared. According to CASMAS, black slavery persists in Mauritania to this day. "In ancient times slavery was common in Mauritania. It became part of armed conflict between ethnic or political groups. Slavery continued among these populations in Mauritania through the eighth century, coming under Islamic authority. From this point forward, only Black Africans have been enslaved in Mauritania." Nor is slavery an isolated problem. "Antislavery leader Bobacar Messaoud [Messaoud ould Boulkheir]," reports CASMAS, "estimate[s] that nearly half the population [of Mauritania] continues to be either enslaved or in slave-like relationships."[25]

Some Muslims also argue that because the slave/master relationship is on the whole much freer, so to speak, than it was in the American South, slavery in Islam should not be tarred with the same moral brush. It is true that in Islam, slaves and masters often marry. They live together in the same house, and a slave may even be wealthier than his master. Slaves must be emancipated under a wide variety of conditions, enumerated in the Qur'an itself.

BBC correspondent David Hecht traveled to Mauritania and found men married to their slaves and treating them with no undue harshness. "The slave/master relationship is a form of kinship," he explained. "Though slaves are mostly black Africans and masters or 'Bidan' have more Arab Berber blood in them, they are all members of the same clans and in some cases the blacks are the chiefs."[26] Hecht adds: "In Mauritania there are no plantations, no big mansions on top of the hill." Mauritania's relatively good treatment of slaves follows a Muslim tradition. Slaves in the House of Islam always enjoyed greater social mobility than they did in other cultures. Indeed, in the Mamluk ("possessed one," or "slave") dynasty that ruled Egypt and Syria from the thirteenth to the sixteenth centuries, many rulers rose from slavery.

There may be some truth to Hecht's analysis, although it provoked a furious response from the Mauritanian former slave and antislavery crusader Messaoud ould Boulkheir: "Freedom is not measured in terms of mansions or tents or in terms of sums of money in bank accounts. Freedom is much simpler and is so much more valuable than anything else."[27] To suggest otherwise is to echo the arguments of slaveholding Southerners who observed before the Civil War that their slaves had it better than some free blacks in the North. Maybe they did. Yet the abolitionist imperative wasn't based on living conditions, but on a perception of the equality of men before their Creator.

Of course, very few Muslim countries practice slavery today. Still, as long as it is explicitly sanctioned by the Qur'an and Islamic law, the possibility of slavery remains for any Muslim reformer who wants to enforce total obedience to Allah's Word and "pure" Islam. And this "pure" Islam will continue to grow in influence as long as the crisis in the Muslim world persists. When all is not right in the House of Islam, Muslim militants can lay blame at the feet of moderates who have supposedly offended Allah, and thereby justify the call for a return to hard-line orthodoxy.

The Quality of Mercy

The Qur'an is as merciless toward Muslim wrongdoers as it is toward infidels. This is clear from even a cursory examination of the draconian penalties it metes out for various offenses. True, penalties of similar ferocity were not unknown for sinners in Christian Europe; but here again, Christian-based principles regarding the dignity of man ultimately mitigated such harshness. In Islam, however, these punishments are written by the Hand of Allah.

The penalty for theft is well known: "As for the man or woman who is guilty of theft, cut off their hands to punish them for their crimes. That is the punishment enjoined by God. God is mighty and wise" (Sura 5:38). This is echoed in Islamic law (as reflected in *Reliance of the Traveller*), which stipulates that the thief's right hand be amputated (forcing the offender thereafter to eat with his left, which is also forbidden), provided that he "has reached puberty; is sane; is acting voluntarily," and steals a certain amount from a place that has taken reasonable security measures. The law also specifies that there must be "no possible confusion ... as to whether he took it by way of theft or for some other reason."[28] Other limbs are to be amputated for further offenses.

As for sexual immorality, "the adulterer and the adulteress shall

each be given a hundred lashes. Let no pity for them cause you to disobey God, if you truly believe in God and the Last Day; and let their
punishment be witnessed by a number of believers" (Sura 24:2). *Reliance
of the Traveller* defines "those whose killing is unlawful" as *not* including
"convicted married adulterers," as well as "non-Muslims at war with the
Muslims, apostates from Islam," not to mention "pigs, and biting dogs."[29]
In addition to amputation and lashing, there is imprisonment within
the home: "If any of your women commit fornication, call in four witnesses from among yourselves against them; if they testify to their guilt
confine them to their houses till death overtakes them or till God finds
another way for them" (Sura 4:15).

Under pressure from strict Muslims, Pakistan adopted laws based
on the Sharia in the late seventies. They reflected Islamic law's ferocity:

> Drinking was to be punished by eight stripes. The punishment for illicit
> sex, for an adult Muslim, was to "be stoned to death at a public place";
> for a non-Muslim, a hundred-stripe public whipping, with the possibil-
> ity of death for rape.[30] "The punishment of stoning to death awarded
> under section 5 or section 6 shall be executed in the following manner
> namely: Such of the witnesses who deposed against the convict as may be
> available shall start stoning him and, while stoning is being carried on,
> he may be shot, whereupon stoning and shooting shall be stopped." For
> theft . . . the punishment for a first offense was amputation—"carried out
> by an authorized medical officer"—of the right hand "from the joint of
> the wrist"' for a second offense, the amputation of the left foot "up to the
> ankle"; for a third offense, imprisonment for life.[31]

The natural human tendency for mercy that God has implanted
into the hearts of all people has prevented the letter of the law from being
followed in all times and places. In fact, journalist Stephen Schwartz
maintains that "for roughly 1,000 years" the letter of the Sharia on punishments like these has been mitigated: "The argument that intentions
were more important than conduct, and that, therefore, a sinful act could
be viewed as a product of human weakness requiring mercy rather than
punishment, triumphed in traditional Islam a long time ago."

There is some truth to this, even though Schwartz overstates the case
when he says that "this is why today the stoning of adulterous women only
exists in a minority of Muslim societies. Saudi Arabia, Pakistan, Afghanistan,
Iran, and 'a few other places' no more represent the entire Muslim world

than Arizona, Indiana, Idaho, and Texas represent the entire U.S."[32] Those nations, of course, are crucially important in the House of Islam precisely because of their universally acknowledged fidelity to Islamic principles. Moreover, violent Muslim groups today agitate for their vision of the purity of Islam not only in the countries that Schwartz mentions, but also in Egypt, Yemen, Somalia, Eritrea, Djibouti, Bosnia, Croatia, Albania, Algeria, Tunisia, Lebanon, the Philippines, Tajikistan, Azerbaijan, Chechnya, Uzbekistan, Kashmir—and, for that matter, the United States.[33]

The larger problem, however, is that if this debate over the interpretation of the Sharia had really been "settled in Islam" a thousand years ago, how did Saudi Arabia, Pakistan and the rest run off the moderate rails?

They did so because the letter of the Qur'an, as well as the Sharia, constantly wars against moderating interpretations. Thus when the Ayatollah Khomeini's "Islamic judge," Ayatollah Khalkhalli, took power in Kurdistan after Iran's Islamic revolution of 1979, a bloodbath followed. Reports V. S. Naipaul:

> In no time, moving swiftly from place to place in the August heat, he had sentenced forty-five people to death. He had studied for thirty-five years and was never at a loss for an Islamic judgment. When in one Kurdish town the family of a prisoner complained that three of the prisoner's teeth had been removed and his eyes gouged out, Khalkhalli ordered a similar punishment for the torturer. Three of the man's teeth were torn out on the spot. The aggrieved family then relented, pardoned the offender, and let him keep his eyes.[34]

The aggrieved family wasn't alone in its horrified reaction to such brutality. Throughout the House of Islam, the heart struggles against the harshness of these dictates. Naipaul reports that even in Iran, "just after the revolution there had been public whippings, as part of the revived Islamic way, but the effect on the public hadn't been good." The Iranian driver who chauffeured Naipaul during his days in Tehran explained that "people didn't like the man doing the whipping. It became hard on him afterwards."[35]

Similarly, a recent Muslim translation of the Qur'an that inserts parenthetical explanatory phrases right into the text renders one of the pertinent verses this way: "Strike the fornicatress and adulteress and the fornicator and adulterer on the body of each one of them a hundred times. (This is the extreme limit,) . . ."[36] But if this cautionary note that the hundred lashes are an "extreme limit" is actually suggested by the Arabic text, it has been missed by other translators.

Because they are founded on the Qur'an, these legal measures are not an exotic element of Muslim tradition, like the burning of heretics in medieval Christianity. On the contrary, they will forever be part of authentic Islam as long as the Qur'an is revered as the perfect Word of Allah. Harsh penalties are still very much in force wherever "pure" Islam holds sway, such as in Saudi Arabia, where, according to an Amnesty International report for 2000,

> At least 123 people were executed and there was an alarming increase in the number of amputations. . . . There were 34 reported cases of amputations during 2000, seven of which were cross amputations (of the right hand and left foot). Flogging continued to be frequently imposed for a wide range of offences. In August, ᶜAbdel Mo'ti ᶜAbdel Rahman Mohammad, an Egyptian national, was reported to have had his left eye surgically removed as punishment ordered by a court in Medina after he had been found guilty of throwing acid in the face of a compatriot and damaging his left eye.[37]

This is the "pure Islam" of the Taliban, of Saudi Arabia, and of everywhere the Sharia holds sway—the Islam that cuts off the hands of thieves, crushes homosexuals under brick walls, stones adulterers and executes converts to Christianity. This is what Islam means in practice, as Naipaul put it in summing up the Islamic bona fides of Khomeini's Iran: "The government had ordered civil servants to break off every day and say their prayers. *It had legislated for Koranic punishments like whipping and stoning to death.* It was talking of levying a Koranic tax, to be paid out to the poor as alms" (emphasis added).[38]

The Case of Nigeria

In the ongoing and convulsive battle over the implementation of Islamic law in several states of Nigeria, Sharia supporters have assured Christian Nigerians that separate, non-Islamic courts will be established for them. However, the fierce resistance to the Sharia they are putting up suggests that they may not consider this promise entirely genuine.

Reliance of the Traveller provides a hint as to why. Within a series of precise regulations governing the conduct of non-Muslims living in

Muslim lands, this manual of Shafi'i and Sunni orthodoxy dictates that Jews and Christians are to be punished "for committing adultery or theft, though not for drunkenness."[39] It specifies that a thief's right hand should be amputated "whether he is a Muslim, non-Muslim subject of the Islamic state, or someone who has left Islam."[40] (Of course, someone who has left Islam, according to the same legal corpus, also deserves the death penalty for apostasy.)

Under Islamic law, non-Muslims living in Muslim lands are also governed by a quite specific set of rules, which we'll examine more closely later on. If the Sharia is to be implemented fully, then must not these laws be implemented for the non-Muslim minority as well?

What's more, all over Nigeria the institution of the Sharia has been accompanied by violence. After all, as the Ayatollah Khomeini said, "Whatever good there is exists thanks to the sword and in the shadow of the sword! People cannot be made obedient except with the sword!"[41] Nigerian Muslims have clashed repeatedly with Christians over the Sharia. In late December 2001, gunmen shot dead the Nigerian justice minister and attorney general, Bola Ige, who according to a Reuters report "appeared to be heading for a showdown with Muslim Sharia courts in Nigeria's north after threatening to intervene to save the life of a mother sentenced to death by stoning for having sex outside marriage."[42]

In Nigeria's Zamfara state, one woman quickly encountered the dark side of the Sharia. She was "found guilty of fornication [and] was given 100 lashes—despite her protests that she had been raped."[43] As a woman she was ineligible under the Sharia to testify in court, even about her own case.

FOUR

Does Islam
Respect Women?

"AFTER ME," SAID THE PROPHET OF ISLAM, "I have not left any *Fitnah* (trial and affliction) more harmful to men than women."[1] Moreover, "evil omen is in three things: The horse, the woman and the house."[2]

Both Muslims and non-Muslims claim that Muhammad has been misunderstood and was not so much of a misogynist as these statements make him sound. "The concept of some Christians about the rights of women in Islam," Muslim scholars Amatul Rathman Omar and Abdul Mannan Omar observe, "is based upon colossal ignorance of the teachings of the Qur'an and Islam."[3] There is no doubt that Muhammad loved women, and at its inception Islam made certain innovations in women's rights. But if some Western analysts are correct, Islam is curiously susceptible to being hijacked: lately by terrorists, and in centuries past by chauvinists.

According to a popular writer on Islam, Karen Armstrong, the women of Muhammad's day "did not seem to have experienced Islam as an oppressive religion, though later, as happened in Christianity, men would hijack the faith and bring it in line with the prevailing patriarchy."[4] After discovering this moral equivalence, Armstrong asserts that "the emancipation of women was a project dear to the Prophet's heart" and enumerates Islam's undeniable achievements for women: "The Quran gave women rights of inheritance and divorce centuries before Western women were accorded such status." But under Christian influence, the Prophet's broadmindedness did not carry over to the generations that followed him:

> The Quran prescribes some degree of segregation and veiling for the
> Prophet's wives, but there is nothing in the Quran that requires the

veiling of all women or their seclusion in a separate part of the house. These customs were adopted some three or four generations after the Prophet's death. Muslims at that time were copying the Greek Christians of Byzantium, who had long veiled and segregated their women in this manner; they also appropriated some of their Christian misogyny.[5]

Maybe it really is true that Islamic misogyny is simply a foreign, Christian influence. On the other hand, perhaps—as in other areas—what was innovative and humane at the beginning of Islam is now antiquated and confining, because Muslims lack a mechanism for bringing what they consider to be the words of Almighty God into line with modern circumstances. Certainly some Muslims have taken to misogyny with gusto, as evidenced by the dreadful tale of the fifteen girls who died in a fire at their school in Saudi Arabia in March 2002. With no men in the school, the girls had taken off their Islamic garb for lessons. The Saudi religious police, the *muttawa,* would not allow them to leave the building because they were not veiled. Death for the girls was preferable to the risk of subjecting the men in the vicinity to impure thoughts.[6]

But this is an extreme case. To discover the facts of the matter, we may begin by looking at what the Qur'an says.

Muslims confronted by Westerners on the issue of women's rights often point to several verses that seem to establish the equality of men and women before Allah. One of them: "Men, have fear of your Lord, who created you from a single soul. From that soul He created its mate, and through them He bestrewed the earth with countless men and women" (Sura 4:1). Another: "I will deny no man or woman among you the reward of their labours. You are the offspring of one another" (Sura 3:195).

Nevertheless, there is still a hierarchy: "Women shall with justice have rights similar to those exercised against them, although men have a status above women" (Sura 2:228). This superiority is divinely ordained: "Men have authority over women because God has made the one superior to the other, and because they spend their wealth to maintain them" (Sura 4:34). Thus, husbands are advised: "Women are your fields; go, then, into your fields whence you please" (Sura 2:223).

Aside from this directive, one could argue that so far we have found nothing stronger than a biblical verse that makes priests and ministers cringe all over the West, St. Paul's "Wives, be submissive to your husbands, as to the Lord" (Ephesians 5:22). Certainly the idea that men are superior to women has been promoted at various times on the strength of this verse, although such a reading is counterbalanced by the concurrent responsibility of the man to love his wife with sacrificial love, "as Christ loved his Church and gave himself up for her" (Ephesians 5:26).

But even if the Apostle did mean that men are superior to women in some respect, it is not in the same measure as we find in the Qur'an, for instance in its instructions about legal testimony: "Call in two male witnesses from among you, but if two men cannot be found, then one man and two women whom you judge fit to act as witnesses; so that if either of them commit an error, the other will remember" (Sura 2:282). That is, one female witness is worth half as much as a man.

The Qur'an teaches that "Good women are obedient. They guard their unseen parts because God has guarded them. As for those from whom you fear disobedience, admonish them and send them to beds apart and beat them" (Sura 4:34).

There is, quite understandably, some disagreement among Muslims about the proper meaning of this verse. Some are uncomfortable with the idea that Allah is telling husbands to beat their wives. In his popular translation of the Qur'an, ʿAbdullah Yusuf ʿAli adds a crucial gloss, rendering the command as "spank them (lightly)."[7] Another group of translators, who liberally mix their parenthetical commentaries into the original text of the Qur'an, go even farther, removing any sense of physical punishment from this portion of Sura 4:34: "As for those women (on whose part) you apprehend disobedience and bad behavior, you may admonish them (first lovingly) and (then) refuse to share their beds with them and (as a last resort) punish them (mildly)."[8] On the opposite end of the spectrum is Mohammed Marmaduke Pickthall's rendering: "As for those from whom ye fear rebellion, admonish them and banish them to beds apart, and scourge them."[9]

Alas, almost all translators of the Qur'an side with Pickthall in rendering the Arabic with at least some notion of physical punishment, and not just the vague "punish them."

What the Hadiths Say

The Sunnah may be a source of the translators' ambivalence. Some hadiths, although they do not appear in Bukhari's collection or in other sources that are generally considered the most sound, recount that the Prophet actually forbade wife beating. In the *Sunan abu-Dawud,* another of the six *Sahih Sittah* or reliable collections, one hadith reads: "Narrated Mu'awiyah ibn Haydah: I said: Apostle of Allah, how should we approach our wives and how should we leave them? He replied: Approach your tilth [field] when or how you will, give her (your wife) food when you take food, clothe when you clothe yourself, do not revile her face, and do not beat her."[10] However, unlike the hadiths that have won general acceptance among Muslims, this one is not repeated in other collections; its attestation is considered weak.

Moreover, also found in *Sunan abu-Dawud* is evidence that the Prophet may have had a change of heart on this matter:

> Iyas ibn Abdullah ibn Abu Dhubab reported the Apostle of Allah as saying: Do not beat Allah's handmaidens, but when Umar came to the Apostle of Allah and said: Women have become emboldened towards their husbands, he (the Prophet) gave permission to beat them. Then many women came round the family of the Apostle of Allah complaining against their husbands. So the Apostle of Allah said: Many women have gone round Muhammad's family complaining against their husbands. They are not the best among you.[11]

Complaining husbands get permission to beat their wives. Complaining wives just get criticized for complaining.

Likewise, the same collection of hadiths has this: "Narrated Umar ibn al-Khattab: The Prophet said: A man will not be asked as to why he beat his wife."[12] Will he not be asked, that is, on Judgment Day? Or in Islamic society? Or both? The hadith doesn't say.

Ultimately, the very existence of Sura 4:34 puts these anti-wife-beating hadiths in doubt. It's unlikely in the extreme that Muhammad himself would have contradicted what he himself had presented to Muslims as the word of Allah, without pronouncing the verse abrogated (as he did with some others).[13]

Nor is wife beating simply of historical interest in Islam, any more than is any other part of the Qur'an. *Reliance of the Traveller* contains the same instructions as Sura 4:34 about how to deal with a disobedient wife: "If she *commits* rebelliousness, he keeps from sleeping ... with her without words, and may hit her, but not in a way that injures her, meaning he may not ... break bones, wound her, or cause blood to flow."[14]

Such directives are not a thing of the past. In 2000 the retired Turk-ish Muslim cleric Kemal Guran sparked a controversy in that secularized Muslim nation with a passage in his booklet *The Muslim's Handbook*. According to the BBC, "the booklet, published by the Pious Founda-tion, which is part of the government's Religious Affairs Directorate, says men can beat their wives as long as they do not strike the face and only beat them moderately." Guran also "suggests that men are naturally supe-rior to women." The plain words of the Qur'an support both points, but apparently some defenders of the Prophet missed Sura 4:34. The BBC article continues: "Sema Piskinsut, who chairs the parliamentary human rights commission, said the booklet was full of inaccuracies, and it mis-interprets the words of prophet Mohammed and Islam."[15]

Maybe Piskinsut is referring not to the Qur'an, but to present-day Islam. Perhaps the charge that Guran "misinterprets the words of prophet Mohammed and Islam" really means that the aged imam is trying to revive a practice that civilized Muslims long ago relegated to the ash-heap of history.

Maybe, but in allowing for wife beating, Guran is by no means alone among Muslims. In the same year that he published *The Muslim's Handbook,* another book giving the same advice caused a similar hulla-baloo in Spain's revivified Muslim community. The Spanish imam Mohamed Kamal Mostafa's book *Women in Islam* "recommends verbal correction followed by a period of sexual abstinence as the best punish-ment for a wife, but does not rule out a beating as long as it is kept within strict guidelines." It further specifies that the husband "should never hit his wife in a state of extreme or blind anger."

> He should never hit sensitive parts of the body such as the face, head, breasts or stomach. He should only hit the hands or feet using a rod that is thin and light so that it does not leave scars or bruises on the body. The husband's aim ... should be to cause psychological suffering and not to humiliate or physically abuse his wife.[16]

For writing this, Mohamed Kamal Mostafa is facing a lawsuit from an association of Spanish women's groups. But what has he done? He has simply restated Sura 4:34—"send them to beds apart and beat them." Thus, the women's groups do not really have a quarrel with the imam, but with the Qur'an. Perhaps the Spanish women should sue the Prophet!

Even a relatively moderate Muslim scholar and apologist, Dr. Jamal Badawi, acknowledges that husbands have the right to beat their wives. Quoting Sura 4:34, Dr. Badawi is clearly embarrassed by this prerogative and tries to explain it away: "Such a measure is more accurately described as a gentle tap on the body, but NEVER ON THE FACE, making it more of a symbolic measure then a punitive one" (emphasis in the original).[17] Likewise, the editors of *Sahih Bukhari* gloss Sura 4:34 in a minimalist fashion, recalling the wording of ʿAbdullah Yusuf ʿAli: "Beat them (lightly[,] your wives, if it is useful) [i.e., without causing them severe pain.]" (brackets in the original).[18]

The concern of these Muslim authorities to limit the force of the husband's beatings is commendable. It's another case of their sentiments being better than their religious convictions: the true God has placed greater compassion in their hearts than Muhammad placed in the Qur'an. But when kind-hearted Muslims like Badawi try to pass off the sanction for wife beating as a "gentle tap," they miss the point. These beatings are not made acceptable because they don't break bones or leave scars. Even if they inflict no physical pain at all, they're indicative of a relationship between a superior and a subordinate, not a holy union of equals.

Even more important, a gentle tap is a subjective thing. In the privacy of his home (and in the heat of the moment), one man's tap is another man's brutal beating. Also, once the book of Allah sanctions wife beating, it has created an understanding of marriage that, for all its superficial resemblance to the Western model, is in fact worlds away from the union in which the couple's "mutual love becomes an image of the absolute and unfailing love with which God loves man."[19]

Domestic Servitude

How far away the House of Islam is from this atmosphere of mutual love is clear from many Muslim sources. A hadith has the Prophet saying, "If a man invites his wife to sleep with him and she refuses to come to him, then the angels send their curses on her till morning."[20] The Prophet does not say anything about why the woman might have refused. *Reliance of the Traveller* echoes Muhammad. This orthodox Shafiʿi source lays down that: "The husband is only obliged to support his wife when she gives herself to him or offers to, meaning she allows him full enjoyment of her person and does not refuse him sex at any time of the night or day."[21]

Another aspect of the traditional role of Muslim women is revealed in Amir Taheri's account of the Ayatollah Khomeini's first meeting with his wife-to-be. Taheri vividly describes the scene: "She could see her suitor, but all Ruhollah could see was a tiny creature covered in black. She did not speak, as a girl whose voice was heard by strangers would be doomed."[22] Alas, the Ayatollah's courtship is not the stuff of great romance; it sounds more like the hiring of a domestic servant. (To his credit, however, Khomeini married only this one time, and by all accounts showed his wife tender and unflagging love.)

Women may be grateful just to be domestic servants, however, for it could be much worse. Numerous hadiths even have Muhammad informing a group of women that their sex will populate hell: "Once Allah's Apostle went out to the Musalla (to offer the prayer) of ʿId-al-Adha or Al-Fitr prayer. Then he passed by the women and said, 'O women! Give alms, as I have seen that the majority of the dwellers of Hell-fire were you (women).'" When the women asked why, he explained, "You curse frequently and are ungrateful to your husbands. I have not seen anyone more deficient in intelligence and religion than you. A cautious sensible man could be led astray by some of you." To support his assessment of female deficiency, he alluded to the Qur'an: "Is not the evidence of two women equal to the witness of one man? [cf. Sura 2:282, above] ... This is the deficiency in her intelligence. Isn't it true that a woman can neither pray nor fast during her menses? ... This is the deficiency in her religion."[23]

The idea that hell will be filled with more women than men appears frequently in the hadiths. To take just one additional example: "The Prophet said, 'I stood at the gate of Paradise and saw that the majority of the people who entered it were the poor, while the wealthy were stopped at the gate (for the accounts). But the companions of the Fire were ordered to be taken to the Fire. Then I stood at the gate of the Fire and saw that the majority of those who entered it were women.'"[24]

In light of these traditions, it's clear why Muslim men have so often fit the stereotype of misogynists who treat women with suspicion, disdain and derision. When they deal with women, they are dealing with a group believed to suffer from severe moral and intellectual shortcomings, not to mention all sorts of physical impurities in a religion obsessed with ritual cleanliness. Women are, moreover, in extra jeopardy of winding up in hell.

But to get there, they had better have permission: Muslim women whose husbands observe Islamic law to the letter must have their husbands' authorization even to venture outside their homes. The Prophet Muhammad said that if a wife leaves the house without her husband's consent, "the angels curse her until she returns or repents."[25]

Polygamy

The Muslim man is free to consort with virtually as many women as he chooses, for Islam also sanctions polygamy. "If you fear that you cannot treat orphans (orphan girls) with fairness, then you may marry other women who seem good to you: two, three, or four of them" (Sura 4:3). This verse has traditionally been understood as permitting a man to have four wives, although divorce and concubinage in Islam allow him a practically unlimited number of women.

Muslims hasten to show critical Westerners the rest of the passage: "But if you fear that you cannot maintain equality among them, marry one only." In fairness, I should point out that the verse continues: "or any slave-girls you may own" (Sura 4:3). Another verse warns men, "Try as you may, you cannot treat all your wives impartially" (Sura 4:129). Muslims who advocate monogamy put these passages together: the Qur'an acknowledges that a man will not be able to treat all his wives impartially, and it tells him that if he cannot do so, he must marry only one wife. Therefore, they say, the Qur'an actually forbids polygamy.

Others who don't go so far point out that the Qur'an restricts a man to four wives (by the assessment of the great majority of scholars) and thus puts a humane restraint upon the practice. Before Muhammad received the Qur'an, they say, men in Arabia sometimes had hundreds of wives. Islam introduced a healthy moderation and thereby raised the status of women.

Muslims claim that polygamy is not condemned in the Bible, so Westerners therefore cannot charge that the custom is inherently immoral. They point to population imbalances and other social factors to argue that in many cases polygamy is a more compassionate alternative than monogamy. Men and women are different, they say: a woman naturally desires only one man, but a man desires many women; so Islam is more realistic than Christianity because it takes this into account. Badawi concludes,

What the Quranic decrees amount to, taken together, is a discourage-
ment of polygamy unless necessity for it exists. It is also evident that the
general rule in Islam is monogamy and not polygamy. However, permission to practice limited polygamy is only consistent with Islam's realistic
view of the nature of man and women and of the various social needs,
problems, and cultural variations.[26]

The Muslim scholar Seyyed Hossein Nasr rails over "the prejudice
of Christianity" against polygamy, a prejudice that has invaded some
overly modernized segments of the House of Islam. "Some," he says,
"have even gone so far as to call it immoral and prefer prostitution to a
social pattern which minimizes all promiscuous relations to the extent
possible."[27] But it is inaccurate, at best, to suggest that polygamy's critics prefer prostitution or promiscuity, and to claim that polygamy minimizes these within Islam.

Nasr begins from the notion, almost universally accepted these
days, of human nature as a steam boiler: when the pressure mounts, let
off some steam. If you're filled with anger, punch a wall or at least a pil-
low. If you're filled with sexual desire, let it out somehow, for holding it
in will injure you. So Islam is more realistic and humane than Christianity because it provides for this letting off of sexual steam in a safe and
secure way—polygamy—as opposed to one that's fraught with physical
dangers and harm to the women involved—prostitution.

In fact, this steam-boiler picture of the soul is a relatively modern
idea, popularized by secular psychology. Sages through the centuries,
Christian and non-Christian, took the opposite view, the one well summed
up by James, the brother of the Lord and first bishop of Jerusalem: "Resist
the devil and he will flee from you" (James 4:7). Accordingly, in the
Catholic tradition, St. Thomas Aquinas taught that habits are eradicated
not by being fed, but by being starved.

Not until modern times was this wisdom rejected on a large scale
anywhere. If it is false, then we would expect to see Nasr's statement
borne out in Muslim countries where polygamy is common: there should
be no prostitution or promiscuity there. Yet recently Muslim Bangladesh
was forced to legalize prostitution, causing "hundreds of sex workers" to
dance in the streets of the capital, Dhaka.[28] Where did these hundreds
of prostitutes come from in a Muslim land? Isn't it likely that their counterparts can be found elsewhere in the Muslim world (despite legal

restrictions) and that Islam's "realistic" approach to sex doesn't render these prostitutes bereft of clients, but all the more popular?

Even if a Muslim man has only one wife (which is the most common arrangement in most Islamic societies), his Qur'an-based permission to take another wife without her consent (as well as to beat her) makes Islamic marriage a fundamentally different institution from marriage in the West. Whether or not they use it, Muslim men have divine permission to commit acts that in a Western context would be considered infidelity.

In Philip Mansel's elegantly written history of Constantinople after the Muslim conquest, he offers a moving case in point involving the daughter of the sultan of the Ottoman Empire:

> Yet even these most powerful and privileged of Ottoman might be tortured by jealousy. Adile Sultan, daughter of the great nineteenth-century reformer Mahmud II, married an army officer, Mehmed Ali Pasha. They were in love. One day at the fashionable meeting-place in the Golden Horn called the Sweet Waters of Europe, she attracted his attention. Since she was thickly veiled, he did not know who she was. He dropped a scented handkerchief at her feet. That night the Pasha found the handkerchief on the pillow beside his sleeping wife.

One day, according to Mansel, Adile Sultan traveled to a mosque far from her home. Taking advantage of the celebrated Oriental hospitality, she stopped for a rest at a mansion along the way. While enjoying coffee and sherbet set out for her, she was astonished to find that her hostess, too, was the wife of Mehmed Ali Pasha! She said nothing, however, and returned home—where, Mansel says, "thereafter she lived in seclusion, writing poems of increasing sadness. When she died in 1898, she was buried beside her husband. They never referred to his infidelity."[29]

This is the story of just one woman, but it doesn't take much knowledge of human nature to recognize that it's a story that is still being repeated the world over. The Qur'an commands a man not to take more than one wife unless he can treat all of them equally, but Muslims have generally understood this to mean equal economic support. An equal distribution of affection wouldn't be possible—even the Prophet favored Aisha over all his other wives. Bukhari reports that one follower of the Prophet was bold enough to ask him, "Who is the most beloved person to you?" Muhammad answered: "Aisha."[30]

What might his other wives have thought?

Inequality of affection can make a polygamous marriage a prison of sorrow. The Prophet's harem wasn't immune. Aisha is forthright about tensions among Muhammad's wives; she is one of the main sources for our knowledge of the celebrated incident, recounted in the last chapter, of Muhammad's dalliance with Mary the Copt on the day reserved for Hafsa. She also reports that "Zainab was competing with me (in her beauty and the Prophet's love)."[31]

So pervasive—naturally—was jealousy in the Prophet's polygamous household that Aisha admits to having been jealous of a dead woman: Khadija, the Prophet's first wife and the only one who had him exclusively to herself.

> Narrated Aishah: I did not feel jealous of any of the wives of the Prophet as much as I did of Khadija (although) she died before he married me; for often I heard him mentioning her; and Allah had told him to give her the good tidings that she would have a palace of *Qasab* (i.e., pipes of precious stones and pearls in Paradise), and whenever he slaughtered a sheep, he would send to her women-friends a good share of it.[32]

Whenever women in the House of Islam have dared to speak about polygamy, the story is the same. Halide Elib, a proto-feminist in the waning days of the Ottoman Empire, said flatly that polygamy "was a curse, a poison which our unhappy household could not get out of its system.... The constant tension in our home made every simple ceremony seem like physical pain, and the consequences hardly ever left me. The rooms of the wives were opposite each other and my father visited them in turn."[33]

A twenty-first-century American Muslim wife was no less aware of the devastating effects of polygamy. April Ray El-Hage, wife of convicted al-Qaeda terrorist Wadih El-Hage, successfully resisted her husband's attempts to take a second wife. She couldn't, of course, deny that he had a right to marry again; to do so would have been, by her own account, "un-Islamic." But here again, her heart was greater than her religion. With her God-given sense that polygamy was wrong, she fought back the only way she could: "I made his life hell.... I was becoming a real b———." It took six months for Wadih El-Hage to relent, but April Ray ultimately won: her husband broke off his engagement to a second woman.[34]

A women's advocate in Egypt, Abu Qomsan, shares April Ray's outlook. She indignantly describes a contemporary Egyptian TV show, *Hag Mitwalli's Family*, that idealizes polygamy: "They make polygamy look very nice, very romantic, very rich like a dream. It is the worst show I have ever seen in my life. It is the worst show Egyptian television has ever made. They destroy all life values. . . . It makes me very angry."[35]

Polygamy encourages seeing women as commodities, which has always been a prevailing view in Islam. This concept reached its apotheosis in the fabled Topkapi palace of the Ottoman sultans, particularly in its harem. Akbar S. Ahmed describes it this way: "It was in the harem that the all-powerful sultan spent most of his life. Every inhabitant of the 230 small, dark rooms was his to command. It is not difficult to imagine the unlimited sensual pleasures available to the sultan (the number of concubines often exceeded a thousand); and only to him." Ahmed goes on to describe the palace's lavish and eclectic furnishings, accented by Qur'anic verses on the walls. "But the Quranic verses underline the fact that in spite of so many quotations from the Quran this was not Islam."[36]

Why not? What in Islam forbade the sultans from keeping such a palace and treating women so?

Apologists like Seyyed Hossein Nasr complain that it isn't fair to attack Islam for its polygamy, "as if polygamy has been practiced with Islam alone."[37] Certainly not; but Islam offers a woman no protection against it. Muslims point to the great Old Testament figures, like David and Solomon, who were polygamous. But neither Jews nor Christians practice polygamy today. They understand their scriptures as teaching a higher morality, including an idea of marriage as a unique and divine bond that cannot be broken.

Divorce

The classic Christian idea of marriage rules out not only polygamy, but divorce as well. Jesus reminds the Pharisees,

> Have you not read that He who made them from the beginning made them male and female, and said, "For this reason a man shall leave his father and mother and be joined to his wife, and the two shall become one?" So they are no longer two but one. What therefore God has joined together, let no man put asunder. (Matthew 19:4–6)

It is true that the West's present-day record on this issue is dismal. In fact, Muslims criticize Westerners of hypocrisy on the matter of polygamy, given that a substantial percentage of Western men nowadays practice serial polygamy through easy divorce and remarriage. Still, Islam cannot take the moral high ground here, either. A Muslim man may divorce a wife if she displeases him in any way (even by protesting a polygamous arrangement). It is almost unheard-of for a Muslim woman to divorce her husband, although it does seem to happen under certain specific circumstances. To achieve the divorce, all a man has to do is pronounce to his wife the famous triple declaration: "You are divorced, you are divorced, you are divorced."[38] That doesn't mean, however, that a Muslim woman can be divorced and put out of her home in a matter of minutes. The Qur'an, in a sura entitled "Divorce," prescribes a waiting period to make sure that the wife is not pregnant: "Prophet (and you believers), if you divorce your wives, divorce them at the end of their waiting period. Compute their waiting period and have fear of God, your Lord. You shall not expel them from their houses, nor shall they go away, unless they have committed a proven vile deed" (Sura 65:1).

An American Muslim woman, Naasira bint Ellison, explains how it works in practice:

> Firstly, many options are taken and tried before coming to the decision of the divorce. If the man and woman decide that they can no longer live together successfully as a husband and wife, the husband (in most cases, not always) pronounces the divorce by saying "I divorce you." At this point the waiting period begins. The waiting period lasts for three menstrual cycles to assure the woman is not pregnant. This period allows the couple time to think about what they are doing and if this is what they really want to do. There are no lawyers involved to antagonize an already delicate situation.

This, she says, is "the most humane and most just system of divorce that exists."[39] Muslims point proudly to Sura 4:128, which forms a foundation stone of this system: "If a woman fear ill-treatment or desertion on the part of her husband, it shall be no offense for them to seek a mutual agreement, for agreement is best."

Aisha's explanation of this verse reveals what kind of "agreement" is meant: "It concerns the woman whose husband does not want to keep her with him any longer, but wants to divorce her and marry some other

lady, so she says to him: 'Keep me and do not divorce me, and then marry
another woman, and you may neither spend on me, nor sleep with me.'"[40]
Thus the "mutual agreement" is rather like one between a beggar and a
king. The woman agrees to give up her conjugal rights and to receive
nothing from her husband, even basic support, as long as she is spared
the shame of divorce. Meanwhile, the husband has his wife's blessing to
marry another woman.

A Muslim husband need not show just cause for divorcing his wife.
One man in Abu Dhabi considered divorcing his wives simply in order
to be able to have more children: "Forty-year-old Salem Jemaa Mabruk
has 27 children, and aims to have 100. He said in an interview in the
daily newspaper *Al-Ittihad* that he might have to divorce some of his four
present wives and seek more energetic ones."[41]

True, there are plenty of married men in the West who divorce in
order to get a more "energetic" wife. Both Islamic divorce law and current Western laws are quite different from the saying of Jesus that shaped
Christendom's understanding of divorce: "For your hardness of heart
Moses allowed you to divorce your wives, but from the beginning it was
not so" (Matthew 19:8). This is one of Jesus' "hard sayings." In light of
the breakdown of the family in the West, Muslim claims to take a more
realistic view of human nature by allowing for divorce and legislating its
parameters could conceivably find real purchase within the former bounds
of Christendom. In fact, despite Jesus' words, almost all Christian com-
munions now allow for divorce and remarriage in one form or another.
Only the Catholic Church still considers remarriage after divorce to be
a grave sin; in Catholicism the granting of annulments is often known
as "divorce by another name," but in fact annulments are granted only
under quite specific conditions. Pope John Paul II reaffirmed this early
in 2002, saying, "Marriage is indissoluble.... [Divorce] ... has devastating consequences that spread in society like the plague."[42]

One observer of Islam remarks that in Egypt, "a great many men"
have taken advantage of Islam's divorce laws and "have married twenty
or thirty women in no more than ten years. By the same token, women
of no great age have married more than a dozen men, one after the other.
It is observable today ... that some men are in the habit of changing
their wife once a month."[43]

Muslim divorce laws can force a woman into virtual prostitution.
The Sharia stipulates that after a man has divorced the same woman three

times, he cannot marry her again until she has married and been divorced by another man.[44] This kind of repeated marriage and divorce is made common in Islam by the way divorce is granted. Consequently, in some places, notably the Iranian holy city of Qom, there are men who make a living as "one-night husbands": they marry thrice-divorced women, consummate the marriage, and divorce them the next day, so the women can now lawfully go back to their families.[45]

UNICEF recently profiled a woman who is a double victim, both of child marriage and of easy divorce:

> Zeinab is 26 years old. She was married at the age of 10, and at 12 gave birth to a girl. However, the trauma of the early delivery was too much for her young, fragile body, whose whole left side became paralyzed. As a result, her husband sent her back to her family. He eventually abandoned her completely and re-married. She and her daughter, now 13, are now living with an aunt and earn some money selling potatoes. But Zeinab cannot afford to send the girl to school.[46]

UNICEF never mentions that Zeinab is a Muslim, although she bears the name of one of the Prophet's wives. In any case, however, she would find no relief from her plight in Islam, which condones child marriage and unilateral male-initiated divorce; nothing in Islamic law and practice prevents Zeinab's story from being repeated all over the Muslim world.

Female Circumcision

The barbarity of female circumcision is practiced within the House of Islam as well as by some Third World non-Muslims. In line with Muhammad's suspicion of women, its stated object is the reduction of female sexual response, so as to restrain a woman's wanton nature. But in fact, the Islamic justification for this custom seems to be weak. It is scarcely found at all in such bastions of Islam as Saudi Arabia, Iraq, Syria, Jordan, Palestine, Turkey, Iran or North Africa.[47] It is observed, however, among Muslims in Egypt, Ethiopia and the rest of East Africa, and elsewhere, and is justified in religious terms. According to Badawi, those who practice it are on shaky Islamic ground: "there is no single text of the Qur'an and Hadeeth which requires female circumcision."[48]

Well, almost none. One hadith comes from about as eminent a source as one can find in Islam: one of Sunni Islam's "Four Great Imams," the foremost collector of hadiths, Ahmad ibn Hanbal (from whom the Hanbali school of Islamic jurisprudence takes its name). This great imam, who was renowned for traveling all over the Muslim world in search of authentic hadiths, quotes Muhammad as saying, "Circumcision is a law for men and a preservation of honour for women."[49] However, despite the respect that ibn Hanbal enjoys among Muslims, there is little mention of this statement of Muhammad elsewhere. *Sunan abu-Dawud* reports a single hadith relating to the practice, and even this one is generally considered "weak," or of doubtful attestation, by most Muslim scholars: "A woman used to perform circumcision in Medina. The Prophet said to her: Do not cut severely as that is better for a woman and more desirable for a husband."[50] Note that he doesn't forbid it, but he does apparently restrict it, ruling out the more barbaric forms that are, nevertheless, still carried out today.

Some important Muslim divines encourage the custom. According to *Reliance of the Traveller,* circumcision is required for both men and women.[51] Sheikh Muhammad Sayyed Tantawi, the grand imam of Egypt's Al-Azhar University (and thus, according to the BBC, "the highest spiritual authority for nearly a billion Sunni Muslims") called circumcision "a laudable practice that did honor to women."[52] Female circumcision is, moreover, deeply ingrained in the societies where it is applied. As one Egyptian said simply, "It is the custom. God wills it."[53]

A Different Understanding of Rape

Numerous reports from the Middle East suggest that the Western understanding of the concept of rape barely exists in the Muslim world. Or more precisely, they know what it is, but under Islamic rules of evidence, it almost never happens. In recent years, Muslims have often charged that non-Muslim soldiers in Bosnia, Kashmir and elsewhere were guilty of raping Muslim women. But inside the House of Islam, the picture is cloudier, not so much because male passions are better controlled but because the Sharia makes the crime of rape virtually impossible to prove.

The testimony of the victim herself is inadmissible. *Reliance of the Traveller* dictates that "if testimony concerns fornication or sodomy, then it requires four male witnesses." It appends to this the commentary of the Muslim legal scholar Sheikh ᶜUmar Barakat, who specifies what these witnesses need to have seen. They must testify, he says, "in the case of fornication, that they have seen the offender insert the head of the penis into her vagina."[54]

Once again, this isn't some long-forgotten medieval law. It remains in force wherever the Sharia rules. Says *Time* magazine, "For a woman to prove rape in Pakistan, for example, four adult males of 'impeccable' character must witness the penetration, in accordance with Shari'a."[55] V. S. Naipaul reports that in that Islamic Republic, "a *pir* or holy man in a provincial town had been charged with raping the thirteen-year-old daughter of one of his followers. The case against him couldn't get far in the sessions court because the new Islamic law under which he was tried required four eyewitnesses to the act."[56]

This law is based on a celebrated incident in Muhammad's life, when his beloved Aisha was suspected of adultery. A revelation from Allah cleared her name, and henceforth required four witnesses to prove sexual sin. Allah asked of Aisha's accusers, "Why did they not produce four witnesses? If they could not produce any witnesses, then they were surely lying in the sight of God" (Sura 24:13).[57]

This law acquitted Aisha, but for other women it has proved a source of immense suffering. It is on the books in Malaysia, where Sisters in Islam, a Muslim feminist group, is trying to get a clear definition of rape written into Malaysian law. Right now, because of the rules of evidence and other factors, rape is difficult to distinguish from adultery and fornication (*zina*). Sisters in Islam points out, reasonably enough, that

> in the real world, rape is unlikely to occur in the open, such that four pious males can observe the act of penetration. If they actually did witness such an act, and have not sought to prevent it, then technically they are abettors to the crime. In reality, unless the rapist confesses to the crime, women can never prove rape at all if rape is placed under syariah [Sharia] jurisdiction as traditionally interpreted.

Some officials are in agreement: in a spring 2000 press release, Sisters in Islam notes with gratitude that they share "the concern expressed by the Deputy Prime Minister that the absence of a definition on rape in syariah law has led to victims of rape being charged for *zina* (illicit sex)."[58]

That is a genuine concern. A Muslim woman who is raped is often afraid to file a complaint with police, for in the absence of four corroborating male witnesses, her testimony can be taken as admission of adultery or fornication (*zina*)—a crime that could cost her her life. Thus, a seventeen-year-old incest victim was charged under the Sharia as a willing participant in the crime. Sisters in Islam points out that the Sharia legal officials who came to this determination fail to understand "the dynamics of power relationship" that prevailed between father and daughter in this case.[59]

In a celebrated case in Nigeria, a Sharia court sentenced a woman named Sufiyatu Huseini to be stoned to death for adultery. She faced a grim fate:

> The method of execution? Sanyinna says the stones themselves will be the size of fists. The logistics, however, are up to the local judge. The villagers may tie Sufiyatu to a tree and stone her straight on, or they may dig a pit deep enough so that she cannot climb out, drop her in, and then rain stones down on her from above. Regardless, the execution is liable to be drawn out: The Sharia forbids the stone-throwers to aim for the head.[60]

Huseini, however, said that Yakubu Abubakar, a neighbor, raped her. Alas, Abubakar claimed not to have met her (a claim that wasn't far-fetched, considering the fact that in strict Muslim society women are largely confined to their homes) and that someone else had fathered the child she claimed was his daughter.

> "Yakubu was exonerated," said Huseini after the trial. "I felt like dying that day because of the injustice." Huseini also claims that she had witnesses to attest to the fact that Abubakar was acquainted with her and admitted to be the father of the child. Says Huseini, "I don't know why they were not listened to."[61]

They were not listened to because they didn't witness the actual act of rape. That is the only testimony that would have saved Sufiyatu Huseini under Islamic law, although ultimately an international outcry resulted in the overturning of her death sentence. Before that, however, the attorney general of the state where Huseini was tried, Aliyu Abubakar Sanyinna, was asked whether he thought the punishment was too harsh. He was dismissive: "It is the law of Allah. By executing anybody that is convicted under Islamic law, we are just complying with the laws of Allah, so we don't have anything to worry about."[62]

Yet human decency and compassion were not entirely absent from the case. Before the death sentence was overturned, the story took a

strange twist: Anthony Olubunmi Okogie, the Roman Catholic archbishop of Lagos, offered himself to Muslim authorities to be executed in
Sufiyatu Huseini's place.[63] Okogie's offer, incidentally, also illustrates how
Muslims read their scriptures differently from Jews and Christians. Yes,
the Old Testament prescribes stoning for adultery, but Jews today do not
stone adulterers. For Christians, the New Testament imperative to mercy
is paramount. How many people have been stoned to death for adultery
in the predominantly Catholic states of South America recently?

Meanwhile, as a result of the misclassification of rape, there are
women in prisons all over the Muslim world who are actually rape victims. In the absence of male witnesses, their complaints were taken as
admissions of guilt. Some estimate that as much as *75 percent* of the
women who now populate Pakistani prisons are there through such
circumstances.[64]

When it comes to rape, blaming the victim is all too common in
the Islamic world. The *Chicago Tribune* reported,

> On May 31, 1994, Kifaya Husayn, a 16-year-old Jordanian girl, was lashed
> to a chair by her 32-year-old brother. He gave her a drink of water and
> told her to recite an Islamic prayer. Then he slashed her throat. Immedi-
> ately afterward, he ran out into the street, waving the bloody knife and
> crying, "I have killed my sister to cleanse my honor." Kifaya's crime? She
> was raped by another brother, a 21-year-old man. Her judge and jury?
> Her own uncles, who convinced her eldest brother that Kifaya was too
> much of a disgrace to the family honor to be allowed to live.[65]

Her brother didn't get off scot-free. He received a fifteen-year prison sentence, later reduced to seven years.

"Honor killing" is, in fact, well rooted in the Islamic world. It is
by no means unheard-of for a woman to be killed by her own family in
order to "prosecute adultery." The absence of clarity about rape puts its
victims at risk of being doubly victimized, while their killers go unpun-
ished. "Just last year," it was reported in 2002, "the male head of a prominent Pakistani family murdered his daughter in a lawyer's office, only to
be acquitted."[66]

By one reading of Islamic law, she had been given justice.

There is a sign of hope, however: in the spring of 2002, two Saudi
Arabian men were convicted of abducting and raping a woman at gun-
point. The *Arab News* story doesn't say whether the classic Islamic

standards of proof were required in this case, but from the circumstances it seems unlikely that they were. The men, however, tasted the severity of Islamic justice anyway: they were summarily beheaded.[67]

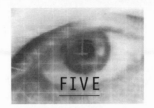

FIVE

Is Islam Compatible with Liberal Democracy?

"AMERICA COUNTS MILLIONS OF MUSLIMS amongst our citizens," said President George W. Bush in the Islamic Center of Washington, D.C., just six days after terrorist attacks destroyed the World Trade Center and a portion of the Pentagon.

> Muslims make an incredibly valuable contribution to our country. Muslims are doctors, lawyers, law professors, members of the military, entrepreneurs, shopkeepers, moms and dads.... This is a great country. It's a great country because we share the same values of respect and dignity and human worth. And it is my honor to be meeting with leaders who feel just the same way I do. They're outraged, they're sad. They love America just as much as I do.[1]

No doubt this is true. A Muslim businessman I know—a kind and thoughtful man—proudly (or prudently) sported an "I love the USA" sweatshirt in the weeks following September 11. There is no indication that he received any flak for this at the mosque on Friday.

But consider a thought experiment: what would happen if these Muslim citizens became a majority in the United States? Although such a possibility is several generations from having the chance to become an actuality, this is more than just idle speculation: Islamic advocates say that theirs is the fastest-growing religion in the world, and it is expanding very quickly in the United States as well. Muslim populations are growing rapidly in Western Europe, and practicing Muslims will shortly outnumber practicing Anglicans in Great Britain, the home of Anglicanism.

Americans who have thought about Muslim demographics are not alarmed. After all, even if the Islamic population continues to increase at a rapid clip, it isn't likely to alter the flow of public discourse. Moreover, the idea of the separation of church and state is well established in the United States. Christians who have attempted to influence political debate in recent decades have learned through hard experience that they must avoid all appearance of trying to "legislate morality." A secular American republic with a Muslim majority would continue as before, no?

It might. There have been notable attempts to establish democracy in an Islamic context. The great opponent of the Wahhabis, the Egyptian modernist Muhammad Abduh (1849–1905), tried to recast traditional Islamic categories to reflect those of the modern West:

> Arguing that Islam was not incompatible with the basics of Western thought, Abdu[h] interpreted the Islamic concept of shura (consultation) as parliamentary democracy, ijma (consensus) as public opinion, and maslah (choosing that ruling or interpretation of the Sharia from which greatest good will ensue) as utilitarianism.[2]

But this doesn't mean that Abduh would have applauded Thomas Jefferson's "wall of separation between church and state."[3] His vision of parliamentary democracy was thoroughly Islamic. His influential disciple Muhammad Rashid Rida (1865–1935) emphasized that "the affairs of the Islamic state must be conducted within the framework of a constitution that is inspired by the Quran, the Hadith and the experiences of the Rightly Guided Caliphs [the leaders of the Muslim community right after the time of Muhammad]."[4]

The Tunisian Muslim journalist and theorist Mohamed Elhachmi Hamdi concurs: "The heart of the matter is that no Islamic state can be legitimate in the eyes of its subjects without obeying the main teachings of the shari'a."[5]

V. S. Naipaul explains, "No religion is more worldly than Islam. In spite of its political incapacity, no religion keeps men's eyes more fixed on the way the world is run."[6] He cites a typical article from the *Tehran Times,* published in the early days of Khomeini's revolution: "Politics is combined with religion in Islam." The writer of the article recommends that Iran and Pakistan join together in a political partnership "with reformation and adaptation to present needs in full conformity with the holy Koran and Sunnah." He concludes that "Iran and Pakistan with a clarity of purpose and sincere cooperation can establish the truth that Islam is a complete way of life."[7]

Mohamed Elhachmi Hamdi insists that "Islam should be the main frame of reference for the constitution and laws of predominantly Muslim countries."[8] According to journalist Dinesh D'Souza, the influential Muslim radical Sayyid Qutb (1906–1966) argued that in an ideal polity, "it is God and not man who rules. God is the source of all authority, including legitimate political authority. Virtue, not freedom, is the highest value. Therefore God's laws, not man's, should govern the society."[9] Likewise the Ayatollah Khomeini in Iran rejected rule "based on the approval of laws in accordance with the opinion of the majority."[10] Only Allah can make laws. In practice, of course, that makes for an autocracy under the Sharia, or pressure for such a political arrangement, wherever Muslims form a majority.

Not only is the Sharia sufficient in itself for the governing of society; it extends to "the totality of religious, political, social, domestic and private life."[11] It governs personal conduct as well as the ordering of society. Islam has always prided itself on rejecting the distinction between that which is rendered unto Caesar and that which is rendered unto God. Muhammad, after all, was a political leader as well as a religious one. All aspects of life in an Islamic state are subject to religious authority. Everything is rendered unto Allah.

An Empire from the Beginning

Muslims count the beginning of the Islamic era not from Muhammad's birth or even from the time of his first revelation. Instead, they date it from the Hegira, when Muhammad left Mecca for Medina to become for the first time, if only on a small scale at that point, head of state and commander of armed forces at once.

Muslims never shared the experience of early Christians, of being a persecuted minority within a hostile regime. (Some would say they tasted this during the period of Western colonialism, but even then they remained the majority in their societies, and the colonial governments generally dared not overtly confront Islam.) State power and religious power were fused in Islam from its inception, centering on the caliph as the leader chosen by Allah for his people. Even though the caliphate is no more since the fall of the Ottoman Empire in 1918 (although fanatical Muslims, including Osama bin Laden, call for its restoration), the Islamic world has always been marked by the centralization of theocracy.

The Ayatollah Khomeini remarked, "What is the good of us [i.e., the mullahs] asking for the hand of a thief to be severed or an adulteress to be stoned to death when all we can do is recommend such punishments, having no power to implement them?"[12] This is why Islam resists democracy. The Qur'an presents the clear and absolute law of Allah (which the mullahs uphold). Why should Muslims be governed instead by fallible human judgment? A state ruled by Islamic law must therefore leave little room for representative government; God's Will is not to be established by voting or public opinion.

V. S. Naipaul found these sentiments echoed all over the Islamic world. "In Islam," a prominent Pakistani Muslim told him, "there is no separation. It's a complete way of life."[13] The noted radical Egyptian Sheikh Muhammad al-Ghazali (1917–1996) even ruled in a fatwa that Muslims who advocated the separation of religion from politics were unbelievers, and pointed out that "there is no punishment in Islam for those Muslims who kill these apostates."[14]

The Sharia is not designed to coexist with alternative systems of governance, including one in which consensus is achieved through the ballot box. Disputed questions are matters for the *ulama,* not for voters. According to Muslim scholar Abdul Qader Abdul Aziz, the Sharia is perfect in itself, and needs no augmentation by puny human legal theorists:

> The perfection of the Shari'ah means that it is not in need for any of the previous abrogated religions [that is, Judaism and Christianity] or any human experiences—like the man made laws or any other philosophy. Therefore, any one who claims that the Muslims are in need of any such canons is considered to be a Kafer, or a disbeliever, for he belied Allah's saying: "This day I have completed your religion for you." [Holy Quran, 5:3] and His saying, . . . Your Lord is never forgetful." [Holy Quran, 19:64]. Equal in Kufr, or disbelief, is the one who claims that the Muslims are in need for the systems of Democracy, Communism or any other ideology, without which the Muslim lived and applied the rules of Allah in matters that faced them for fourteen centuries.[15]

To conclude our thought experiment, this means that the values at the heart of American law and society would change with a Muslim majority. In Europe, increasing Muslim populations may herald a substantial change in those societies. Sharia advocate Mohamed Elhachmi Hamdi notes that "even in the United States and Europe, there are supreme values that are embodied in the constitutions and the laws of those lands," but the Muslim world has its own set of values. Islam "has been playing this role [i.e. giver of values and laws] for the last 1,400 years, mostly for the good of Muslims, and there is no need to replace it with a set of Western values."[16] He is, of course, arguing against replacing Islamic values with Western ones in the Islamic world; but as Muslim populations expand in Europe, the call for Islamic values will be carried westward with them.

Autocracy Even Without the Sharia

The House of Islam today is still in disarray from the period of Western colonialism, and its governments range from Sharia-based Islamic republics to more or less secular regimes based on Western models. But the rule is autocracy.

Searching for Islamic democracies, Middle East scholar Bernard Lewis uses political scientist Samuel P. Huntington's criteria for what makes a democratic state:

> [Y]ou can call a country a democracy when it has made two consecutive, peaceful changes of government via free elections. By specifying two elections, Huntington rules out regimes that follow the procedure that one acute observer has called "one man, one vote, once." So I take democracy to mean a polity where the government can be changed by elections as opposed to one where elections are changed by the government.…
>
> [By this criterion] predominantly Muslim regions show very few functioning democracies. Indeed, of the 53 OIC [Organization of the Islamic Conference] states, only Turkey can pass Huntington's test of democracy, and it is in many ways a troubled democracy. Among the others, one can find democratic movements and in some cases even promising democratic developments, but one cannot really say that they are democracies even to the extent that the Turkish Republic is a democracy at the present time.[17]

Lewis continues: "Predominantly Muslim societies (Turkey, as we saw earlier, being the great exception) are ruled by a wide variety of authoritarian, autocratic, despotic, tyrannical, and totalitarian regimes." These he classifies into five major types:

• Traditional autocracies, "like Saudi Arabia and the Gulf sheikhdoms, where established dynastic regimes rest on the traditional props of usage, custom, and history." These are the states, aside from those in the fourth category below, that most explicitly base their legitimacy and law on the Qur'an and Muslim tradition. They are also, as we saw in chapter three, among the most repressive governments in the world—excepting only Marxist/Leninist dinosaurs like North Korea, Cuba and China.

• "Modernizing autocracies. These are regimes—one thinks of Jordan, Egypt, and Morocco in particular—that have their roots in traditional autocracy but are taking significant steps toward modernization and democratization. None really fits the description of liberal democracy as given above, but none is anything like a total autocracy, either." These states are caught on the fault line between the Western world and Islam, having bought into Western notions of how to constitute a society, and paying the price for it. All of these states currently suffer from increasing violence by radical Muslim groups that want to make them over into full-fledged Islamic states.

• "Fascist-style dictatorships," found today in Syria and Iraq. Radical Muslims of bin Laden's ilk hold Syria's Bashar Assad (and his late father) and Iraq's Saddam Hussein in contempt for their un-Islamic ways. According to journalist Dilip Hiro, Muslim radicals have been "murderously hostile" to the Assad regime in Syria.[18] This is chiefly because the present Syrian and Iraqi regimes are an odd hangover from the occupation of Muslim lands by European colonizers in the nineteenth and early twentieth centuries. At that time many Muslims adopted Western styles of dress and Western ways of thinking (while others reacted in the opposite fashion, by returning to the pure religion of the Qur'an and Sunnah). Saddam Hussein with his rumpled uniform and cult of personality is a sartorial and ideological stepchild of mid-twentieth-century Europe's uniformed strongmen: Hitler, Stalin, Mussolini.

• "Radical Islamic regimes. There are two of these so far, Iran and Sudan. . . . Egypt has a potent radical Islamic movement, but the Egyptian political class also has a remarkable knack for maintaining itself in power. Moreover," Lewis concludes, writing before the Taliban and Osama bin Laden had burst into the world's awareness, "the threat to the sovereign state posed by pan-Islamic radicalism has been greatly exaggerated."[19]

• The Muslim former Soviet republics of central Asia, which Lewis characterizes as being in a period of transition. These republics are a way station from Soviet autocracy to Islamic autocracy (or perhaps secularism), and all display to varying degrees the tensions of Islamic states the world over: the tug-of-war between secularism and the Sharia.

In Azerbaijan, for example, Shi'ite Muslims from neighboring Iran have fomented discord against the secular government; in May 1996 the nation's Islamic Party leader was arrested in espionage charges. Kyrgyzstan is another secular state. It has taken stern measures against militant Muslim groups (which it refers to collectively as "Wahhabis"), but it also shows indications of adopting the political aspects of Islam: for example, the government frowns on conversions from Islam to Christianity.

Fifty-three states, one struggling democracy. The judgment of one experienced observer of the Arab world, is devastating.

> Arabs have been organizing their society for half a century or so of independence, and have made a wretched job of it. A whole range of one-man rulers, whether hereditary monarchs or presidents, have proved unable or unwilling to devise political regimes that allow their people to have any say in their destinies. . . .
>
> Perhaps Islam and representative democracy are two beautiful but incompatible ideals. Arab states have not built the institutions that are indispensable for dealing with contemporary problems. In Islam, state authority and religious authority have always gone together. Nobody so far has been able to devise some way of separating them and thus laying the foundations of a civil society.[20]

SIX

Can Islam Be Secularized and Made Compatible with the Western Pluralistic Framework?

MAYBE BEFORE THE WEST IS ISLAMICIZED, Islam will be secularized.

Can this happen? In a certain way this question recalls Mark Twain's celebrated remark when he was asked if he believed in infant baptism. "Of course I believe in infant baptism!" Twain replied. "I've seen it with my own eyes."

Of course Islam can be secularized. You can see it with your own eyes. There are millions of secularized Muslims in the world today. The Egyptian reformer, secular nationalist and political theorist Muhammad Abduh, whose influence is still felt in the House of Islam, was anxious to reconcile Islam with the modern world. He went so far as to assert that polygamy and easy divorce (as well as slavery) were not fundamental elements of Islam, and could be discarded.[1] He revived the ancient Mu'tazilite respect for human reason, and even asserted that women's rights and religious freedom were core Islamic ideas.

Although during his lifetime his influence was felt mostly among academics, many Muslims have followed Muhammad Abduh's lead. As Bill Clinton put it,

> A quarter of the world's population is Muslim—from Africa to Middle East to Asia and to the United States, where Islam is one of our fastest-growing faiths. There are over 1,200 mosques and Islamic centers in the United States, and the number is rapidly increasing. The six million Americans who worship there will tell you there is no inherent clash between Islam and America.[2]

In Clinton's view there is no inherent clash because he believes in the lure of secularism, and in its power to draw Muslims (and Christians and Jews, and everyone else) away from their religion.

That lure is real. When American journalist Charles Glass was kidnapped and held hostage in Beirut by the Hezbollah in 1987, he experienced firsthand how pervasive American pop culture has become, even among those who have dedicated themselves to destroying America as the Great Satan: "The guards were all young," Glass relates. "They liked Michael Jackson and Madonna. One of them was disappointed when I told him Madonna was American, but he said he liked her anyway."[3] In this the terrorists reflect the ambivalence so well expressed by the twelfth-century Persian poet Mujir:

> In one hand the Qur'an, in the other a wineglass,
> sometimes keeping the rules, sometimes breaking them.
> Here we are in this world, unripe and raw,
> not outright heathens, not quite Muslims.[4]

Dinesh D'Souza reports that "in the Middle East, American dolls have become so popular that an official of the Arab League frets that Barbie—with her miniskirts and career aspirations—is not a suitable role model for Muslim children."[5]

V. S. Naipaul noted the same ambivalence, remarking that attraction to the West in Islamic societies was "more than a need for education and skills. But the attraction wasn't admitted; and in that attraction, too humiliating for an old and proud people to admit, there lay disturbance."[6] This ambivalence is found even among the most ferocious proponents of terrorism:

> Jamia'at Ulama-e-Islam is one of the most extreme Islamic movements in Pakistan, and its leader—a ferocious old man with a white beard—is currently summoning the faithful onto the streets to overthrow the government of President Musharraf and launch a holy war. But two of his sons are studying in the United States. He says that they will be better able to understand their enemy. This humbug reveals the inner ambiguity common to his kind. He knows, and we know, that he is supplying them with a brighter future, as any father would.[7]

Secularization brings other concepts with it. The idea of human rights, born in Christianity, has now become virtually universal. Muhammad Abduh and other Islamic modernists such as Jamal al-Afghani and Muhammad Iqbal have helped such Western ideas find a welcome in the Islamic world. In the Islamic Republic of Iran, the populace that overthrew the hated shah for growing too Western and un-Islamic is showing signs of growing restive after twenty-plus years of Islamic orthodoxy and absolutism. When the Taliban withdrew from Kabul, Afghanis joyfully played music for the first time in years.[8] Just as in the nineteenth century the arrival of Western ideas led to the emancipation of the *dhimmis,* so now the House of Islam is home to all sorts of Western notions, including feminism and secularism.

Some even go so far as to call for the adoption of secularism as the only way out of increasingly intractable interreligious squabbles. Shi'ite minorities, for example, after suffering under the Wahhabis in Saudi Arabia and other Sunnis in Iraq, Pakistan and elsewhere, might find secularism welcome—or at least so goes the argument.

The Western Model

In *What Went Wrong: Approaches to the Modern History of the Middle East,* Bernard Lewis proposes that Muslim states follow the Western secularist model in order to solve some of these difficulties. He invites Muslims to learn from Christian experience:

> Secularism in the Christian world was an attempt to resolve the long and destructive struggles of church and state. Separation, adopted in the American and French Revolutions and elsewhere after that, was designed to prevent two things: the use of religion by the state to reinforce and extend its authority; and the use of the state power by the clergy to impose their doctrines and rules on others. This is a problem long seen as purely Christian, not relevant to Muslims or for that matter to Jews, for whom a similar problem has arisen in Israel. Looking at the contemporary Middle East, both Muslim and Jewish, one must ask whether this is still true—or whether Muslims and Jews may perhaps have caught a Christian disease and might therefore consider a Christian remedy.[9]

This advice is not acceptable to Mohamed Elhachmi Hamdi. "There is nothing new about this 'remedy,' which is one that the West has tried before to impose on Islamic countries, albeit without major success," Hamdi writes. For him and other Muslims of like mind, the Sharia is not negotiable. "A secular government might coerce obedience, but Muslims will not abandon their belief that state affairs should be supervised by the just teachings of the holy law."[10]

Indeed, the assumption that Western cultural hegemony means the battle has already been won and Muslims can be secularized is premature. As Naipaul observed in Pakistan, "Every Friday every man, whatever his condition, heard from the mullahs that the laws of men were not to be obeyed if they went against the teachings of the Koran."[11] A Christian preacher might say similar words on any given Sunday from any pulpit in America, but they wouldn't mean exactly the same thing; for as we have seen time and time again, the Bible and the Qur'an are fundamentally different. Islam rejects the idea of a separation of church and state—a notion harmonious with Jesus' own words about rendering to Caesar that which is Caesar's and to God that which is God's. Anyone, therefore, who thinks that Muslims can become another species of Methodist or Presbyterian—the Middle Eastern analogue of civic-minded Americans, committed to democracy and tolerance—will be disappointed. The open-minded and tolerant Islam of Abduh and his followers repeatedly founders upon the plain words of the Qur'an, which every Muslim is continuously exhorted to read and love.

Working from the words of the sacred book, many Muslims reject the notion that all human beings have rights—a cardinal principal of the secular state. As we saw earlier, Iran's delegate to the United Nations, Sa'id Raja'i-Khorassani, declared in 1985 that "the very concept of human rights was 'a Judeo-Christian invention' and inadmissible in Islam."[12]

Even so, it is one thing to call the concept inadmissible and another to expel it from the House of Islam. Today there are Muslim organizations dedicated to promoting secular Islam. The Institute for the Secularization of Islamic Society (ISIS) declares boldly that "Islamic society has been held back by an unwillingness to subject its beliefs, laws and practices to critical examination, by a lack of respect for the rights of the individual, and by an unwillingness to tolerate alternative viewpoints or to engage in constructive dialogue." Consequently, the institute hopes to "promote the ideas of rationalism, secularism, democracy and human rights within Islamic society." The ISIS stands for the whole panoply of Western rights that are generally held in disfavor in the House of Islam: "freedom of expression, freedom of thought and belief, freedom of intellectual and scientific inquiry" and, most ominously of all for the mullahs, "freedom of conscience and religion—including the freedom to change one's religion or belief—and freedom from religion: the freedom not to believe in any deity."[13]

As reasonable as all this may sound to Westerners, however, it is unlikely that such a program will find much support among Muslims. Because it would entail the abandonment or restriction of full enforcement of the Sharia, for many Muslims secularism is tantamount to apostasy. By standing for these ideas—ideas that are taken for granted everywhere in the West—the members of the ISIS risk death. Apostasy is a capital crime under the Sharia, and when these men stand for the "freedom to change one's religion or belief," they are placing themselves outside the law of Islam.

They risk suffering the fate of Rashad Khalifa, an early victim of Islamic terror on American soil. According to Middle East expert Daniel Pipes,

> Khalifa, an Egyptian biochemist living in Tucson, Arizona, analyzed the Koran by computer and concluded from some other complex numerology that the final two verses of the ninth chapter do not belong in the holy book. This insight eventually prompted him to declare himself a prophet, a very serious offense in Islam (which holds Muhammad to be the last of the prophets). Some months later, on January 31, 1990, unknown assailants—presumably orthodox Muslims angered by his teachings— stabbed Khalifa to death. While the case remains unsolved, it sent a clear and chilling message: Even in the United States, deviancy leads to death.[14]

Pipes relates this in his review of Ibn Warraq's *Why I Am Not a Muslim* (1995). The ISIS website contains numerous reviews of this book and trumpets Ibn Warraq as a prime example of the secular Muslim. No doubt he is, and not just for his skeptical writings about Islam and the Prophet Muhammad; he is also an exemplary secular Muslim because his true identity is a secret. Secular Muslims, after all, risk death from hardliners who consider them to have fallen away from the faith. "Ibn Warraq" is a pseudonym that protects the author from those who are ready to carry out the Prophet's death sentence on apostates.

Ibn Warraq's pseudonymous status is emblematic of the difficult challenge facing those who would call for the secularization of Islam, whether from within or from without. As soon as they mention looking at the Qur'an as a historical document, or mitigating the binding force of the Sharia, another vocal party is ready to denounce them as apostates and enemies of Islam. How, then, can the House of Islam ever implement Bernard Lewis's benign and well-reasoned prescription for secular-

ism, when a not inconsiderable party of Muslims will fight this prospect
to the death as a nationwide apostasy?

The Example of Turkey

Consider the case of Turkey. In the aftermath of World War I, Mustafa
Kemal, who called himself Ataturk, or Father of the Turks, established
the first secular government in a Muslim society—leading the sheikh
who famously visited Osama bin Laden on video in 2001 to refer to "infidels like the Turks."[15] Ataturk declared that "the civilized world is far
ahead of us. We have no choice but to catch up. It is time to stop nonsense, such as 'should we or should we not wear hats?' We shall adopt
hats along with all other works of Western civilization. Uncivilized people are doomed to be trodden under the feet of civilized people."[16] Hats
were more than just a symbol: because of their brims, they interfered
with the prostrations that were and are an essential element of Muslim
prayer. By outlawing turbans and mandating hats, Ataturk was striking
at the very heart of Turkish Islamic society.

Within a relatively brief period the great Islamic empire that had
been the seat of the caliphate and the lodestar of the Muslim world became
a Western-style modern state. The unity of the polity was based on racial,
not religious grounds (resulting in the murder and exile of millions of
Armenians and a substantial number of Greeks, who fared better even
as *dhimmis* than they did under the nationalistic and secular Turkish government). According to Islamic scholar Caesar Farah, Ataturk accomplished this transformation by rapidly "abolishing the caliphate, placing
restrictions on the observances of the faith, introducing secular marriage
procedures, and neglecting Islamic places of devotion and worship." He
"pursued a deliberate policy of downplaying religion in the life of the
state when under the Ottoman, the last Islamic empire, it was central."[17]

This is exactly the dream of moderate, Western-influenced and
Western-friendly Muslims and their non-Muslim patrons. Ataturk labored
to erect a truly Jeffersonian wall of separation between church and state.
If the notion of a modernized, secularized Islam has any viability, it should
show in Turkey, its principal research-and-development project.

But there was resistance to Ataturk's program in Turkey virtually
from the beginning. Scholar Paul Dumont notes that "the expeditious
secularization imposed on the country by Mustafa Kemal and his

entourage created a shock wave through the country which has not yet died out."[18] The chief opposition to Kemalism, as secular rule in Turkey came to be known, was fundamentally religious. Rank-and-file Turks, according to Ataturk's biographer Andrew Mango, believed that "misery was the fruit of impiety, prosperity the reward of obedience to the law of Islam."[19]

In this reaction to Ataturk's reforms, Turks were repeating an assessment of Turkish affairs that was common long before turbans were abolished. After the Ottoman conquest of Constantinople in 1453, observes historian Philip Mansel,

> Islam itself presented one potential challenge to the Ottoman capital. Islam is a religion with revolutionary implications. Rulers are considered legitimate only if they enforce the *sheriat* [this is the Turkish form of the word *sharia*], the holy law of Islam based on the teachings of the Koran. The *sheriat* was considered above, rather than a product of, the state.... Conflict between dynastic power and Islam emerged throughout the history of the city.[20]

Instances of this conflict fill Ottoman history. In the early seventeenth century, "extremist" preachers began, in the name of pure Islam, to inveigh against the secular elements of Westernized Istanbul. Mansel continues: "They denounced not only coffee, tobacco, silk and dancing, but also such dervish practices as pilgrimages to tombs." (The tombs of Sufi saints are popular objects of veneration in the Muslim world, especially among Shi'ites but also to varying degrees throughout Islam. This veneration is well established in Islamic practice, but has always been subject to attack from purists, who contend that even to pray in front of the tomb of a saint is to associate partners with Allah and compromise Islamic monotheism.) These preachers and their followers "were so threatening that for most of 1651 the Oecumenical Patriarch took refuge in the French embassy."[21]

This movement ultimately threatened the sultan, who put an end to it. But the sultan's grand vizier had learned its chief lesson: on his deathbed he advised the sultan to rule with "an appearance of religion and justice."[22]

Over two hundred years later, the spiritual children of these preachers vied with Ataturk's secularists for control of the tottering empire. When the absolute rule of the sultan became a kind of constitutional monarchy in 1908, Muslim leaders were furious.

> A preacher called "Blind Ali" denounced the constitution in the mosque
> of Fatih. On 7 October 1908 he led a large Ramadan crowd to Yildiz to
> see the Sultan, who appeared at a window. Blind Ali told him: "We want
> a shepherd! A flock cannot exist without a shepherd!" The fundamental-
> ists demanded the rule of *sheriat,* the prohibition of taverns, theatres and
> photography, and an end to Muslim women's freedom to walk around
> the town.[23]... A fundamentalist newspaper, Volkan, was started in Novem-
> ber with the programme "to spread the light of divine unity in the capi-
> tal of the Caliphate." ... On 3 April 1909 the Society of Muhammad was
> established and held meetings in Aya Sofya [the conquered Hagia Sophia
> cathedral] hostile to the [reformist] Committee: "Forward! If we fall as
> martyrs, do not retreat!"

At that time, Muslim leaders were divided over the fundamentalist agenda,
much as they are today. Mansel concludes: "Many sufis and imams supported it; senior *ulama* remained loyal to the constitution."[24] But as
always, those who were against the new republican arrangements justified their actions on the basis of the fundamental tenets of Islam.

Religious uprisings have been a feature of the Turkish secular state
virtually since its inception, and those desiring to restore Islam to centrality in public life have made steady gains. By the 1950s, says Farah, the
secular authorities "found it prudent henceforth to play up to Islamic
loyalties and allow the ulama and other religious leaders a freer hand."[25]

This prudence, however, wasn't enough to satisfy the proponents
of a restored Islamic regime. The Turkish politician Necmettin Erbakan
led pro-Islamic forces against the Kemalist regime for three decades. He
was forthrightly anti-Kemalist: "only Islam, he argued, could shield the
country from succumbing to unhealthy Western values."[26] He even served
as prime minister of the Kemalist state for a brief and tumultuous period
(June 1996 to June 1997), during which he did what he could within
Turkey's existing structures to restore Islam. Fierce opposition limited
his effectiveness, but he was able to do enough that the American secretary of state, Madeline Albright, expressed her displeasure with the "drift
of Turkey away from secularism."[27]

The army (which is the bastion of Kemalist secularism in Turkey)
ultimately forced Erbakan from power, but the struggle for Turkey's soul
continues. The former mayor of Istanbul, Recep Tayyip Erdogan, is one
of the most prominent of a new generation of antisecularists. Meanwhile,
Turkey is home to a number of Islamic "brotherhoods." The Nurcus,

followers of the Islamic theorist Said Nursi (1876–1960), claim about five million followers (many of them Turkish emigrants in European countries) and continue to fight against Kemalism on Islamic grounds, along with other Muslim groups including the Suleymancis, the Nur community and the Fethullah Gulen group. The late Cemalettin Kaplan ("The Black Voice") even founded an "Anatolian Islam Federal Republic" with himself as caliph; the current caliph is his son Metin Muftuoglu, although not all members of this group have accepted his rule.[28] Some of these groups have received funding from Iran and other militant Islamic sources.[29]

Turkey's experience reinforces a primary lesson of Islamic history: there will always be some Muslims who will not rest until all traces of secularism and other Western influences are eradicated from their societies. This is not because of resentment of the West's power or wealth, but because of an abiding interest in guarding and maintaining the purity of the House of Islam.

Secularization Defied

It was the same story in Iran. The attempts by several shahs to follow Ataturk's lead and modernize Iran along Western lines were ultimately torpedoed by Khomeini's Islamic Revolution of 1979, which restored traditional Islam's strict dress code and swept away "music and most other 'satanic arts'" as well as alcoholic beverages.[30] Westerners were mystified by the spectacle of women wearing traditional Muslim garb, demonstrating against the shah who had tried to give them greater rights. But those who searched for economic or political causes for this revolution, or who were puzzled by the apparent popularity of the dour, scowling Ayatollah Khomeini, failed to recognize that "in the Muslim world, Islam is the only key to the hearts and minds of the people."[31] When Khomeini spoke to the Iranian people, he didn't talk about economics. His message was that it was time to restore the purity of Islam.

The tension between Islam and secularism didn't start with Shah Muhammad Reza Pahlavi and Khomeini. "In 1906," says Amir Taheri, supporters of a constitution for Persia (Iran's ancient name) took "as a model the French Revolution's charter of human rights. Had they succeeded in imposing that model, as the *mashru'eh* mullahs [supporters of a traditional Islamic theocracy] feared, the road would have been paved for the secularization of the Iranian state."[32] One of these anticonstitutionalist mullahs was arrested, tried and sentenced to death by the government that was newly in place. Just before he was hanged, he managed one last sermon: "Either this system must go or Islam will perish."[33]

Long after his death, the mullah's cry would drive the shah from his Peacock Throne.

This pattern is repeated throughout the Islamic world. Every government that goes too far in implementing Western principles encounters religious resistance. This was the case with Iraq's relatively secular Saddam Hussein, who received a tremendous boost to his legitimacy from the Persian Gulf War:

> The *ulama* [Islamic religious leadership] had resisted a declining status and continued to insist on their moral obligation to ensure that government actions meet Islamic requirements. . . . And on the eve of the launching of the war, the secular banner of Iraq was embroidered with the Islamic battle cry "God is Great" in order to rally more Islamic sentiment. Being an observing Muslim, like most of his Sunni followers, Saddam's demonstration of loyalty to the faith was accelerated by the war. Since the end of the war, Islam's role in society and politics has received greater emphasis, and that is in a state once conceived as secular, socialist, democratic, and pan-Arab nationalist in character.[34]

Pakistan also, in Farah's words, has struggled since its independence "to reconcile modern Western style institutions with the *Shari'ah* of Islam."[35] It was founded as a secular state, but Islamic activists resisted its secular character from the beginning. In 1956, eight years after independence, it was proclaimed an Islamic Republic. Amid a great deal of ongoing unrest, Prime Minister Zulfikar Ali Bhutto promised in 1977 to implement the Sharia. Shortly thereafter, President Muhammad Ziaul-Haq, who had taken power in a bloody coup, declared that the Sharia was above Pakistan's civil law. Unrest has continued, and the small Christian community in Pakistan has suffered considerably under the Sharia. The Christian Ayub Masih, sentenced to death on a questionable charge of blasphemy, would never even have been arrested under the nation's original "Westernized" law.

The same situation prevails in Sudan, where the Sharia was adopted in 1983, setting the stage for the persecution and enslavement of the nation's Christians, which continues to this day. In Algeria, proponents of the Sharia won a ballot-box victory in 1992 by calling for "a renewal based on Islam to combat the festering problems of unemployment, lack of economic well-being, and social inequalities stemming from vestiges of colonial rule."[36] They were prevented from taking power at that time, but they have by no means given up their vision of a land made great again by the purity of Islam.

Desire to restore the purity, and thus the glory, of the *umma* is also the impetus behind the rise of Osama bin Laden and other Muslim terrorists today. Setbacks in the Islamic world commonly result in the diagnosis that the defeat resulted from insufficient religious fidelity. In 1948, the Egyptian Islamic radical Sayyid Qutb surveyed the House of Islam and wrote passionately, "We only have to look in order to see that our social situation is as bad as it can be." Yet "we continually cast aside all our own spiritual heritage, all our intellectual endowment, and all the solutions which might well be revealed by a glance at these things; we cast aside our own fundamental principles and doctrines, and we bring in those of democracy, or socialism, or communism."[37]

In other words, the key to success is more Islam. This has always been the reaction in times of crisis. According to Bernard Lewis, as far back as the sixteenth and seventeenth centuries, Ottoman officials looked at the weaknesses in their society and government and came to the conclusion that "the basic fault ... was falling away from the good old ways, Islamic and Ottoman; the basic remedy was a return to them."[38]

V. S. Naipaul discovered this kind of diagnosis to be very much alive in modern Pakistan, where "failure led back again and again to the assertion of the faith."[39] He quotes an article in the *Pakistan Times* by A. H. Kardar, "the former cricket captain of Pakistan, and an Oxford man." Says Kardar of modern Pakistan: "Clearly, the choice is between materialism and its inseparable nationally divisive political manifestoes, and the Word of God."[40] Dinesh D'Souza reconstructs this way of thinking: "The Koran promises that if Muslims are faithful to Allah, they will enjoy prosperity in this life and paradise in the next life." When the House of Islam is not prospering, it is solely because "Muslims are not following the true teaching of Allah!"[41] A new severity invariably follows.

If Islamic orthodoxy were differently constituted, it wouldn't be so vulnerable to exploitation by fanatics and demagogues who invoke religious principles as the basis of their legitimacy—but that's precisely the problem. And it's a problem that calls for careful examination by everyone who believes that the House of Islam can easily be secularized and fit into place as another ingredient in a global multicultural society.

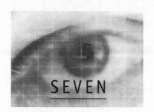

SEVEN

Can Science and Culture Flourish under Islam?

THIS CYCLE OF DEFEAT FOLLOWED BY CALLS FOR religious revival not only marks a great deal of Islamic history, but also colors the Muslim approach to science and culture.

Islamic cultural achievements are legendary. While Europe trampled the glories of pagan Greece and Rome and degenerated into the savagery of the Dark Ages, Islam was becoming a beacon to the world. "For while [the caliphs] al-Rashid and al-Mamun were delving into Greek and Persian philosophy," says the historian Philip K. Hitti, "their contemporaries in the West, Charlemagne and his lords, were reportedly dabbling in the art of writing their names."[1]

Islam burst forth from Arabia in the seventh century with awesome energy, as a great and terrible force that swept all before it and quickly established its superiority. "Only a hundred years after the death of Muhammad," Hitti observes, "his followers were the masters of an empire greater than that of Rome at its zenith, an empire extending from the Bay of Biscay to the Indus and the confines of China and from the Aral Sea to the lower cataracts of the Nile."[2] By the time of the great Caliph Harun al-Rashid (786–809), the Islamic imperial capital of Baghdad "had grown from nothingness to a world center of prodigious wealth and international significance, standing alone as the rival of Byzantium."[3]

Not only did the Muslims of the seventh through the twelfth centuries build a great empire; they also fashioned a grand civilization that led the world in technology, science, literature, philosophy and more. Hitti concludes: "No people in the early Middle Ages contributed to human progress as much as did the Arabs."[4]

Medieval Islamic Achievements

In astronomy, Muslims refined the astrolabe, allowing for tremendous breakthroughs in our knowledge of the heavens. Abu Raihan al-Biruni (973–1048) developed precise methods for determining the positions of the sun and even completed groundbreaking work on longitude and latitude, long before the rest of the world caught on. Hitti also notes that one will find "under the roll of Islam's most distinguished astronomers the celebrated name of Umar al-Khayyam [1048–1131]—the author of the even more celebrated *Rubaiyat.*"[5]

In architecture, Muslims built some of the grandest structures the world has ever seen, including the Taj Mahal and the Blue Mosque. Hitti describes Jerusalem's Dome of the Rock as "an architectural monument of such noble beauty that it has scarcely been surpassed anywhere."[6] He calls the eighth-century Umayyad Mosque in Damascus a "jewel of architecture which still attracts lovers of beauty."[7]

Nor were Islamic architectural achievements restricted to these grand edifices, as the English traveler Robert Byron confirmed in his charming 1933 book *The Road to Oxiana.* Traveling from Beirut through Jerusalem, Iraq, Iran and Afghanistan, he uncovers (between adventures) unknown marvels of Islamic art and architecture hidden away in remote mosques. In Isfahan in Iran, for instance, he tours the Mosque of Sheikh Lutfullah, where the interior "pageant of colour and pattern," he says, "must astonish the European ... because he can previously have had no idea that abstract pattern was capable of so profound a splendour."[8] Even the poor black-and-white accompanying photo in the current edition of his book discloses a structure that is indeed breathtaking. In Yezd he enters the Friday Mosque and finds "fourteenth-century mosaics in perfect condition."[9] Afghanistan's Shrine of Khoja Abu Nasr Parsa in Balkh (Bactria) possesses "an unearthly beauty."[10] And Byron finds comparable gems virtually everywhere he goes.

In medicine, Caliph al-Rashid's Islamic empire saw the establishment of the *umma*'s first hospital. His son Abdullah al-Mamun (813–833) broke new ground in establishing professional standards for physicians and pharmacists, which later caliphs continued to require. "Following a case of malpractice," according to Hitti, "a distinguished physician was ordered by the caliph in 931 to examine all practicing physicians and grant certificates only to those who satisfied the requirements. Over eight hundred and sixty such men in Baghdad passed the test and the capital rid itself of quacks."[11]

Abu Bakr ar-Razi (865–925), known in the West as Rhazes, wrote an encyclopedia of medical information and a book of alchemy that, rendered into Latin, became principal bases for the understanding of medicine and chemistry in medieval Europe. Another Muslim famous for his philosophical work, Ibn Sina or Avicenna (980–1037), authored a medical textbook that was preeminent with European doctors from the twelfth to the seventeenth centuries.[12] Still another philosopher/physician, Ibn Rushd, known as Averroës (1128–1198), contributed a notable medical text as well.

In mathematics, the ninth-century theorist Muhammad ibn Musa al-Khwarzimi (790–850) "composed the oldest work on arithmetic and the oldest work on algebra, which was translated into Latin and used until the sixteenth century as the principal mathematics textbook of European universities and served to introduce into Europe the science of algebra, and with it the name."[13] The word *algebra* comes from the title of his mathematical treatise *Al-Jabr wa-al-Muqabilah,* and *algorithm* is derived from his name.

In literature, *The Thousand and One Nights* has had untold influence on later writing of all kinds: history, fiction, fantasy, memoir. And that (along with the *Rubaiyat* of Umar al-Khayyam, immortalized by Edward FitzGerald's English translation) is just the work that's best known in the West. A wealth of fine Persian and Arabic poetry stands with the greatest literary achievements of any culture of any period. It would be impossible to list all the classics of Islamic literature, but I would be remiss if I didn't mention at least the twelfth-century Sufi Farid ud-Din Attar's *The Conference of the Birds,* a splendid and wise allegory of the mystical journey. The eminent Sufi poet Jalaluddin Rumi (1207–1273) has likewise inspired mystics for centuries, and is enjoying a new vogue today among New Agers.

Virtually from the beginning of Islam, the poetic tradition was strong, especially in mystically minded Persia. There was the sensual Persian poet Abu Nuwas (750–810); the poet/chronicler Abu Tammam Habib ibn Aus (805–845); the magnificent panegyrist al-Mutanabbi (915–965), whose poetry was so highly regarded that he came to be known by this surname, which means "one who pretends to be a prophet";[14] the epic poet Abolqasem Ferdowsi (932–1025), who attracted attention in the

English-speaking world in the nineteenth century through translations by the English poet Matthew Arnold; the lyric poet Hafiz (1325–1390); the heterodox Turkish Sufi Nesimi (d. 1417);[15] and a host of others who are worth reading even in the driest scholarly translation.

In addition to the poets, there were prose writers. The prolific scholar Abu ᶜUthman ᶜAmr ibn Bahr al-Jahiz (776–868), whom Bernard Lewis calls "the greatest master of the essay and indeed of Arabic prose," wrote more than two hundred books over the course of his long life, encompassing a multitude of subjects including politics (*The Institution of the Caliphate*), zoology (the seven-volume *Book of Animals*), cuisine *(Arab Food),* and practical living *(Sobriety and Mirth; The Art of Keeping One's Mouth Shut).*[16] Muhammad Abu Ja'far al-Tabari (839–923) completed a universal history as well as a respected commentary on the Qur'an. Another historian, al-Baladhuri (d. 892), contributed a key early history of the Arabs.

Somewhat later, Ibn Khaldun (1332–1406) was centuries ahead of his time in his studies of sociology and economics. His *Muqaddimah* stands as the earliest attempt at a systematic analysis of the study of history that "takes due cognizance of the physical facts of climate and geography as well as of moral and spiritual forces."[17] To Bernard Lewis, he was "the greatest historian of the Arabs and perhaps the greatest historical thinker of the Middle Ages."[18]

In music, the Sufis of Egypt, Tunisia, Morocco, Iran and Turkey created a rich and varied tradition. The ninth-century philosopher al-Kindi even wrote treatises on musical theory, which "indicate that measured song, or mensural music, was known to the Moslems centuries before it was introduced into Christian Europe."[19] Hitti notes that "the refined and dazzling court of Harun al-Rashid patronized music and singing, as it did science and art, to the extent of becoming the center of a galaxy of musical stars."[20]

Music As Treason

Oddly enough, however, orthodox Sunni Islam in its traditional form bans musical instruments and frowns on music in general. These strictures have always been widely ignored, but they are very much on the books. *Reliance of the Traveller,* the Islamic legal manual that embodies Sunni orthodoxy, quotes the Prophet:

Allah Mighty and Majestic sent me as a guidance and mercy to believers and commanded me to do away with musical instruments, flutes, strings, crucifixes, and the affair of the pre-Islamic period of ignorance.

On the Day of Resurrection, Allah will pour molten lead into the ears of whoever sits listening to a songstress.

Song makes hypocrisy grow in the heart as water does herbage.

"This Community will experience the swallowing up of some people by the earth, metamorphosis of some into animals, and being rained upon with stones." Someone asked, "When will this be, O Messenger of Allah?" and he said, "When songstresses and musical instruments appear and wine is held to be lawful."

There will be peoples of my Community who will hold fornication, silk, wine, and musical instruments to be lawful.[21]

Muslim rigorists still try to enforce these strictures of the Prophet whenever and wherever they attempt to reestablish the fullness and purity of Islamic practice. The reformer Muhyi al Din Aurangzeb (1658–1707) made a campaign against music a central element of his effort to purify Islam in India.[22] In our own day, young John Walker Lindh, as he learned more about his new religion, ultimately realized that he had to stop listening to his beloved rap records. The Indonesian militant group Laskar Jihad considers music "a distraction from God."[23] The Taliban was criticized worldwide for actually enforcing the legal ban on music.

In the Malaysian state of Kelantan, reports Aid to the Church in Need, "there was a new law forbidding songs, dances and even the sound of church bells. Such activities, according to the government controlled by Islamic fundamentalists, were contrary to religion. Singing and dancing, especially in the evening, could lead to 'immoral' activities."[24] Iran's Ayatollah Khomeini remarked several years ago with his characteristically flamboyant vehemence:

Music corrupts the minds of our youth. There is no difference between music and opium. Both create lethargy in different ways. If you want your country to be independent, then ban music. Music is treason to our nation and to our youth.[25]

Indeed, Khomeini's vision of Islam was singularly joyless—by his own account:

Allah did not create man so that he could have fun. The aim of creation was for mankind to be put to the test through hardship and prayer. An Islamic regime must be serious in every field. There are no jokes in Islam. There is no humor in Islam. There is no fun in Islam. There can be no fun and joy in whatever is serious.[26]

Yet even Khomeini betrayed something of the *umma*'s longstanding ambivalence toward song and sensual experience. While thundering against music, he wrote some delicate little examples of Shi'ite poetry—which with its mystical bent is firmly in the tradition of classical Persian verse, and bears many similarities to the Sufi mystical tradition. It is strange but true that this sonnet came from the pen of the irascible and fantastic old man:

> Oh, I desire a cup of wine from the Beloved's own hands.
> In whom can I confine this secret?
> Where am I to take my grief?
> I have yearned a lifetime to see the Beloved's face;
> I am a frenzied moth circling the flame,
> A wild rue seed pod roasting in the fire.
> See my stained cloak and this prayer-rug of hypocrisy;
> Can I, one day, tear them to shreds at the tavern door?
> If the Beloved allowed me one sip from the Jug of Love, intoxicated,
> I would break loose from the bonds of my existence.
> Old as I am, one signal of hope from those eyes would turn me young
> again.
> Graciously bestow me this favour, and I will transcend this earthly
> abode.[27]

Openness to Other Cultures

Muslims built their great medieval civilization with an attitude of openness to what they could learn from non-Muslims. Bernard Lewis has remarked upon "the unique assimilative power of Arab culture, sometimes misrepresented as merely imitative."[28] Islam in its glory days never hesitated to borrow from other cultures. Indeed, all great civilizations have done this, taking up and improving upon what came before them.

The architectural design of mosques, with their imposing domes, is the pride of Islam. While the calligraphy that decorates the walls is a

Muslim invention (and, indeed, a uniquely beguiling art form), the shape of mosques is derived from the structure of the Byzantine church, whose dome is meant to represent the cosmos in miniature. According to historian Bat Ye'or, the first of these magnificent mosques, the seventh-century Dome of the Rock, was "of Byzantine conception and execution."[29]

The astrolabe, though perfected by Muslims, was developed long before the Angel Gabriel commanded Muhammad to recite the words of Allah. *The Thousand and One Nights* owes a debt to the *Iliad,* just as Avicenna, Averroës and the other Muslim philosophers built upon the work of a Greek pagan.

The preservation of Aristotle's thought during a time when the Christian West largely neglected its pagan heritage was not an achievement of Muslims alone. The Arab-speaking world became acquainted with Aristotle through the work of a fifth-century priest named Probus of Antioch.[30] During the ninth-century reign of Caliph al-Mamun, the importance of learning from non-Muslims was so universally recognized that translation became a virtual industry. Many of those who did the translating were non-Muslims, including the Christian Hunayn ibn-Ishaq (809–873), whom Hitti calls "the sheikh of the translators."[31] According to historian Elias B. Skaff, he "translated most of the works of Aristotle and Galen into Syriac, which his son and nephew rendered into Arabic. He is also said to have translated Hippocrates' medical treatises and Plato's *Republic.*"[32]

Christians also contributed to the Muslim ascendancy in medicine and other sciences in the early period, as Bat Ye'or shows:

> The first known scientific work in Arabic was a treatise on medicine, written in Greek by Ahrun, a Christian priest from Alexandria, and translated from Syriac into Arabic in 683 by Masarjawayh, a Jewish doctor from Basra (Iraq).... Ibn Bakhtishu (d. ca. 771), a Nestorian physician summoned to Baghdad by the caliph al-Mansur, established a hospital there, where his son (d. 801) became the leading practitioner. Yuhanna b. Masawayh (777–857), a Jacobite physician, translator, and ophthalmologist, wrote the first treatise on ophthalmology in Arabic.[33]

Muslims combined what they derived from non-Muslims with their own labors to build something new, and something great. Seyyed Hossein Nasr sums up the guiding principle of this achievement: "Coming at the end of the prophetic cycle, Islam has considered all the wisdom of traditions before it as in a sense its own and has never been shy of borrowing from them and transforming them into elements of its own worldview."[34]

The borrowings, of course, went both ways. Most famous to Westerners among the achievements of the Islamic civilization of the Middle Ages are the works of the eminent Muslim philosophers who had a tremendous influence upon the Christian philosophers of medieval Europe. Averroës, Avicenna and others blazed new intellectual trails during a time when scarcely any significant Christian philosophy was being done. For later Christian thinkers like St. Albert the Great and St. Thomas Aquinas who made extensive use of Aristotle, the work of these Muslims in explicating Aristotle's writings was an essential reference point.

Philosophy

In Antiquity and the Middle Ages, philosophy was much more closely tied to science and other disciplines than it is now. (Aristotle was a naturalist; Avicenna and Averroës were physicians.) Thus, the waning of Muslim philosophy provides a window on some of the reasons why Islamic civilization itself went into decline.

From its origins, philosophy in Islam, just as in Christendom, strove mightily—and with notable success—to reconcile faith and reason. Islamic philosophy, according to Muslim apologists Mohamed Azad and Bibi Amina, "recognized no theoretical limits other than those of human reason itself; and it assumed that the truth found by unaided reason does not disagree with the truth of Islam when both are properly understood." Hitti observes that "it is to the eternal glory of medieval Islam that it succeeded for the first time in the history of human thought in harmonizing and reconciling monotheism ... with Greek philosophy."[35] Islamic philosophers struggled to harmonize the Qur'an with the necessary truths they were deriving by the light of reason. "To the Moslem thinkers," says Hitti, "Aristotle was truth, Plato was truth, the Koran was truth; but truth must be one. Hence arose the necessity of harmonizing the three, and to this task they addressed themselves."[36]

Some philosophers, however, considered this effort misguided. Abu Yusuf Yaqub ibn Ishaq al-Sabbah al-Kindi (801–873), a physician and philosopher, suggested that "prophets and philosophers have different and independent ways to the highest truth available to man."[37] Philosophers needn't labor to reconcile the pure truths of philosophy with the Qur'an, he thought. Another physician/philosopher, Rhazes, even went so far as to say that *only* philosophy leads to the highest truth.[38]

Avicenna (Abu Ali al-Husain ibn Abdallah ibn Sina), whose influence spread into the West, was somewhat more circumspect. He distinguished between "the faculty of prophetic knowledge (the 'sacred' intellect)" and "revelation (imaginative representation meant to convince the multitude and improve their earthly life)."[39] But if revelation was only "imaginative representation," the door to skepticism lay open. This was too much for more religiously inclined Muslims. Avicenna's views, according to the historian of philosophy Wilhelm Windelband, were "regarded with jealous eyes by Mohammedan orthodoxy, and the scientific movement experienced such violent persecutions in the tenth century that it took refuge in the secret league of the 'Pure Brothers.' Avicenna himself was also persecuted."[40]

The growing rift between philosophy and orthodox Islam ultimately developed into an open war, in which the philosophers were greatly outnumbered. The orthodox party's champion was a Sufi, Abu Hamid al-Ghazali (1058–1128), whose classic work *The Incoherence of the Philosophers* took brilliant aim at virtually the entire Islamic philosophical tradition—and scored a direct hit.

For al-Ghazali, most philosophy was simply a veil for heresy. Many philosophers, he said, were teaching truths that they themselves had discovered and that had no more attestation than their own word. They were denigrating the holy Qur'an. They were guilty of "denial of revealed laws and religious confessions" as well as "rejection of the details of religious and sectarian [teaching], believing them to be man-made laws and embellished tricks."[41] Indeed, the teachings of these philosophers (chiefly the outstanding Muslim thinkers al-Farabi and Avicenna) "challenge the [very] principles of religion."[42]

Al-Ghazali was no anti-intellectual, and his quarrel was not so much with philosophy per se as with heresy. He employs quite sophisticated philosophical arguments in *The Incoherence of the Philosophers* in order to refute the philosophers' pretensions. He takes issue particularly with the idea that Allah's revelation consisted of mere "imaginative representation," i.e., parable rather than literal truth. Discussing the Qur'an's depictions of heaven and hell, he insists that "what has come down [in the law] describing paradise and the fire and the detailing of these states has attained a degree [of explicit statement] that does not [render it] subject to metaphorical interpretation." That is, the Qur'an is true to the letter. Discussing the possibility of the resurrection of the body, he says simply, "The religious law has declared [the resurrection]. It is [in itself] possible, and, hence, must be believed."[43]

According to Tilman Nagel, a scholar of Islam, al-Ghazali "was inspired by a notion that we frequently see in Islam's intellectual history: the notion that everything human beings can possibly know is already contained in the Koran and the hadith; only naïve people can be made to believe that there is knowledge beyond them."[44] And whatever contradicts the Qur'an must give way.

With chilling fidelity to Islamic law, al-Ghazali poses a final question at the end of *The Incoherence of the Philosophers:* "If someone says: 'You have explained the doctrines of these [philosophers]'; do you then say conclusively that they are infidels and *that the killing of those who uphold their beliefs is obligatory?"*[45] He then answers this himself: "Pronouncing them infidels is necessary in three questions": their teachings that the world existed eternally, that Allah does not know particular things but only universals, and that there is no resurrection of the body. Al-Ghazali doesn't say that the philosophers should not be killed, because Islamic law says they should be. *Reliance of the Traveller* declares, "When a person who has reached puberty and is sane voluntarily apostatizes from Islam, he deserves to be killed."[46]

Al-Ghazali's masterwork heralded the beginning of the decline of Islamic philosophy, although the victory of the views he represented was not immediate. To counter him there arose another great Muslim philosopher whom the West knows as Averroës (Abul-Waleed Muhammad ibn Rushd). This rationalist took al-Ghazali to task, most notably in his reply to *The Incoherence of the Philosophers,* which he entitled *Incoherence of the Incoherence,* where he insisted that those who pursue philosophy "need not adjust its certain conclusions to what theologians claim to be the correct interpretation of the divine law."[47]

But the damage was done. Islamic philosophy became suspect to a large party of those who considered themselves guardians of religious orthodoxy. Indeed, even before al-Ghazali it was suspect. In his *History of Islamic Theology,* Nagel says, "All attempts to incorporate the philosophical tradition into a way of thinking that was based on Islam failed. Playing with philosophy could be an enjoyable pastime, but even as early as the tenth century the general opinion among the educated was that no faithful Muslim and faithful follower of the Sharia could practice it seriously."[48]

A rationalist school of Islamic philosophy would continue. The Ash'arite sect followed the Mu'tazilites in trying to secure a place for rationalism in the study of the Qur'an, but by the twelfth century, says Nagel, "the few who practiced rationalist—that is to say, largely Ash'arite—theology were considered troublemakers who dared criticize the Prophet's *sunna*."[49] As late as the seventeenth century, the Persians Muhammad Baqir Mir Damad (d. 1631) and his disciple Mulla Sadra (Sadr al-Din Muhammad al-Shirazi, 1572–1640) did work of tremendous significance—when they weren't being rebuked by the *ulama* for, among other things, daring to interpret the Qur'an allegorically.

Although Islamic philosophy lived on, it never regained the influence it had in the early centuries. And however deserving they may have been, no Muslim philosopher after Averroës gained the worldwide attention that the early Islamic philosophers justly attracted.

Closing to the Outside World

Although al-Ghazali himself probably would have disapproved of such a development, *The Incoherence of the Philosophers* helped reinforce an anti-intellectual strain of thought that was present in Islam from the beginning. This anti-intellectualism developed from core theological propositions: The Qur'an is the perfect book. What other book do I need? What other book is worth reading?

This kind of thinking is summed up by a story told of Caliph ᶜUmar, one of the Companions of the Prophet, when he conquered Alexandria in the seventh century. In a notorious episode that may contain as much legend as fact (Bernard Lewis holds that it didn't happen), he ordered that city's famous library burned to the ground. "If what [the books] say agrees with the Koran, they are superfluous," explained the caliph. "If what they say disagrees with the Koran, they are heretical."[50]

ᶜUmar may not have said it, but many other Muslims thought it. As Lewis puts it, during the heyday of Islamic culture "in the Muslims' own perception, Islam itself was indeed coterminous with civilization, and beyond its borders there were only barbarians and infidels."[51] Such an attitude may have contributed to the decline of Islamic thought and culture, which Hitti describes thus:

> In no branch of pure or physical science was any appreciable advance made after Abbasid days.[52] The Moslems of today, if dependent on their own books, would indeed have less than their distant ancestors in the eleventh century. In medicine, philosophy, mathematics, botany and other disciplines a certain point was reached—and the mind of Islam seemed to stand still.... In fact the whole Arab world had by the beginning of the thirteenth century lost the intellectual hegemony it had maintained since the eighth.[53]

Osama bin Laden's biographer Yossef Bodansky suggests that Islamic anti-intellectualism was in part a defensive reaction to the House of Islam's unprecedented defeats in the First Crusade (1099) and in Spain at around the same time. Muslims had never known defeat on this scale, and their theology gave them only one way to interpret it—as a religious failing:

> The result of these setbacks was a backlash. Ruthless military commanders emerged to lead the armies of the believers to reclaim the lands of Islam. Most famous were Saladin, the Kurd who defeated the Crusaders in 1187 to 1192, and Abdul Mumin from Morocco, who defeated the Christian armies in Spain in 1146 to 1163 and again in 1195. But as these and other military leaders rose to power, the once glorious Islamic culture and civilization crumbled. Having consolidated power by the strength of their swords, the new conquerors-turned-rulers had to prove their uniqueness— their "Islamness." They revived religious extremism as the source of their legitimacy while accusing their enlightened and sophisticated predecessors of causing the Muslim world's earlier defeats.[54]

Throughout Islamic history this temptation to uphold Islam against enlightenment and sophistication has competed with the openness to other cultures that first helped make Islamic civilization great. Jordan's late King Hussein summed up what happened when he said, "Islam was very open as it spread throughout the world. It made major contributions. Then, in the tenth century or so, Islam changed course and went into decline."[55] From around the time of the Crusades onward, the idea that non-Muslims might know something that Muslims could benefit from learning fell so far out of Islamic consciousness that in the eighteenth century, when the Ottoman state employed Western experts in various fields, "for Muslims, in Turkey and later elsewhere, this brought a shocking new idea—that one might learn from the previously despised infidel."[56]

Civilizational Suicide

We saw in chapter one how the rationalist Mu'tazilite sect rose and fell in medieval Islam. The demise both of philosophy and of Mu'tazilism (and other rationalist movements such as the Ash'arites) was only part of this larger trend. Bodansky outlines what the Iranian scholar Fereydoun Hoveyda calls the "anti-intellectual rage" that swept through Islam during the Middle Ages. Clearly the impetus for such a reaction came from the Qur'an and Islamic tradition, or it wouldn't have been so strong or long lasting.

> "The Koran contains all the truth required in order to guide the believer in this world and open for him the gates of Paradise," argued the new religious elite—a principle still guiding today's Islamists. By the time this anti-intellectual movement was well established in the twelfth century, the Muslim world had committed what Hoveyda calls "civilizational suicide": incited and excited by the lure of brute force, the community of believers willingly agreed to abandon and deny its own cultural and scientific achievements and commit itself to a process of self-destruction that still unfolds.

That self-destruction is not metaphorical:

> Aspiring to power, new generations of extremist and militant forces have repeatedly demonstrated their supremacy by ordering the destruction of cultural treasures of previous generations. For example, in 1192 the ulama— the religious leadership—in Cordova, Spain, publicly burned the books of the main scientific-medical library, including a rare study of astronomy, because these books were a "horrible calamity" to Islam.[57]

In modern Iran this contempt for culture has taken the form of a bizarre popular recasting of the nation's pre-Islamic history. In the 1920s, Shah Reza Khan's attempts to restore Persian national pride met only bewilderment and anger. Amir Taheri explains:

> Most Iranians had all but forgotten their pre-Islamic past. . . . Persepolis, whose majestic ruins dominated the plain of Morghab near Shiraz, was not recognizable to the average Iranian as the once glorious capital of the

Achaemenean empire. It was called Takht-e-Jamshid (Jamshid's Throne) and believed to be a relic of a mythological past. The tomb of Cyrus the Great at Pasargadae was believed to be the resting place of King Solomon's mother. Outside the small Zoroastrian community all ancient Persian names had been replaced by Arab Islamic ones."[58]

Rather than evoke pride, this past greatness inspired contempt, as the creation of infidel predecessors.

After centuries of this kind of thinking, Islamic philosophy, once a brilliant testimony to the dynamic force of the religion and a vital contribution to world thought, is in the popular mind but a distant memory. Now it is the province of a few academics—and of types such as the "two turbaned, sunburnt medicine men" whom V. S. Naipaul encountered in a bazaar in Iran. They offered him folk remedies with illustrious pedigrees: they were developed, said the hawkers, by "Avicenna, Galen, and 'Hippocrat.'" Naipaul was amazed: Avicenna! "In this dusty pavement medical stock," he writes, "was a reminder of the Arab glory of a thousand years before, when the Arab faith mingled with Persia, India, and the remnant of the classical world it had overrun, and Muslim civilization was the central civilization of the West."[59]

It is indicative of the present state of affairs that after this episode, in all his other travels through the House of Islam, Naipaul rarely encountered Avicenna again.

Is Allah's Hand Chained?

There is a strange and telling passage in the Qur'an that is emblematic of how Muslims came to view philosophy, with its reliance on human reason instead of the great truths revealed to Muhammad—and, indeed, all knowledge derived from unaided reason: "The Jews say: 'God's hand is chained.' May their own hands be chained! May they be cursed for what they say! By no means. His hands are both outstretched: He bestows as He will" (Sura 5:64).

"God's hand is chained"!

Scholars have wondered for fourteen centuries what Muhammad might have heard Jews saying to make him think they believed that God was bound by any laws. But that is how Muslims have regarded the Jewish

CAN SCIENCE AND CULTURE FLOURISH UNDER ISLAM?   127

and Christian concept of a rational, knowable universe, and the natural philosophy built on that belief.

Jews and Christians believe that God created the universe to operate according to reliable, observable laws. While he can suspend those laws, ordinarily he does not do so; he is not bound, but freely chooses to uphold the laws that he created. This way of thinking provided a foundation for the edifice of modern science: Christian mathematicians and astronomers knew their investigations would lead to knowledge of truth, because they believed that God had established the universe according to laws that could be ascertained. St. Thomas Aquinas explained:

> since the principles of certain sciences—of logic, geometry, and arithmetic, for instance—are derived exclusively from the formal principals of things, upon which their essence depends, it follows that God cannot make the contraries of these principles; He cannot make the genus not to be predicable of the species, nor lines drawn from a circle's center to its circumference not to be equal, nor the three angles of a rectilinear triangle not to be equal to two right angles.[60]

This is simply saying that God has established a rational, orderly universe in which the law of noncontradiction prevails.

But to the Muslim who found all knowledge in the Qur'an and suspected philosophers of infidelity, that was tantamount to saying, "God's hand is chained." Allah, they argued, could not be thus restricted. He was free to act as whimsically as he pleased. If one could not rely on the universe to obey observable laws, and if reliable knowledge was found only in the revelation, science could not flourish.

Stanley Jaki, a Catholic priest and a physicist, attributes contemporary Muslim unrest to this turning away from reason and natural law. He says, "What is occurring in the Muslim world today is a confrontation, not between God and the devil, identified with capitalism or Communism, but between a very specific God and science which is a very specific antagonist of that god, the Allah of the Koran, in whom the will wholly dominates the intellect." Jaki explains that it was al-Ghazali, among others, who "denounced natural laws, the very objective of science, as a blasphemous constraint upon the free will of Allah."[61] He adds that "Muslim mystics decried the notion of scientific law (as formulated by Aristotle) as blasphemous and irrational, depriving as it does the Creator of his freedom."[62]

Relatively early in its history, then, much of the House of Islam determined that Allah's hand would not be chained. Philosophy and science came to be widely seen as essentially worthless endeavors that only confuse man and distract him from the Qur'an.

The decline of Islamic culture began when orthodox Muslims consolidated their victory over those who would learn from non-Muslims, and those who would pursue knowledge by the light of reason. Henceforth, Muslim divines would teach that believers should heed only the revealed law of Allah, and would strictly subordinate science and philosophy to the lineaments of divine revelation as they saw it. The consequences have been far-reaching. Jaki details just a few of them:

> More than two hundred years after the construction of the famed Blue Mosque, W. Eton, for many years a resident in Turkey and Russia, found that Turkish architects still could not calculate the lateral pressures of curves. Nor could they understand why the catenary curve, so useful in building ships, could also be useful in drawing blueprints for cupolas. The reign of Suleiman the Magnificent may be memorable for its wealth of gorgeously illustrated manuscripts and princely paraphernalia, but for no items worth mentioning from the viewpoint of science and technology. At the Battle of Lepanto the Turkish navy lacked improvements long in use on French and Italian vessels. Two hundred years later, Turkish artillery was primitive by Western standards. Worse, while in Western Europe the dangers of the use of lead had for some time been clearly realized, lead was still a heavy ingredient in kitchenware used in Turkish lands.[63]

Seeds of Resentment

In the face of increasing Western prosperity, the Muslim ambivalence toward intellectual endeavor and the non-Muslim world threatens to become explosive. The Palestinian scholars Hisham Sharabi and Mukhtar Ani ask pointedly: "Why has Arab society failed to modernize? Why have Arab countries failed to cope with some of the most basic social tasks?" They call for sweeping social change, according to David Pryce-Jones, but do not specify "what practical steps, what modalities, they have in mind for implementing this drastic prescription."[64]

What steps can they realistically suggest? If a significant party of Muslims believe that science and modernity are somehow in their very nature un-Islamic, any attempts at large-scale reform will run into a brick wall. For there will always be a vocal and militant group demanding that the faith be implemented in its purity—whatever the cost.

Even so, Stanley Jaki remains optimistic: "Today the impossibility of making ends meet without science forces the Muslim world to reconsider its notion of Allah. It is an agonizing process, which, in spite of the bloodshed, may, in the long run, bring a more rational mentality to troubled parts of the world."[65]

Can Islam possibly "reconsider its notion of Allah"? It won't be easy, for that notion comes straight from the perfect Word of Allah, universally and eternally valid.

Yet at the same time, the technological superiority and cultural hegemony of the West make it an object of envy: Islamic civilization is supposed to be superior to that of unbelievers, but at this stage of human history it clearly isn't. As we have noted earlier, even radical Muslims regard Western society with ambivalence.[66] In Islam, says Naipaul,

> The West, or the universal civilization it leads, is emotionally rejected. It undermines; it threatens. But at the same time it is needed, for its machines, goods, medicines, warplanes, the remittances from the emigrants, the hospitals that might have a cure for calcium deficiency, the universities that will provide master's degrees in mass media. All the rejection of the West is contained within the assumption that there will always exist out there a living, creative civilization, oddly neutral, open to all to appeal to. Rejection, therefore, is not absolute rejection. It is also, for the community as a whole, a way of ceasing to strive intellectually. It is to be parasitic; parasitism is one of the unacknowledged fruits of fundamentalism.[67]

But will the parasite kill the host?

From such resentment and envy arises Osama bin Laden, who may not be able to build something like the World Trade Center, but he can sure knock it down. If the West's technological superiority can't be matched, it can at least be assaulted. Osama respected technology enough to teach his followers how to wreak destruction on a grand scale, but not enough to sponsor large-scale educational efforts in Islamic countries. In a sense, then, the terrorist attacks of September 11 are a new round, in a new and especially virulent form, of the struggle between strict Islamic orthodoxy and human reason. The problem the West faces is that unless and until Islamic orthodoxy is radically redefined (with the overwhelming agreement of the *umma*), it will not finally call off the struggle.

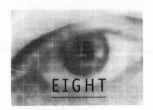

EIGHT

The Crusades: Christian and Muslim

"THIS CRUSADE, THIS WAR ON TERRORISM, is going to take a while," said George W. Bush on September 16, 2001.

Crusade!

There he went again: exposing the same old imperialist West, still bent on dominating Islam just as in the Middle Ages. When the President of the United States used the C-word, Osama bin Laden saw his opening. In a fax sent the following week to the al-Jazeera news network of Qatar, he denounced "the new Jewish and Christian crusader campaign that is led by the Chief Crusader Bush under the banner of the cross."[1]

Absurd as this was, bin Laden was not alone in thinking thus. The Taliban's Mullah Muhammad Omar gleefully remarked, "President Bush has told the truth that this is a crusade against Islam."[2] Other Muslims were similarly affronted. Najeh Bkeirat, an official at Jerusalem's Al-Aqsa Mosque, huffed: "Bush is using an ancient savage slogan. His statement reflects his limited cultural knowledge. Bush is making enemies, not only among Islamic activists, but also among ordinary Muslims and Christians alike."[3] It seemed that everyone, not just Muslims, was offended. The White House issued a hasty retraction and never again dared use the word.

But the Crusades are ancient history, aren't they? What bearing could they possibly have on today's political situation?

Pundits across the Western world hastened to explain that in the House of Islam, memories are long. A grievance like the Crusades still burns in the collective Muslim consciousness. No less a figure than former President Bill Clinton observed that Muslims seethe over the Crusades even today:

Indeed, in the first Crusade, when the Christian soldiers took Jerusalem, they first burned a synagogue with 300 Jews in it, and proceeded to kill every woman and child who was Muslim on the Temple mound [*sic*]. The contemporaneous descriptions of the event describe soldiers walking on the Temple mound, a holy place to Christians, with blood running up to their knees. I can tell you that that story is still being told today in the Middle East and we are still paying for it.[4]

East and West, Muslim and Christian, secular and religious—commentators were united about the Crusades: they were an illegitimate land grab, an imperialist war against the indigenous population of the Holy Land, and an affront to the basic human right to religious freedom.

Almost no one stood up to defend the Crusades, and to be sure, in some ways they can't be defended. Bill Clinton's lurid description of the First Crusade has some truth to it. Undeniably there were abuses and atrocities. And in fact, the West has questioned the Crusades—something probably not possible if the shoe were on the Islamic foot—almost since they were launched. Virtually all Westerners have learned to apologize for the Crusades. Less noted is the fact that these campaigns have an Islamic counterpart for which no one is apologizing and of which few are even aware.

Over a hundred years ago, Mark Twain voiced common Western assumptions in *Tom Sawyer Abroad,* when he had Tom explain to Huck Finn that he wants to go to the Holy Land to liberate it from the Muslims.

> "How," Huck asks, "did we come to let them git holt of it?"
>
> "We didn't come to let them git hold of it," Tom explains. "They always had it."
>
> "Why, Tom, then it must belong to them, don't it?"
>
> "Why of course it does. Who said it didn't?"[5]

But was Tom Sawyer right?

The Christian Middle East

Islam originated in Arabia in the seventh century. At that time Egypt, Libya and all of North Africa were Christian and had been so for hundreds of years. So were Palestine, Lebanon, Syria and Asia Minor. The churches that St. Paul addressed in his letters collected in the New Testament are located in Asia Minor (now Turkey) as well as Greece. North of Greece, in a buffer zone between Eastern and Western Europe, were lands that would become the Christian domains of the Slavs.

Antioch and Constantinople (Istanbul), in modern Turkey, and Alexandria, in modern Egypt, were three of the most important Christian centers of the first millennium. The theological schools of Antioch and Alexandria vied for influence in the Church at large, and Christian teachings about the Person and natures of Jesus Christ were hammered out between them at the great ecumenical councils of Ephesus (431) and Chalcedon (451). (Both Ephesus and Chalcedon are now in Turkey.) The latter council was held at Chalcedon, right across the Bosporus from Constantinople, for the convenience of the Eastern Roman Emperor, whose seat was in Constantinople and who was deeply interested in the proceedings.

Virtually all of the great early Fathers of the Church hailed from these areas. St. John Chrysostom, whose liturgy is still celebrated by the Orthodox and Byzantine Catholic Churches, was from Antioch. When news of his eloquence and holiness spread far and wide, he was compelled to become archbishop of Constantinople, the imperial city. St. Athanasius, the main force behind the Nicene Creed, which virtually all Christians—Catholic, Orthodox and Protestant—still profess, was archbishop of Alexandria. St. Augustine, author of two of the foundation stones of Western civilization, the *Confessions* and the *City of God,* was a North African.

There were also St. Basil the Great, St. Mary of Egypt, St. Anthony the Great, St. Cyril of Jerusalem—the list goes on and on. Western Christians, if they are aware of Eastern Christianity at all, tend to think of it as an exotic outpost, but in the first five centuries of Christianity, the East led the way in both the growth of the Church and her theological development. Nor were those great saints minorities in a pagan world. These were Christian lands.

Where Did the Christians Go?

Yes, say the textbooks, these were Christian centers, and great ones, too. But then Muhammad and his Muslim armies arose out of the desert, and these lands became Muslim. Some historians say that the inhabitants of the lands conquered by the early Muslims were happy to be free of their corrupt Byzantine rulers, and welcomed the invaders.

Nonetheless, it is undeniable that Muslims won these lands by conquest and, in obedience to the words of the Qur'an and the Prophet, put
to the sword the infidels therein who refused to submit to the new Islamic
regime. Those who escaped this fate lived in humiliating second-class
status. Conversion to Islam became the only way to have a decent life.
Not surprisingly, the Christian populations of these areas steadily
diminished.

How did it happen? One of the few historians who is telling this
story today is Bat Ye'or, an Egyptian who now resides in Europe. In her
eye-opening book *The Decline of Eastern Christianity under Islam,* she
recounts facts that both the West and the Muslim world would prefer to
sweep under the rug. For instance:

> Sophronius [Bishop of Jerusalem], in his sermon on the Day of Epiphany
> 636, bewailed the destruction of churches and monasteries, the sacked
> towns, the fields laid waste, the villages burned down by the nomads who
> were overrunning the country. In a letter the same year to Sergius, patri-
> arch of Constantinople, he mentions the ravages wrought by the Arabs.
> Thousands of people perished in 639, victims of the famine and plague
> that resulted from these destructions.[6]

That's how it happened in one place and time. But the story was
repeated, again and again, wherever Muslim armies were triumphant.

Here is a contemporary account of the Muslims' arrival in Nikiou,
an Egyptian town, in the 640s:

> Then the Muslims arrived in Nikiou. There was not one single soldier to
> resist them. They seized the town and slaughtered everyone they met in
> the street and in the churches—men, women and children, sparing nobody.
> Then they went to other places, pillaged and killed all the inhabitants
> they found.... But let us now say no more, for it is impossible to describe
> the horrors the Muslims committed when they occupied the island of
> Nikiou.

In addition to massacres, this process involved exile and enslavement, all
based on a broken treaty:

> Amr oppressed Egypt. He sent its inhabitants to fight the inhabitants of
> the Pentapolis [Tripolitania] and, after gaining a victory, he did not allow
> them to stay there. He took considerable booty from this country and a

large number of prisoners.... The Muslims returned to their country with booty and captives. The patriarch Cyrus felt deep grief at the calamities in Egypt, because Amr, who was of barbarian origin, showed no mercy in his treatment of the Egyptians and did not fulfill the covenants which had been agreed with him.

Once the Muslims were entrenched in power, they began to levy the *jizya,* the tax on non-Muslims:

Amr's position became stronger from day to day. He levied the tax that had been stipulated.... But it is impossible to describe the lamentable position of the inhabitants of this town, who came to the point of offering their children in exchange for the enormous sums that they had to pay each month, finding no one to help them because God had abandoned them and had delivered the Christians into the hands of their enemies.[7]

An eyewitness of the Muslim conquest of Armenia in 642 tells what happened when they took the town of Dvin: "The enemy's army rushed in and butchered the inhabitants of the town by the sword.... After a few days' rest, the Ismaelites [Arabs] went back whence they had come, dragging after them a host of captives, numbering thirty-five thousand."[8]

On the island of Cos a few years later, the Muslim general Abu al-A'war, according to another contemporary account, "laid waste and pillaged all its riches, slaughtered the population and led the remnant into captivity, and destroyed its citadel."[9]

According to the Orthodox patriarch Michael the Syrian (1126–1199), Muslims conquered Cilicia and Caesarea of Cappadocia in the year 650 in this way:

They [the Taiyaye, or Muslim Arabs] moved into Cilicia and took prisoners ... and when Mu'awiya arrived he ordered all the inhabitants to be put to the sword; he placed guards so that no one escaped. After gathering up all the wealth of the town, they set to torturing the leaders to make them show them things [treasures] that had been hidden. The Taiyaye led everyone into slavery—men and women, boys and girls—and they committed much debauchery in that unfortunate town; they wickedly committed immoralities inside churches.[10]

Even Muslim chroniclers of the time make no secret that this kind of activity went on. The Muslim historian Ibn al-Athir (1160–1233), in his world history entitled *The Complete History,* includes this account of eighth- and ninth-century Muslim incursions into Spain and France:

> In 177 [17 April 793], Hisham, [Muslim] prince of Spain, sent a large army commanded by Abd al-Malik b. Abd al-Wahid b. Mugith into enemy territory, and which made forays as far as Narbonne and Jaranda [Gerona]. . . . For several months he traversed this land in every direction, raping women, killing warriors, destroying fortresses, burning and pillaging everything, driving back the enemy who fled in disorder. He returned safe and sound, dragging behind him God knows how much booty.

Were these escapades a source of shame for the Muslim chronicler? Hardly. He concludes his account of them by noting proudly: "This is one of the most famous expeditions of the Muslims of Spain." (Similarly, a thirteenth-century Persian Muslim wrote of Islamic victories with "no idea of what is cruel and what is not cruel," as Naipaul puts it.)[11] Ibn al-Athir goes on to tell more:

> In 223 [2 December 837], Abd ar-Rahman b. al-Hakam, sovereign of Spain, sent an army against Alava; it camped near Hisn al-Gharat, which it besieged; it seized the booty that was found there, killed the inhabitants and withdrew, carrying off women and children as captives. . . . In 246 [27 March 860], Muhammad b. Abd ar-Rahman advanced with many troops and a large military apparatus against the region of Pamplona. He reduced, ruined and ravaged this territory, where he pillaged and sowed death.[12]

In Amorium in Asia Minor in 838, says Michael the Syrian, "there were so many women's convents and monasteries that over a thousand virgins were led into captivity, not counting those that had been slaughtered. They were given to the Moorish slaves, so as to assuage their lust."[13]

In *The Decline and Fall of the Roman Empire,* Edward Gibbon recounts the Muslim drive into the heart of France, which was turned back at Tours in 732. They pushed "above a thousand miles from the Rock of Gibraltar to the banks of the Loire: the repetition of an equal space would have carried the Saracens to the confines of Poland and the Highlands of Scotland; the Rhine is not more impassible than the Nile or the Euphrates and the Arabian fleet might have sailed without a naval combat into the mouth of the Thames." Had that happened, says Gibbon, "perhaps the interpretation of the Koran would now be taught in the schools of Oxford and her pulpits might demonstrate to a circumcised people the sanctity and truth of the revelation of Mahomet."[14]

"The blood ran in rivers"

Centuries later, when Muslim armies resumed their expansion in Europe after a period of relative decline—which included, most notably, the loss of Sicily in 1091, the capture of Jerusalem by the Crusaders in 1099, and the steady erosion of power in Spain—they maintained the same pattern of behavior. On May 29, 1453, the city of Constantinople, the jewel of Christendom, finally fell to an overwhelming Muslim force after weeks of resistance by a small band of valiant Greeks. According to Steven Runciman, the preeminent historian of the Crusades, the Muslim soldiers "slew everyone that they met in the streets, men, women, and children without discrimination. The blood ran in rivers down the steep streets from the heights of Petra toward the Golden Horn. But soon the lust for slaughter was assuaged. The soldiers realized that captives and precious objects would bring them greater profit."[15] The options for Christians after conquest had been spelled out by the pioneering sociologist Ibn Khaldun in the fourteenth century: "It is [for them to choose between] conversion to Islam, payment of the poll tax, or death."[16] The historian of jihad Paul Fregosi puts it succinctly: "It was a case of 'your money or your life'!"[17]

It is true that these sins of the Muslims do not excuse the sins that Christians committed against them in return. One massacre doesn't cancel out another. But clearly what we now call "human rights abuses" have not come only from the Western side, and the recent defensiveness of the West before the House of Islam and the world on this issue is hardly justified by the facts.

It is also important to point out once again that the Crusaders who pillaged Jerusalem were transgressing the bounds of their religion in all sorts of ways. As for the Muslim armies who murdered, raped, pillaged and enslaved—what Islamic principles were they violating? After all, they were following the example of their Prophet:

> It has been narrated on the authority of Ibn ʿUmar that the Jews of Banu Nadir and Banu Quraizi fought against the Messenger of Allah, who

expelled Banu Nadir, and allowed Quraiza to stay on, and granted favour
to them until they too fought against him. Then he killed their men, and
distributed their women, children and properties among the Muslims,
except that some of them had joined the Messenger of Allah who granted
them security. They embraced Islam. The Messenger of Allah turned out
all the Jews of Medina, Banu Qainuqa' . . . and the Jews of Banu Haritha
and every other Jew who was in Medina.[18]

In light of the violence with which Muhammad spread Islam (including
forced conversions), there is a certain menace in his celebrated invitation to the Byzantine emperor Heraclitus: "Embrace Islam and you will
be safe."[19] Heraclitus didn't, and Byzantium wasn't.

In fact, the portions of ancient Christendom that are now universally considered to be part of the House of Islam only became so in the
same way as the Arabian Jewish tribes became Muslim: by being bathed
in blood.

Christendom Responds

The jihad and the Crusade are often seen as synonymous. When President Bush called for his "crusade," one Pakistani exclaimed, "He has used
the Christian word for jihad."[20]

Well, not precisely.

Western Christendom, which emerged relatively unscathed from
the Islamic onslaught, was distracted by internecine squabbles and did
not rise to the defense of its beleaguered coreligionists until five centuries
after the first Muslim conquests, when Pope Urban II called the First
Crusade in the year 1095. There followed centuries of intermittent conflict, through which the Muslims steadily rolled back the boundaries of
Christendom.

The circumstances of the First Crusade were these: Christian pil-
grims to the Holy Land were being molested by Muslims and prevented
from reaching the holy places. Some were killed. This was the impetus
that finally moved Western Christianity to try to recover just one small
portion of the Christian lands that had fallen to the Muslim sword over
the previous centuries. Bernard Lewis observes,

> At the present time, the Crusades are often depicted as an early experi-
> ment in expansionist imperialism—a prefiguration of the modern

European empires. To the people of the time, both Muslim and Christian, they were no such thing. When the Crusaders arrived in Jerusalem, barely four hundred years had passed since that city, along with the rest of the Levant and North Africa, had been wrested by the armies of Islam from their Christian rulers, and their Christian populations forcibly incorporated in a new Muslim empire. The Crusade was a delayed response to the jihad, the holy war for Islam, and its purpose was to recover by war what had been lost by war—to free the holy places of Christendom and open them once again, without impediment, to Christian pilgrimage.[21]

The lands in dispute during each Crusade were the ancient lands of Christendom, where Christians had flourished for centuries before Muhammad's armies called them idolaters and enslaved and killed them. Whatever evils Christians committed during their course, the Crusades were at base a defensive action, a belated attempt by Western Christians to turn back the tide of Islam that had engulfed the Eastern Church.

And the effort was insufficient: all the Crusades essentially failed. The most successful was the first, and all it accomplished was to establish a few tottering Latin domains in Palestine and the surrounding regions. The Crusaders were far from home; their Muslim foes were not. These Christian principalities didn't last long.

By Christian lights, many Crusaders undeniably sinned. On the Temple Mount, as Bill Clinton reminded the world, they transgressed the strict boundaries of the Just War doctrine. But this doesn't mean that their cause itself was wrong. Insofar as the Crusades were fought to protect Christians in the Holy Land and to turn back the Muslims who had conquered so much of Christendom, they represented a just cause.

There is no reason to accept the permanence or inevitability of the incorporation of the Middle East and North Africa into the House of Islam—just as Muslim armies did not accept that those territories would be permanently Christian. Yet an assumption of historical necessity is the basis on which Muslims scold Christians (and Westerners in general) about the Crusades, which they call an incursion into Muslim lands. If Westerners had no right to invade these putative Muslim places, then Muslims had no right to conquer them to begin with. If they continue to insist that the Crusades were wrong, Muslims should also be willing to withdraw from the Middle East and North Africa. But this is to enter the realm of fantasy. Still, at the very least, Westerners should know the record of how those areas became Muslim, and they should insist that jihad be judged according to the same moral standards as the Crusades.

"When accusing the West of imperialism," says historian Paul Fregosi, "Muslims are obsessed with the Christian Crusades but have forgotten their own, much grander Jihad." Conventional wisdom locates the beginning of Christian/Muslim hostility in the Crusades; according to Amin Maalouf in *The Crusades through Arab Eyes,* the sack of Jerusalem in 1099 was "the starting point of a millennial hostility between Islam and the West." But the reality is somewhat different. Fregosi remarks that "the Jihad is more than four hundred years older than the Crusades." Comparing the Muslim occupation of Christian lands in Europe, the Middle East and North Africa to European colonialism, he finds that the latter was much briefer and less culturally pervasive. "Yet, strangely, it is the Muslims ... who are the most bitter about colonialism and the humiliations to which they have been subjected; and it is the Europeans who harbor the shame and the guilt. It should be the other way around."[22]

The Long Muslim March

Right or wrong, the Crusades are a historical fact. Yet long after they had become a distant memory in the West, the warriors of jihad continued to press into the heart of Europe. After the fall of Acre in 1291, no more Crusades were mounted. Through the next four centuries, however, Muslim armies solidified their hold on southeastern Europe and kept advancing whenever and wherever it was possible to do so.

Muslim incursions into Europe from the east were finally stopped at the gates of Vienna, a defeat which heralded the beginning of the long decline of the Ottoman Empire. The date of that event is one that no doubt still stings in the mind of Osama bin Laden: September 11, 1683.

It would be naïve to think that between 1683 and 2001, jihad somehow became an antiquated or rejected concept. As the Muslim world was outstripped technologically and ultimately even colonized by the West, conditions became unfavorable, for a variety of reasons, to the enlargement of the House of Islam. Muslim states were relatively powerless, and the ensuing frustration and resentment contributed to the rise of Islamic militancy. Analysts who ascribe Islamic fundamentalism in our own day to various cultural and socioeconomic factors are thus partially right.

Nevertheless, the seeds of jihad are always present within Islam. As we shall see in the pages ahead, the theology of jihad has never been discarded or even modified. Indeed, this theology is written into the charter of Islam, and is therefore, in the eyes of most Muslims, valid until the end of the world.

NINE

Is Islam Tolerant of Non-Muslims?

WHILE CHRISTENDOM HAS GOTTEN A BAD NAME for its treatment of non-Christians, Islam's reputation in this regard is not so bleak. Bernard Lewis acknowledges that the Muslim record of tolerance is poorer than that of the modern, secular West, but he asserts that Muslim regimes historically have far surpassed their Christian counterparts on this score. "There is nothing in Islamic history," he says, "to compare with the Spanish expulsion of Jews and Muslims, the Inquisition, the *Auto da fé*'s, the wars of religion, not to speak of more recent crimes of commission and acquiescence."

Does this mean that Christians and Jews actually lived well in the House of Islam? Not exactly: "There were occasional persecutions, but they were rare, and usually of brief duration, related to local and specific circumstances." Nevertheless, Lewis concludes, "Within certain limits and subject to certain restrictions, Islamic governments were willing to tolerate the practice, though not the dissemination, of other revealed, monotheistic religions."[1]

One moving indication of this tolerance came at the fall of the Ottoman Empire, when the new secular rulers of Turkey abolished the caliphate. The last caliph, exiled to Switzerland, was made to wait all day at Istanbul's railroad station for the Orient Express that would take him there. The Jewish station manager did his best to make the caliph, an old and broken man, comfortable during the wait, explaining:

> The Ottoman dynasty is the saviour of the Turkish Jews. When our ancestors were driven out of Spain, and looked for a country to take them in, it was the Ottomans who agreed to give us shelter and saved us from extinction. Through the generosity of their government, once again they

received freedom of religion and language, protection for their women, their possessions and their lives. Therefore our conscience obliges us to serve you as much as we can in your darkest hour.[2]

Most modern Westerners would assume this is essentially the whole story, and that the Muslim record is one of tolerance from beginning to end. But the truth, as always, is more complicated.

The Roots of Muslim Tolerance

The limits and restrictions on the tolerance of non-Muslims that Lewis mentions were well defined virtually from the beginning of Islam. According to the Muslim historians A. Zahoor and Z. Haq, in the year 628 the Prophet Muhammad himself granted a charter of privileges to the Christian monks of St. Catherine's Monastery on Mt. Sinai. It is not certain whether Muhammad himself actually issued this document, but nonetheless it is revealing of several aspects of the Muslim attitude toward Christians during the time of the great Islamic conquests.

In this charter, the Prophet says of Christians, "Verily I, the servants, the helpers, and my followers defend them, because Christians are my citizens; and by Allah! I hold out against anything that displeases them. No compulsion is to be on them."

This echoes the famous "tolerance verse" of the Qur'an: "There shall be no compulsion in religion" (Sura 2:256). Muslims and others use this verse to compare Christianity's record of forced conversions unfavorably with that of Islam. Yet if some Christians in certain times and places have thought that people should be converted by force, no branch of Christianity has ever taught such an idea. In fact, on this matter the principles of both religions are good, and the practice less so. At various points in their history, both Christians and Muslims have failed to live up to their stated ideals very well.

The Muslim record of granting tolerance and freedom of religion is stained by many events and practices, including the *devshirme,* the seizure of Christian children for slavery. These lads were given the choice of Islam or death. According to a historian of the janissaries, the Ottoman crack troops recruited from Christian families through the *devshirme,* "no child might be recruited who was converted to Islam other than by his own free will—if the choice between life and death may be called free will."[3]

The charter with the monks of St. Catherine's also stipulates that

no one is to destroy a house of their religion, to damage it, or to carry anything from it to the Muslims' houses. Should anyone take any of these, he would spoil God's covenant and disobey His Prophet. Verily, they are my allies and have my secure charter against all that they hate.... Their churches are to be respected. They are neither to be prevented from repairing them nor the sacredness of their covenants.

The pact even covers defense: "No one is to force them to travel or to oblige them to fight. The Muslims are to fight for them."

Drs. Zahoor and Haq assert that "This charter of privileges has been honored and faithfully applied by Muslims throughout the centuries in all lands they ruled."[4]

With the Christians of Najran, a Christian town in Yemen, Muhammad concluded a similar pact. This one (although the present text is not likely to be fully reliable) includes more specifics. It forbids the removal of any bishop, priest or monk, excuses the Christians from "tithes," and dictates that "no image or cross shall be destroyed." It even declares that the Christians of Najran "shall continue to enjoy everything great and small as heretofore." Again, Dr. Zahoor claims that "Muslims have faithfully applied the terms of this treaty to their non-Muslim citizens."[5]

These agreements are tolerant indeed. If Zahoor and Haq are correct in saying that Muslims have always held to them scrupulously in their relations with their Christian and Jewish minorities, then the House of Islam truly deserves its reputation for tolerance. So let's look at the record.

Because the Muslim world expanded so quickly when its armies overwhelmed the ancient Christian communities of the Middle East, Islam had to face the problem of religious minorities early on. As with most other aspects of Islam, it developed a specific and comprehensive code of laws for the treatment of these minorities.

Reliance of the Traveller, the legal code from the Shafi'i school of Islamic jurisprudence that broadly represents Islamic orthodoxy, sets forth these laws in detail. They include the payment by the *dhimmis,* or conquered non-Muslims—chiefly Jews and Christians—of the "non-Muslim poll tax," the *jizya.* This tax comes directly from the Qur'an, which mandates that Muslims must "fight against such of those to whom the Scriptures were given as believe neither in God nor the Last Day, who do not forbid what God and His Apostle have forbidden, and do not embrace the true Faith, *until they pay tribute* [*jizya*] *out of hand and are utterly subdued*" (Sura 9:29; emphasis added). The code sets the annual rate of the *jizya* at a minimum of one dinar, which the text explains is equivalent to 4.235 grams of gold. "The maximum is whatever both sides agree upon." Why the *dhimmis* would agree to anything above the minimum if they had a choice is left unexplained.

Reliance of the Traveller adds that the *jizya* "is collected with leniency and politeness, and it is not levied on women, children, or the insane."[6] But just as one man's tap is another man's beating, so leniency and politeness vary from culture to culture. For the collection of the *jizya* in practice often differed sharply from what the law books instructed. Michael the Syrian reports that under Caliph Marwan II (744–750), leniency and politeness evidently gave way to pressing economic concerns. A contemporary writer said that "Marwan's main concern was to amass gold and his yoke bore heavily on the people of the country. His troops inflicted many evils on the men: blows, pillages, outrages on women in their husbands' presence."[7] This was not a singular case. One of Marwan's successors, al-Mansur (754–775), says Michael, "raised every kind of tax on all the people in every place. He doubled every type of tribute on Christians."[8]

Bat Ye'or, the leading historian of the religious minorities under Islam, paints a grim picture of the collection of the *jizya* in eighth-century Egypt:

> "They mercilessly struck honorable men and old hoary elders." These evils afflicted the whole Abbasid empire. In Lower Egypt, the Copts, crushed and ruined by taxation and subjected to torture, rebelled (832). The Arab governor ordered their villages, vines, gardens, churches, and the whole region to be burned down; those who escaped massacre were deported.[9]

And Paul Fregosi expresses the Muslim perspective trenchantly: "Christianity, whether as a religious entity to be protected within the Ottoman empire or as a religious entity to be assailed outside the empire, was always first and foremost a cow to be milked."[10]

As for politeness, the *jizya* had to be paid in public, in a bizarre and degrading ceremony that required the Muslim tax official to hit the *dhimmi* on the head or the back of the neck. This ritualized violence symbolized, of course, the subjugation of the *dhimmis.* The twelfth-century Qur'anic commentator Zamakhshari, in fact, directed that the *jizya* should be collected "with belittlement and humiliation."[11]

Is this merely ancient history? Hardly. According to Bat Ye'or, the performance of this blow "survived unchanged till the dawn of the twentieth century, being ritually performed in Arab-Muslim countries, such as Yemen and Morocco, where the Koranic tax continued to be extorted from the Jews."[12]

Reliance of the Traveller also sets down that the *jizya* is not to be collected from women and children. But once again, reality was different: "The poll tax was extorted by torture," says Bat Ye'or. "The tax inspectors demanded gifts for themselves; widows and orphans were pillaged and despoiled."

> In theory, women, paupers, the sick, and the infirm were exempt from the poll tax; nevertheless, Armenian, Syriac, and Jewish sources provide abundant proof that the *jizya* was exacted from children, widows, orphans, and even the dead. A considerable number of extant documents, preserved over the centuries, testify to the persistence and endurance of these measures. In Aleppo in 1683, French Consul Chevalier Laurent d'Arvieux noted that ten-year-old Christian children paid the *jizya.* Here again, one finds the disparity and contradiction between the ideal in the theory and the reality of the facts.[13]

The alternative was slavery. The seventeenth-century European traveler Jean-Baptiste Tavernier found that:

> Armenians, too poor to pay their poll tax, were condemned to slavery together with their wives and children. At Cyprus where [Tavernier] put into port in 1651, he learned that: "during the last three or four months, over four hundred Christians had become Muhammadans because they could not pay their *kharaj,* which is the tribute that the Grand Seigneur levies on Christians in his states." In Baghdad, in 1652, the Christians incurred such expenses "that, when they had to pay their debts or their *kharaj,* they were forced to sell their children to the Turks to cover it." Historical sources on collective groups, official documents, individual behavior which history has fortuitously preserved—all provide abundant evidence that the *dhimmis'* offspring were regarded as a reservoir of slaves for economic or political purposes.[14]

Many of these abuses of the *jizya* were clearly against Islamic law. The laws of the *jizya* themselves, moreover, are still on the books, ready to be enforced wherever and whenever the Sharia is implemented. That fact should worry any non-Muslim in a country with a Muslim majority; and those who wonder why Christians fight Muslims in Nigeria or Lebanon and resist the implementation of the Sharia should take note.

Subject People

Steven Runciman says that Christians in the Ottoman Empire "were never allowed to forget that they were a subject people."[15] Muslims seem to have invented the idea of making despised minorities wear distinctive clothing: the *dhimmis* were also to be "distinguished from Muslims in dress, wearing a wide cloth belt (*zunnar*)."[16] In practice, this led to a blizzard of laws regulating clothing for Christians and Jews, and in some places Christians even had to wear a sort of modified tonsure by shaving the fronts of their heads.[17] According to Philip Hitti,

> The Caliph al-Mutawakkil in 850 and 854 decreed that Christians and Jews should affix wooden images of devils to their houses, level their graves even with the ground, wear outer garments of honey color, i.e. yellow, put two honey-colored patches on the clothes of their slaves ... and ride only on mules and asses with wooden saddles marked by two pomegranate-like balls on the cantle.[18]

Often the Muslim authorities buttressed these laws with others that restricted or denied altogether the *dhimmis'* access to public baths and other public spaces. In some places, Christians and Jews could go to the baths, but only if they wore small bells on their fingers and toes so that, even when unclothed, they could be identified and duly shunned.[19] *Reliance of the Traveller* also dictates that *dhimmis* "are not to be greeted with [the standard Muslim greeting,] 'as-Salamu ᶜalaykum' [Peace be with you]" and "must keep to the side of the street."[20] Other laws assigned distasteful duties to the *dhimmis,* such as the removal of dead animals and the cleaning of public toilets.

Many of these laws remained in effect until late in the nineteenth century or even into the twentieth. They began to give way only when notions of individual human rights filtered into the House of Islam from Western colonizers and brought about a certain relaxation of the *dhimmis'* plight.

The effects of such laws were manifold. A *dhimmi* could never blend into the crowd. He had to keep to the side of the street and could not be greeted the way ordinary people were greeted; he was an inferior, and unclean. These wretched fellows could become a target for Muslim wrath anytime, anywhere. After all, the principle behind these laws was that anyone who remained a Jew or a Christian in a Muslim milieu must be deliberately perverse, with a heart so set against Allah as to refuse to acknowledge the manifest truth and superiority of Islam. Such people were natural targets for popular resentment, and the *dhimmis* often were subject to random violence.

Disquietingly, this violence was more common wherever Muslims became more fervent, for their scripture and laws reinforced hatred of Christians and Jews. Michael the Syrian writes that the Syrian rabble-rouser Nur al-Din tried to curry favor among the local Muslims by being especially harsh toward Christians: "He did his utmost to harass the Christians in every way in order to be considered by Muslims as an assiduous observer of their laws."[21] When Mongol armies entered Syria in 1281, "the sultan Qalawun reacted by forcing all the Christians at the service of the state to convert to Islam"—no doubt to purify the polity and perhaps stave off the threat.[22]

Reliance of the Traveller adds to the humiliation by stipulating that *dhimmis* "may not build higher than or as high as Muslims' buildings." They are "forbidden to openly display wine or pork ... recite the Torah or Evangel aloud, or make public display of their funerals and feastdays." A commentator referred to in the text adds that they may not "ring church bells or display crosses." They are, furthermore, "forbidden to build new churches."[23]

Not only were *dhimmis* forbidden to build new churches, but because they were thought to be obstinately rejecting the truths of Islam, their existing houses of worship were always under threat:

> Churches and synagogues were rarely respected. Regarded as places of perversion, they were often burned or demolished in the course of reprisals against infidels found guilty of overstepping their rights. The exterior of these buildings looked dilapidated and the extreme wretchedness of the interiors was often the consequence of looting or was intended to discourage predatory attacks. This state of decay—also an obligatory social component of the *dhimmi* servile status—is often mentioned in *dhimmi* chronicles and described by European consuls and, later, by foreign travelers.[24]

These churches and synagogues were dilapidated because Muslims widely believed that, as one Islamic jurist reported, "the Prophet made this declaration: 'No churches are to be built in Muslim lands, and those that have fallen into ruin shall not be repaired.' "[25]

This, of course, contradicts what the Prophet is supposed to have told the monks of St. Catherine's. It is unclear which tradition is authentic; for that matter, they could both be inauthentic. Muslims on both sides of this issue invoke the tradition they find most useful.

Life in Peril

The life of a *dhimmi* was cheap and tenuous. Jews and Christians lived in constant fear of harassment and persecution, particularly when the House of Islam suffered some setback that could be blamed by the aroused rabble on the impure ones in their midst. Although *dhimmi* status was supposed to confer the protection of the Muslim authorities, in practice this was often ignored:

> In 1261, Muslims of Mosul [in Iraq] pillaged and killed all those who did not convert to Islam. Several monks and community leaders and others from the common people recanted. The Kurds then descended from the mountains and attacked the Christians of the region, massacring many of them; they pillaged the convent of Mar Matai, only withdrawing after extorting a heavy ransom from the monks. In 1273, brigands from Ayn Tab and Birah in Syria infiltrated the region of Claudia (upper Euphrates) and led a great part of the population—women and a multitude of youth— into captivity. In 1285, a horde of about six hundred brigands—Kurds, Turks and Arab nomads—fell on Arbil, pillaging and massacring the dhimmis in the surrounding villages. After devastating the whole Mardin region, they left with a considerable booty in flocks and enslaved women and children.[26]

Because of the inflexible nature of Islamic law, even minor incidents could be deadly. A typical case unfolded late in the 1600s when, according to the historian Philip Mansel, "a Greek boy was heard imitating the muezzin's call to prayer. Having thereby inadvertently made a profession of Islam, he was asked by Turkish passers-by to live as a Muslim. When he refused, he was put in prison, and finally executed—hailed by the Greeks as another martyr."[27]

Nor was he the only one. Runciman recounts that "as late as the

1780s a Greek boy who had been adopted by Muslims and brought up in their faith was hanged at Janina for reverting to the faith of his fathers."[28] Countless Christians and Jews were arrested over the centuries for insulting Islam or the Prophet. In 744, the patriarch of Antioch, Stephen III, was accused of denouncing Islam, and his tongue was cut out.[29] Some avoided this or a worse fate at the price of their faith. After the terrible massacres of Armenians in 1915 and 1916, "a small number escaped death by converting to Islam."[30]

Since non-Muslims' testimony weighed less than that of Muslims, a trumped-up accusation could mean death. Says Runciman, "Any lawsuit involving a Christian and a Muslim was heard in a Muslim court, according to Koranic law; and few Muslim judges were prepared to give a judgment in favour of an unbeliever."[31] Ayub Masih, a Christian jailed in Pakistan on a charge that he mentioned Salman Rushdie's *The Satanic Verses,* can testify that this situation hasn't changed.

Preview of Genocide

Occasionally also, Muslim authorities found it politically expedient to arouse the fury of the populace against the *dhimmis,* who were thought to be bringing Allah's disfavor upon the larger community. In a harbinger of the Armenian genocide that would take place twenty years later, the Ottoman sultan Abdul Hamid in 1895 initiated a series of bloody strikes against the restive Christian Armenians in eastern Anatolia. The Armenians had made the mistake of imbibing Western notions of human rights and beginning to question their *dhimmi* status.

According to Lord Kinross, historian of the Ottoman Empire, Hamid "briefed agents, whom he sent to Armenia with specific instructions as to how they should act." Their mission was to arouse "religious fanaticism among the Moslem population," which they accomplished by telling them that "under the holy law the property of rebels might be looted by believers, encouraging Moslems to enrich themselves in the name of their faith at the expense of their Christian neighbors, and in the event of resistance, to kill them."[32]

The Armenians were offered, "at the point of a bayonet, the choice between death and forcible conversion to Islam," an Ottoman practice that had been "previously renounced" in the mid-nineteenth century, "under British pressure."

Each operation, between the bugle calls, followed a similar pattern. First into a town there came the Turkish troops, for the purpose of massacre; then came the Kurdish irregulars and tribesmen for the purpose of plunder. Finally came the holocaust, by fire and destruction, which spread, with the pursuit of fugitives and mopping-up operations, throughout the lands and villages of the surrounding province. The murderous winter of 1895 thus saw the decimation of much of the Armenian population and the devastation of their property in some twenty distinct districts of eastern Turkey. Often the massacres were timed for a Friday, when the Moslems were in their mosques and the myth was spread by the authorities that the Armenians conspired to slaughter them at prayer. Instead they were themselves slaughtered, when the Moslems emerged to forestall their design. The total number of victims was somewhere between fifty and a hundred thousand, allowing for those who died subsequently of wounds, disease, exposure, and starvation.[33]

In the town of Urfa, home to a sizable Christian minority, the Armenians (after enduring a siege that dragged on for two months) asked for protection from the government. In response, the Turks slaughtered all the men in the town. One group of Armenian youths was taken to a sheikh, who "had them thrown down on their backs and held by their hands and feet. Then, in the words of an observer, he recited verses of the Koran and 'cut their throats after the Mecca rite of sacrificing sheep.'" A contingent of troops (along with a mob of enflamed civilians) stormed the cathedral, where a large crowd had gathered for sanctuary. Crying, "Call upon Christ to prove Himself a greater prophet than Muhammad," they murdered the men and burned the women and children alive in the cathedral.

Eight thousand men, women and children were dead in Urfa by the time the afternoon bugle call signaled that the troops' work was done for the day.[34]

The *Devshirme*

Another source of the fear in which *dhimmis* lived in the Ottoman Empire was the notorious *devshirme*. Begun in the fourteenth century by Sultan Orkhan and continued until late in the seventeenth century, this was the seizure and enslavement of 20 percent of the Christian children in various predominantly Christian areas of the empire. These boys were given the choice of Islam or death and, after rigorous training, were enrolled in the janissary corps, the emperor's elite fighters. At first these unfortunate boys were torn from their homes and families only at irregular intervals—sometimes every seven years and sometimes every four—but after a time the *devshirme* became an annual event.[35] By the time it ended, around 200,000 boys had been enslaved in this manner.[36]

The tragedy of this, strangely enough, is in the eye of the beholder. Some families actually hoped that their sons would be chosen for the janissaries, for this at least was a way out of the miserable life of the *dhimmi* and a chance to advance in Ottoman society. Nevertheless, historian Godfrey Goodwin paints an inescapably grim, if romanticized, picture of how these young Christians were recruited:

> Whatever ambitions families might or might not have, it was an unhappy day when the troops trudged into the village, hungry and thirsty. The priest was ready with his baptismal rolls and so were the boys with their fathers; in theory mothers and sisters were left to weep at home. Then each of the recruits had to be examined both physically and mentally. . . . Once the selection process was completed, the roll was drawn up in duplicate. . . . Now was the time for tears and some farewells must have been poignant but the boys tramped the dusty roads side by side with friends and all had the excitement of starting out on an adventure. They could dream of promotion and fortune while the peasants returned to their fields, doubtless to weep longer than their sons.[37]

Threats, uncertainty, enslavement, high taxes, humiliation, persecution—all this ultimately had its desired effect: in not too long a period, the once-vibrant Christian majorities in the lands of Muslim conquest became despised and cowering minorities.

The Islamicization of One City

The transformation of Constantinople after its conquest in 1453 is a case in point. Prior to this, it had been the center of Eastern Christianity and the second city of all Christendom, the chief rival to Rome in splendor and authority. Its Hagia Sophia cathedral, built by Emperor Justinian in the sixth century, was the grandest and most celebrated church in Christendom until the construction of St. Peter's in the Vatican.

But the Muslim conquerors, much like the Taliban who blew up Afghanistan's towering Buddhist statues in 2001, treated the city's wealth of beauty as an unclean thing. According to Hoca Sa'deddin, the tutor of the sixteenth-century sultans Murad III and Mehmed III, "churches which were within the city were emptied of their vile idols and cleansed from the filthy and idolatrous impurities and by the defacement of their images and the erection of Islamic prayer niches and pulpits many monasteries and chapels became the envy of the gardens of Paradise."[38]

Philip Mansel reveals the extent of this "cleansing":

> The repeated transformation of churches (in all forty-two) into mosques asserted the supremacy of Islam. They led to the plastering-over of Christian mosaics and frescos, the expulsion of icons and the insertion of an oval prayer niche facing south-east to Mecca to the right of the former high altar facing south to Jerusalem. In the 1490s the late Byzantine church of St Saviour in Chora, with its incomparable mosaics of the life of Christ, became the Kariye Cami [Mosque]. In Galata in 1545 the cathedral of St Michael was torn down and replaced by the han [a guest house or hotel] of the Rustem Pasha. In 1586 the seat of the Patriarch himself, the resplendent church of the Pammacaristos, was taken, on the excuse that, when Mehmed II had visited the Patriarch Gennadios, he had prayed there. It was renamed Fethiye Cami, the Mosque of Victory, since the empire had just conquered Azerbaijan.[39]

Mansel adds that the patriarch of Constantinople relocated to a small church in the Phanar district of the city. His headquarters are still there today. "Low, and without a visible dome, the mother church of Orthodox Christianity is smaller than most English churches. . . . The contrast with the glory of the sultans' mosques in Constantinople and of the Catholic counterpart, St Peter's in Rome, is remarkable."[40]

The de-Christianization of Istanbul has only accelerated in secular Turkey. The city had a population nearly 50 percent Christian as recently as 1914, just before the secularists took power, but is now 99.99 percent Muslim.[41] Islamic rule was better for Christians than the hegemony of Turkish nationalism. While Islam mandated coexistence (within the limits we have seen) with the Christian population, Turkish nationalists evidently feel themselves bound by no such strictures as they endeavor to perfect their Turkish state.

Score Sheets

So, is Bernard Lewis right? Did Muslims treat Christians and Jews better than Christians treated Muslims and Jews? It is difficult to compare such things. Indeed, how can it be done? By a casualty count? An estimate of lost earnings? A survey of the psychological damage inflicted on the victims? By tallying up the killings, exiles, forced conversions, humiliations and the like? On those scores, both sides have a lot to answer for. But this much is clear: the conventional wisdom that religious minorities had a better quality of life in the House of Islam than in Christendom is at least open to question.

Historian Paul Johnson identifies a disparity between theory on the one hand and economic and social necessity on the other:

> In theory ... the status of the Jewish *dhimmi* under Moslem rule was worse than under the Christians, since their right to practise their religion, and even their right to live, might be arbitrarily removed at any time. In practice, however, the Arab warriors who conquered half the civilized world so rapidly in the seventh and eighth centuries had no wish to exterminate literate and industrious Jewish communities who provided them with reliable tax incomes and served them in innumerable ways.[42]

Both Christians in Christendom and Muslims in the House of Islam at times saw unbelievers as having forfeited all human rights and persisting in deliberate rejection of the truth—a willful obstinacy that deserved punishment. Christian mistreatment of religious minorities was based partly on crude theological reasoning—that Jews were killers of Christ, and so on. But such ideas were subsequently rejected and stigmatized among Christians. Today, in Christianity generally—Catholic, Orthodox and Protestant—the idea of the universal dignity of all people, unbelievers as well as believers, has taken firm root. Indeed, that idea has been one of the Church's great gifts to secular society, and one of the singular discoveries of the West. In Islam, by contrast, the theory about infidels has not changed, and it can always cause more pain for human beings when given the opportunity.

By many accounts, Jews had it better in Muslim countries than in Christian ones during the Middle Ages. Yet by the dawn of the modern age, the great majority of Jews lived in the West, not within the confines of Islam. One reason for this is that while Christian teachings about human rights ultimately eased the plight of religious minorities in the West, the hardening of Muslim attitudes toward infidels created the opposite situation in Islamic lands.

This hardening became evident in the House of Islam at the end of the colonial period. In 1962, when the French colonists left and Islam became the state religion of Algeria, numerous churches were converted to mosques. But this wasn't simply a matter of the occupation of abandoned real estate. New laws forbade Christians to practice their religion openly. Muslims showed that they meant business in 1978, when the Roman Catholic episcopal vicar of Algiers, Monsignor Gaston Jaquier, was murdered—"probably," according to Aid to the Church in Need, "for no other reason than that he had gone out openly wearing his pectoral cross."[43]

Likewise in Tunisia, "in the early 1950s, half of the inhabitants of Tunis were Catholics, but with the declaration of independence some 280,000 Tunisian Catholics were expelled. Today there are no more than a tenth of this number and most of the churches are closed or not in use."[44]

What is the situation today? In Islamic states, non-Muslims are still despised, hemmed in by discriminatory laws, and in peril of their lives.

V. S. Naipaul was told by an Iranian Baha'i he met on an airplane during his travels through the world of Islam, "These Muslims are a strange people. They have an *old* mentality. Very *old* mentality. They are very bad to minorities."[45] In his account of the Iranian revolution, Amir Taheri tells about how a young Ayatollah Khomeini tried unsuccessfully to begin a persecution of the Baha'is. Taheri says matter-of-factly, "The Baha'is are considered a heretical sect by the mullahs, and could thus be automatically punished by death."[46]

At the same time, Muslims may sometimes call upon the principle of toleration when it's expedient. Naipaul encountered a man who, while in London, won the right for his daughter to wear Muslim dress to school instead of the school uniform. Naipaul relates, "The law provided for freedom of religion, he said. He meant the law of England, the other man's law."[47] In other words, Western values can be used when convenient, if not honored in practice.

Today, Christians are enslaved in Sudan and harassed (by means of the Sharia) in Pakistan. That's just the tip of the iceberg; there are hundreds of similar cases all over the Muslim world. It is worthwhile to recount at least some of them, for these stories have been widely ignored in the mainstream Western media.

The Fate of Infidels Today

Perhaps worst off are converts from Islam to Christianity, for virtually all Muslim legal authorities agree that anyone who renounces Islam deserves to die. The Prophet himself decrees death for "the one who turns renegade from Islam (apostate) and leaves the group of Muslims."[48]

All the major collections of hadiths agree that the Prophet said something like this, and it has been a cornerstone of Islamic law from the beginning. Says *Reliance of the Traveller:* "when a person who has reached puberty and is sane voluntarily apostatizes from Islam, he deserves to be killed." Although the right to kill an apostate is reserved in Muslim law to the leader of the community and other Muslims can be punished for taking this duty upon themselves, a Muslim who kills an apostate need pay no indemnity and perform no expiatory acts (as he must in other kinds of murder cases under classic Islamic law).[49]

Some Muslims still manage to become Christians. One of these is the Sudanese Al-Faki Kuku Hassan, whom news reports describe as "a former Muslim sheikh who converted to Christianity in 1995." Hassan was arrested for apostasy in March 1998 and held, despite international protests, until his declining health (he suffered a stroke in spring 2001) led to his release on May 31, 2001.[50]

Muhammad Sallam, an Egyptian convert to Christianity, was arrested in 1989 and tortured; he was arrested again in 1998 and spirited away to an unknown destination. Two other converts to Christianity, Dr. Abdul-Rahman Muhammad Abdul-Ghaffar and Abdul Hamid Beshan Abd El Mohzen, were held in solitary confinement for extended periods in the late 1980s. A female convert from Islam, Sherin Saleh, was married shortly after her conversion, only to have her marriage annulled by the government under the Islamic law forbidding a Muslim woman to marry a Christian man.[51]

In Kuwait, Hussein Ali Qambar converted from Islam to Christianity, and then was "denounced in secret, for apostasy, by his wife and radical Islamic family, after he had received baptism in 1995." An Islamic court condemned him to die, although he seems later to have returned to Islam, thus nullifying the death sentence. However, Professor Anh

Nga Longva of the University of Bergen, Norway, visited Kuwait in 1997 and found passions running high over the Qambar case:

> I found a surprisingly strong consensus across the liberal/islamist divide. Practically everyone agreed that Qambar's conversion was a serious crime and as is the case with all crimes, it had to be punished. They also agreed that depriving him of all his civil rights was an adequate punishment. The only topic which gave rise to some disagreement and a subdued sense of unease within some circles was the question of the death penalty.

Intriguingly, Longva reports that those who were indignant over Qambar's conversion invoked the same Qur'anic verse he would have used to argue that Qambar was within his rights to become a Christian: "Those who opposed [the death penalty for Qambar] based their position on the Qur'anic verse (2:257) that says 'no compulsion is there in religion.' But more often than not, the same verse was quoted in front of me to show that precisely because Islam is such a tolerant religion, there are no possible excuses for apostasy." Longva quotes the disquieting summation of a Kuwaiti jurist: "We always remind those who want to convert to Islam that they enter through a door but that there is no way out."[52]

In Morocco, authorities jailed Christian converts as well as a Salvadoran Baptist musician, Gilberto Orellana, who was accused of converting a Muslim to Christianity.[53]

Even in relatively tolerant Jordan, where freedom of religion is guaranteed by the constitution, "Muslims who convert to other religions suffer discrimination both socially and on the part of the authorities, since the government does not fully recognise the legality of such conversions and considers the converts to be still Muslims, subject to the Sharia, according to which they are apostates and could have their property confiscated and many of their rights denied them."[54] Christians who are not converts from Islam don't have it much easier.

Saudi Arabia, the holy land of Islam, has been especially harsh on religious minorities. Even foreigners must submit to draconian religious laws:

> In 1979, when the Muslims requested the intervention of a special French unit into the Kaaba, against a group of Islamic fundamentalists who were opposed to the government, the soldiers of the intervention force of the French national police (GIGN—Groupe d'intervention de la Gendarmerie

nationale) were obliged to undergo a rapid ceremony of conversion to Islam. Even the Red Cross was obliged, during the course of the Gulf war, to drive around without the symbol of the Cross and not to display its banner.[55]

Adds former U.S. Foreign Service officer Tim Hunter, who served in Saudi Arabia from 1993 to 1995, "On occasion they beat, even tortured, Americans in Jeddah for as little as possessing a photograph with a Star of David in the background or singing Christmas carols.... The Muttawa [Saudi religious police] chained, beat and cast clergy into medieval-style dungeons."[56]

Amnesty International reports that an Indian named George Joseph, who was working in Saudi Arabia, "was reportedly arrested outside his home in May [2000] as he returned from a Catholic service with a religious cassette tape."[57] Christians are, after all, "forbidden to reside in the Hijaz, meaning the area and towns around Mecca, Medina, and Yamama, for more than three days," says *Reliance of the Traveller*.[58] This prohibition goes all the way back to the second caliph, ʿUmar (634–644), one of the Companions of the Prophet.[59] It is often interpreted as pertaining to the whole of Saudi Arabia. So the Saudi authorities were on firm legal ground when they held Joseph incommunicado, beat him, and ultimately deported him.

Maybe Joseph got off easy. The Saudis still hold at least eight foreign nationals, ignoring all inquiries from their governments about their status. All were employees in good standing at Saudi companies, but they committed the crime of holding Christian worship services in private homes. Their fate remains unclear.[60]

In Egypt, Coptic Christians, who officially make up 6 percent of the population but who claim a substantially larger percentage, live in constant peril from Muslim militants. The ordeal of Suhir Shihata Gouda exemplifies the experience of Egyptian Christians.

> Suhir ... was kidnapped on February 25th [1999] by a group of Muslims who forced her to marry a Muslim man, Saed Sadek Mahmoud. After Suhir failed to return home from school, her distraught father rushed to Abu-Tisht police station to report the incident, but instead of assisting him, a police officer began assaulting Suhir's father, Shihata Gouda Abdul-Noor, beating and cursing him. Three days later, Suhir's father and brother returned to the police station to ask for help and they were subjected to

the same abuse, as a result of which the father had to be admitted to hospital for treatment.

Suhir herself managed to escape, but was recaptured "and beaten for running away and is currently under heavy guard." Her Muslim "husband" accompanied a mob to her father's house. There the mob threatened to kill all the Christian men in Suhir's home village and carry off all the women if her family took legal action.[61] (In Pakistan, a fourteen-year-old girl named Gloria Bibi suffered much the same fate: she was kidnapped in 1996 "by a young Muslim who forced her to convert to Islam before marrying her.")[62]

Bishop Wissa of Egypt's Coptic Orthodox Church painted a grim picture in an interview with the Protestant organization Prayer for the Persecuted Church in May 2000:

> One man in his 20s was in the field working when he was approached by armed Muslims. He was asked to renounce Christianity and to verbally say the two statements of faith that would convert him to Islam. When he refused and did the sign of the cross, he was shot in the head and killed.
>
> Another young man had a tattoo on his arm of St. George and the Virgin Mary. They also asked him to renounce his faith. When he refused, they cut off his arm that had the Christian tattoos and chopped it up. They finished him off with their daggers and then burned his body.
>
> A 17-year-old boy, who is a deacon at the church, was going to look for his sister in the fields. He too was asked to renounce his faith, and when he refused, he was shot. After they killed him, they asked the young girl to lay next to her brother and they killed her right there.

The Egyptian government, caught between the Sharia and the laws of a secular republic (Egypt is currently, after all, an "Arab Republic," not an "Islamic Republic"), could not entirely ignore these acts of murder. They compensated each of the families of these victims with eight hundred dollars.

The father of another victim, however, got nothing. His son was on his way to school when Muslim militants stopped the school bus on which he was riding and ordered the Christians to separate from the Muslims. They demanded that the boy renounce his faith. When he refused, says Bishop Wissa, "they killed him with an axe, and then they drove over his body with their car." Authorities called the death a vehicular accident and denied the father compensation—just as they did previously when Muslim militants destroyed his shop.[63]

Muslim militants in Algeria have targeted that country's small group of Catholics for years. In 1994 they killed a priest, a nun and four missionaries; in 1995, two nuns; in 1996, a bishop and fourteen monks. Many of those who were murdered were trying to establish friendly relations with the Muslim community. Bishop Pierre Claverie of Oran, killed in 1996, "had dedicated his life to promoting dialogue between Islam and Christianity; he was known as the 'Bishop of the Muslims' and had studied Islam in depth—indeed to such an extent that . . . the Muslims themselves would consult him on the subject."[64]

Compass Direct, a global Protestant news service, reported in early 2002 that in Malawi, two local Christians "have been stoned, threatened with machetes and warned by local Muslim leaders that they will be sent back to their original villages as corpses if they continue to hold meetings in their houses."[65]

According to Aid to the Church in Need, in Bangladesh "on April 28, 1998, a crowd—instigated by the Islamists—ransacked and partly burnt down the Catholic girls' college of St Francis Xavier, the churches of Santa Croce and St Thomas in the capital, and the Baptist church in Sadarghat. Some priests, nuns and even ordinary workers have been threatened with death." The occasion for this violence seems to have been a dispute over land:

> The reason for the conflict was a plot of land belonging to the Church which the adjacent mosque wanted for itself. Seven thousand people, incited via a loud-hailer with claims that the mosque had been invaded by Christians and Jews, broke into the St Francis Xavier College, burning books, smashing crucifixes and statues of Our Lady, breaking down doors, windows and ransacking the dormitories.[66]

In a notorious incident in Peshawar, Pakistan, Muslim gunmen killed fifteen Christians at Sunday worship on October 28, 2001. Since then other Christians have been attacked and killed in Peshawar; five people were killed and forty wounded in another church attack on March 17, 2002. The entire Pakistani Christian community was terrorized by an al-Qaeda threat to kill "two Christians in retaliation for every Muslim killed in the U.S. military strikes in Afghanistan."[67]

Pakistani schoolteacher Cadherine Shaheen was harassed on the job, "pressured to convert to Islam." Finally she was told that she would have to convert to Islam or leave the school. Soon she was accused of blasphemy. All the area mosques posted copies of a poster bearing her name and picture. "You have to understand," says Shaheen. "This was a death sentence for me. It's considered an honor for one of the Muslim men to kill a blasphemer. Just before me, the Muslims murdered a school principal accused of blasphemy. I was next."

Shaheen went underground, whereupon Pakistani police arrested her father and brothers. Her father, age 85, was traumatized and soon died. Cadherine made her way to the United States. "It's horrible for Christians in Pakistan," she says. "The Muslims take our land, rob our homes, try to force us to accept Islam. Young girls are kidnapped and raped. Then they're told that if they want a husband who will accept them after that defilement, they must become Muslim."[68] Egyptian girls report being subjected to similar harassment.[69]

Even in the relatively secular Iraq of Saddam Hussein, where Deputy Prime Minister Tariq Aziz is a Chaldean Catholic Christian, the small Christian community faces random violence from the Muslim majority. In 1996 and 1997, Kurds killed over thirty Christians in northern Iraq. Christians are routinely pressured to marry Muslims.[70]

Muslim militants despise Libya's Muammar Qaddafi as much as they do Saddam Hussein. Qaddafi has imposed a heretical form of Islam upon Libya, rejecting the Sunnah and hadith. But that doesn't mean he's any more tolerant toward Christians: "The majority of the Christian churches were closed following the revolution of 1969, despite the fact that the words of the Constitution guarantee the liberty of religion. After expelling the Italian and Maltese Catholics, Qaddafi turned the cathedral in the capital into a mosque."[71]

Since the Turkish occupation of northern Cyprus in 1974, churches have been despoiled of icons, which have flooded the market in Greece. The Turks have taken over many churches for secular uses, and even tried to convert the fourth-century monastery of San Makar into a hotel. Christian Cypriots are forbidden to come near the building, much less to enter it.[72]

Secular Turkey is little better: Muslim militants seem determined to drive all Christians out of the country. In Tur-Abdin in southwest Turkey in 1960, there were 150,000 Christians; today there are just over 2,000. There is also terrorism: "on December 3, 1997, a bomb exploded in the headquarters of the Ecumenical Patriarch, injuring a deacon and damaging the church."[73]

In Nigeria, over two thousand people have been killed in Muslim-Christian riots in the city of Jos. All over Nigeria, Muslim militants continue to try to impose the Sharia over the whole country, despite its sizable Christian population. A report warned that in Jos, "the conflict could recur, since Muslim militants are still bent on attacking Christians."[74]

In Indonesia, the violent repression of Christians in East Timor is by no means the only case of oppression of non-Muslims. Compass Direct reports that a militant Muslim group, Laskar Jihad, and its allies are waging war on Christians on a large scale. In Java in 1996, Muslims destroyed thirteen churches. Aid to the Church in Need reported an incident emblematic of the differences between Islam and Christianity: "Eight Sisters of the Little Child Jesus, on arriving in Cileduk, a suburb of Java, were attacked by stone-throwing Muslims; they responded by building a care centre for children, an old people's home and a school."[75]

Thirteen more churches were torched in Djakarta in 1998 by mobs shouting, "We are Muslim gentlemen and they are Christian pigs" and, paraphrasing the Qur'an, "Kill all the pagans!" One Muslim shouted at an army offer who was trying to protect some Christians to "stand aside and allow Islamic justice to take its course."[76]

Have the people who commit such acts "hijacked" Islam? As we have seen, it would be hard to make a case that they are bad Muslims. They are simply obeying the Qur'anic injunctions to "slay the unbelievers wherever you find them" (Sura 9:5), for "Muhammad is God's Apostle. Those who follow him are ruthless to the unbelievers but merciful to one another" (Sura 48:29).

There will be many more such stories, for Islam supports and perpetuates hatred of Christians. Some traditions even suggest that Christians are the worst of all unbelievers—as does one hadith about the lawfulness of marrying unbelieving women:

> Narrated Nafi': Whenever Ibn ʿUmar was asked about marrying a Christian lady or a Jewess, he would say: "Allah has made it unlawful for the believers to marry *Al-Mushrikat* (ladies who ascribe partners in worship to Allah), and I do not know of a greater thing, as regards to ascribing partners in worship, etc., to Allah, than that a lady should say that Jesus is her Lord although he is just a slave from the slaves of Allah."[77]

In fact, the worse off the House of Islam is, the more threatened are its Christian minorities. When things are going wrong, Muslims tend to blame the infidels among them for calling down the wrath of Allah. So they purify the land and court Allah's favor by killing them. That may be why Christians in Pakistan and elsewhere have been having a harder time of it lately, when passions are enflamed throughout the House of Islam. That is also why Christians and Jews will always be in danger of persecution in Islamic lands. Until Muslims in general come to view the Qur'an and the hadiths the way Christians and Jews regard some portions of the Old Testament, as limited in their modern application by their historical context, it is unlikely that this situation will change.

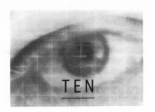

TEN

Does the West Really Have Nothing to Fear from Islam?

THERE ARE NOT TWO, BUT THREE CERTAINTIES in human affairs: death, taxes, and jihad. If the West faces any long-term threat from Islam, it stems from the latter, much-abused concept.

Muslim commentators complain that nothing (except, possibly, the status of women) is more misunderstood and misrepresented in the West than the concept of jihad. The Council on American-Islamic Relations (CAIR) went so far as to claim that it "does not mean 'holy war.'"[1] Journalist Ahmed Rashid blames the misunderstanding on those universal whipping boys, the Crusaders: "In Western thought, heavily influenced by the medieval Christian Crusaders—with their own ideas about 'holy war'—jihad has always been portrayed as an Islamic war against unbelievers." He insists that "militancy is not the essence of jihad."

What is, then? "The greater jihad as explained by The Prophet Muhammad," says Rashid, "is first inward-seeking: it involves the effort of each Muslim to become a better human being, to struggle to improve him- or herself."[2] This much is undisputable.

Muhammad Sa'id al-Buti, a theology professor at Damascus University, insists that "the essence and core of Jihad ... [has] nothing to do with fighting." He supports this assertion with a pair of hadiths: "Allah's Messenger himself confirms and clarifies this fact by his hadith (saying) 'A most excellent Jihad is when one speaks a word of truth in the presence of a tyrannical ruler.' He also says, 'A most excellent kind of Jihad is to carry on against your own self and whim for the sake of the Lord.'"[3]

If that's what CAIR means in saying that jihad doesn't denote "holy war," they are absolutely right. This spiritual and ascetical struggle is indeed commonly known in Islam by the term Rashid uses for it: the greater jihad.

But even as they grouse about purposeful Western misunderstand-
ings, Rashid and al-Buti acknowledge that there is also a lesser jihad.
This is where the AK-47's come in.

Lesser jihad cannot be separated from the waging of war. Even
Rashid and al-Buti grant this. Jihad can, says Rashid, "become the means
to mobilize . . . political and social struggle."[4] How? By leafleting or holding seminars? Perhaps, but al-Buti is more explicit. He notes the example of the Prophet and his Companions in "waging armed struggle against
those who wanted to resist the Islamic *da'wah* [proclamation of the Islamic
message] which followed the norm of communication and dialogue."[5]
Even CAIR acknowledges that jihad includes "the struggle to improve
the quality of life in society, *struggle in the battlefield for self-defense* . . . or
fighting against tyranny or oppression" (emphasis added).[6]

In noting that the battlefield jihad must be waged only in self-
defense, CAIR is following Muhammad Abduh and others who tried to
bring Islam into line with modern sensibilities. In his commentary on
the Qur'an, ᶜAbdullah Yusuf ᶜAli states that "war is permissible in self-
defence, and under well-defined limits."[7] Unfortunately, however, not
all currents of Islam have flowed in this direction.

"I have been ordered to fight"

According to classic Islamic theology, Muslims can legitimately wage war
against those who resist the proclamation of Islam. In his book *Jihad in
Islam: How to Understand and Practice It,* al-Buti (whose theories have
ignited some controversy in the Muslim world) considers at great length
the question of whether this armed struggle can be undertaken "to avert
belligerency" or "to put an end to infidelity."[8] In other words, is jihad
purely defensive, or can it be offensive? (Al-Buti, however, carefully defines
"to avert belligerency" in a way that allows for a preemptive strike against
a perceived imminent attack.)

Al-Buti bases his discussion of this question on the Qur'an and
these hadiths from Bukhari and Muslim, which have justified Islamic
belligerency for centuries:

> Narrated Ibn ᶜUmar: Allah's Messenger said: "I have been ordered (by
> Allah) to fight against the people until they testify that *La ilaha illallah,
> wa anna Muhammad-ar-Rasul-Allah* (none has the right to be worshipped

but Allah and that Muhammad is the Messenger of Allah), and perform *As-Salat* [Iqamat-as-Salat (prayers)] and give *Zakat* so if they perform all that, then they save their lives and property from me except for Islamic laws, and then their reckoning (accounts) will be (done by) Allah."[9]

It is reported on the authority of Abu Huraira that he heard the Messenger of Allah say: I have been commanded to fight against people, till they testify to the fact that there is no god but Allah, and believe in me (that) I am the messenger (from the Lord) and in all that I have brought. And when they do it, their blood and riches are guaranteed protection on my behalf except where it is justified by law, and their affairs rest with Allah.[10]

After a thorough discussion of these hadiths and other elements of Muslim tradition, al-Buti concludes that Muslim forces should not attack unbelievers. They should fight when attacked, or when an attack seems imminent, but that's all. In this conclusion he sides with three of the four major Sunni schools of Islamic jurisprudence, the Hanafi, Maliki and Hanbali; by his account, all agree that military jihad should only be undertaken to ward off an attack or potential attack.

But of course, that is precisely what Osama bin Laden says that the September 11 attacks were doing. His justifications for his actions have always been theological. In his World Islamic Front statement of February 23, 1998, he laid out a litany of American offenses and then declared:

All these crimes and sins committed by the Americans are a clear declaration of war on Allah, his messenger, and Muslims. And ulama have throughout Islamic history unanimously agreed that the jihad is an individual duty if the enemy destroys the Muslim countries. This was revealed by Imam Bin-Qadamah in "Al-Mughni," Imam al-Kisa'i in "Al-Bada'i," al-Qurtubi in his interpretation, and the shaykh of al-Islam in his books, where he said: "As for the fighting to repulse [an enemy], it is aimed at defending sanctity and religion, and it is a duty as agreed [by the ulama]. Nothing is more sacred than belief except repulsing an enemy who is attacking religion and life."[11]

Certainly other imams have disputed his interpretation, although most Muslims who avowed that the September 11 attacks were illegal according to Islam focused on the killing of the innocents—which, as we have seen, bin Laden also has disputed. But the point here isn't that bin Laden is right and others are wrong; it's that his interpretation is firmly rooted in Islamic law. Other bin Ladens can and will use the same laws to make more trouble. The problem, in other words, is that the *theory* of jihad allows for the unchecked growth of militant groups in Islam—growth which outmanned and outgunned Islamic moderates are powerless to stop, because to do so would be to turn against Islam itself.

What's more, the other major Sunni school, the Shafi'i, and the smaller Zahiri school favor offensive jihad. The Shafi'is and Zahiris, according to al-Buti, "proclaimed that the fundamental cause of Jihad is to terminate Paganism."[12] This would mean that jihad must continue as long as there are unbelievers, at least according to the Shafi'is. Making war on unbelievers is one of the responsibilities of the Muslim *umma*. The Shafi'i manual *Reliance of the Traveller* stipulates that jihad is "a communal obligation" to "war against non-Muslims."

> The caliph makes war upon Jews, Christians, and Zoroastrians (N: provided he has first invited them to enter Islam in faith and practice, and if they will not, then invited them to enter the social *order* of Islam by paying the non-Muslim poll tax (jizya)—which is the significance of their paying it, not the money itself—while remaining in their ancestral religions (O: and the war continues) until they become Muslim or else pay the non-Muslim poll tax.... The caliph fights all other peoples until they become Muslim.[13] ["N" and "O" denote references to commentaries by Sheikh Nuh ʿAli Salman and Sheikh ʿUmar Barakat, respectively. These parenthetical comments are included within the main text of *Reliance of the Traveller,* as they appear here.]

Since the fall of the Ottoman Empire there has been no caliph, but this doesn't mean that no Muslim will dare to declare jihad. Bin Laden has taken it upon himself to declare jihad on his own. (Other Muslim clerics have, however, denied his right to do this.)

The Shafi'is, in any case, are no fringe group, nor are they newly minted. The Shafi'i juridical rite has been around for more than a millennium: it was founded upon the teachings of the Imam al-Shafi'i, who flourished in the ninth century, and is particularly strong today in Egypt, Syria, India and Indonesia. It was once widespread in Arabia, only to be displaced by the even more militant Wahhabis.

Moreover, the niceties of theory and theological debate aside, there is little doubt that on matters of jihad the Shafi'is find substantial agreement from, for example, the Wahhabis (who profess the Hanbali school of jurisprudence) and many others. Even if they disagree on the textbook occasions for jihad, enough Muslims believe that they have ample cause nowadays to "combat belligerency" that Americans should prepare themselves for a long, hard war.

Those who claim that jihad is primarily a struggle against sin, or that it only resorts to arms in a defensive mode, are correct, then—but only partially. Likewise, those who think that militant Islam is a Wahhabi creation fail to recognize that even some of the Islamic groups that the Wahhabis condemn as heretics allow for Wahhabi-like militancy among their adherents.

Three Territories

Traditional Islamic thought divides the world into three spheres: *dar-al-Islam, dar-al-Sulh* and *dar-al-harb*—that is, the House of Islam, the House of Truce and the House of War.

The House of Islam, of course, is the territory where Islamic law holds sway. Dependent upon it is the House of Truce, the area where non-Muslims live in covenant with Muslim rulers; this area, then, is the abode of the *dhimmis*. (Dr. Mustafa Ceric, a high-ranking Bosnian Muslim cleric, defines *dar-al-Sulh* as more of an intermediary area, where "the situation is such that Islam or the shariah cannot be implemented fully, but the government should endeavour to put it into practice as much as possible.")[14]

About the House of War there is no disagreement. "Non-Muslims," explains Bat Ye'or, "are *harbis*, inhabitants of the *dar-al-harb*, the lands of war, so called because they are destined to come under Islamic jurisdiction, either by war (*harb*) or by the conversion of their inhabitants." The jihad that aims to increase the size of the *dar-al-Islam* at the expense of the *dar-al-harb* is not a conventional war that begins at a certain point and ends at another. Jihad is a "permanent war" that "excludes the idea of peace but authorizes temporary truces related to the political situation *(muhadana).*"[15]

This is a point that few, if any, Western commentators have remarked upon. A jihad such as that declared against the United States by bin Laden is not the sort of war that ends with the victory of one side and the defeat of the other, heralded by the signing of a peace treaty and the other trappings of the conclusion of modern warfare. Instead, it's just an episode in the ongoing Muslim struggle against the unbelieving world.

Karen Armstrong acknowledges that "Muslim jurists ... taught that, because there was only one God, the whole world should be united in one polity and it was the duty of all Muslims to engage in a continued struggle to make the world accept the divine principles and create a just society." The House of War "should be made to surrender to God's rule. Until this had been achieved, Islam must engage in a perpetual warlike effort." But, she says, "this martial theology was laid aside in practice and became a dead letter once it was clear that the Islamic empire had reached the limits of its expansion about a hundred years after Muhammad's death."[16]

The problem is that however much of a dead letter it became in practice during times of weakness in the House of Islam, no one laid it aside in principle. No one seems to have told the warriors of jihad who besieged Europe through the seventeenth century that the Islamic empire had already reached the limits of its expansion centuries before. No one seems to have told the modern-day warriors and apostles of Islam from Bosnia to the Philippines that jihad is a dead letter, and that Islam isn't doing any more expanding. Historian Paul Fregosi observes that from the time of Muhammad, "the purpose of Jihad became, and basically still is, to expand and extend Islam until the whole world is under Muslim rule."[17]

Jihad will no more end with Osama bin Laden than it began with him. As the *Encyclopedia of Islam* put it in 1913, "Islam must be completely made over before the doctrine of jihad can be eliminated."[18] If anything about the future is certain, it is that whatever the ultimate outcome of the war on terrorism may be, there will be more jihads as long as there are people who take the Qur'an as the word of Allah and the Sunnah as second only to the Qur'an as a reliable guide to behavior.

Demographic Jihad

On the other hand, if demographic trends continue, jihad may not be necessary. The Islamicization of the West will happen, but in a slower, less dramatic way.

The population in the Muslim world is skyrocketing, while in the lands that once were Christendom it is aging and diminishing. According to the CIA, in the twenty-first century "the population of the region that served as the locus for most 20th Century history—Europe and

Russia—will shrink dramatically in relative terms; almost all population growth will occur in developing nations that until now have occupied places on the fringes of the global economy." Moreover, "of the 1.5 billion people that the world population will gain by 2020"—less than twenty years from now—"most will be added to states in Asia and Africa." Those growing fastest will be Muslim nations, including some of those that are currently the most militant. "Many developing nations will experience substantial youth bulges: the largest proportional youth populations will be located in Pakistan, Afghanistan, Saudi Arabia, Yemen, and Iraq."[19] In Europe, meanwhile, the population bulge is among the aged.

In 2000, Catholic, Orthodox and Protestant Christians comprised 30 percent of the global population and Muslims 19 percent. But one estimate predicts that if present trends continue, by 2025 Muslims will substantially outnumber Christians, comprising 30 percent of the world's people, with Christians constituting 25 percent.[20]

Demographic predictions are always risky. But these predictions aren't pulled out of thin air: populations are already exploding in the Muslim world, just as they are already declining in the West. A recent news item from Saudi Arabia is emblematic of current trends: the 133-year-old Hussein Rashid al-Sowaikat al-Baqami died on May 8, 2002, leaving behind "the last of his nine wives, 23 sons and 113 grandchildren."[21] A story from the Gaza Strip is similar: "The Gaza Strip's oldest resident, Haj Abdullah Kadurah, died last week at the age of 128. For the last 70 years he had served as a muezzin [caller to prayer] of the Tufeh neighborhood mosque, located next to his home. Kadurah is survived by more than 240 children, grandchildren, great-grandchildren, and great-great-grandchildren."[22]

Granted, not every Muslim lives twelve decades and leaves behind hundreds of descendants, but these two men are emblematic of larger demographic trends. By contrast, imagine a Westerner, born at the same time as Haj Abdullah Kadurah, who had a now-typical two-child family, as did all of his descendants. In five generations he would have a total of 30 descendants, compared with Kadurah's 240.

Where will all these people go?

To Europe, where the population decline has made jobs plentiful and immigrants more welcome than ever. They have already gone there in great numbers. In France, Islam is the second-largest religion in the country: there are now about four million Muslims in France, or about

7 percent of the nation's total population. The Muslim population in
Germany is approaching 4 percent. There are also about a million Muslims in Italy and half a million in the formerly Muslim land of Spain.

All these populations are increasing rapidly, as exemplified by the
growth of Islam in the Netherlands. According to the U.S. State Department's International Religious Freedom Report,

> Only 49 Muslims lived in the country in 1879. After 1960 the number of
> Muslims began to rise due to the arrival of migrant workers, primarily
> from Morocco and Turkey. Family unification increased their numbers
> to 234,000 Moroccans and 279,000 Turks by 1998. Additional Muslims
> came from the former Dutch colony of Suriname. In the past decade,
> Muslim numbers further increased due to the large numbers of asylum
> seekers from countries such as Iran, Iraq, Somalia, and Bosnia. By 1998
> about 700,000 persons, or 4.4 percent of the population, were Muslim—
> the majority Sunni.[23]

As these numbers continue to expand among Europe's aging, secularized populations, Europe will be, in the words of the CIA, "less willing to face up to global hotspots"[24]—and presumably even less willing
when to do so will entail making war against the homelands of large segments of its population.

Of course, while Muslim enclaves in European cities have already
aroused concern, a great many of these immigrants will experience the attraction not only of secularism, but of liberal democracy. The great majority of
them, once removed from the heightened emotions and fanaticism of the
contemporary House of Islam, will become productive citizens, hardly dis-
tinguishable from their neighbors. Human nature is the same the world over.
Even so, fanaticism and rage dominate so much of contemporary Islamic
discourse that it would be naïve to assume that all of the Muslims stream-
ing into Europe are likely to assimilate peacefully into Western culture.

The ideology of multiculturalism, in fact, dictates that they not
assimilate, but rather cling proudly to their Islamic beliefs and traditions.
The multiculturalist imperative also coincides neatly with the traditional
Muslim view of non-Islamic cultures. Philip Hitti explains that Muslims
"call the era before the appearance of Muhammad the Jahiliyah period,
a term usually rendered as 'time of ignorance' or 'barbarism.' "[25]

V. S. Naipaul encountered this attitude in his travels through the
House of Islam. For many Muslims, he observes, "The time before Islam

is a time of blackness: that is part of Muslim theology. History has to serve theology." Naipaul explains how at least some Pakistani Muslims, far from valuing the nation's renowned archaeological site at Mohenjo-Daro, see it as a teaching opportunity for Islam:

> A featured letter in *Dawn* offered its own ideas for the site. Verses from the Koran, the writer said, should be engraved and set up in Mohenjo-Daro in "appropriate places": "Say (unto them, O Mohammed): Travel in the land and see the nature of the sequel for the guilty. . . . Say (O Mohammed, to the disbelievers): Travel in the land and see the nature of the consequence for those who were before you. Most of them were idolaters."[26]

Likewise in Iran: "In 637 A.D., just five years after the death of the Prophet, the Arabs began to overrun Persia, and all Persia's great past, the past before Islam, was declared a time of blackness."[27] We have also seen the fruit of this assumption in our own time in Cyprus, where Muslims attempted to use the fourth-century monastery of San Makar as a hotel; in Libya, where Muammar Qaddafi turned Tripoli's Catholic cathedral into a mosque; and in Afghanistan, where the Taliban dynamited the Buddhas of Bamiyan.

Are All Religions Created Equal?

It is not true that all religions are basically identical, or that all are essentially peaceful. It would be too pessimistic to say that there are no peaceful strains of Islam, but it would be imprudent to ignore the fact that deeply imbedded in the central documents of the religion is an all-encompassing vision of a theocratic state that is fundamentally different from and opposed to the post-Enlightenment Christian values of the West.

Even in Pakistan, where Christians have suffered so terribly, they are unafraid to tell the whole truth about Islam. The website of the *Pakistan Christian Post* featured an article entitled "Lesson for Christian Women on Marriage to Any Muslim Man." It cautions Christian girls considering marriage to Muslims that "there is an old saying 'Love is blind but marriage is an eye opener.' This could never be truer than with regard to the young western woman marrying into Islam. So take warning!"[28] The author then explores Islamic law regarding marriage and the status of women: women are inferior, unclean, subject to corporal punishment and polygamy, and so on.[29]

But it seems to be easier to say things like that in Muslim Pakistan, where Christians live under the constant threat of arrest and assault, than in the West. In Western Europe and North America, the fact that Islam at its core contains elements that are not peaceful or benign has become the truth that dares not speak its name.

Instead, the news media indulges in puerile and outrageously inaccurate comparisons like this one by ABC reporter Jami Floyd: "Since September 11, the word 'terrorist' has come to mean someone who is radical, Islamic and foreign. But many believe we have as much to fear from a home-grown group of anti-abortion crusaders."[30] On June 7, 2002, the *New York Times* ran an op-ed piece alleging that Americans are "distracted by our own stereotypes, searching for Muslim terrorists in the Philippine jungle ... and forgetting that there are blond, blue-eyed mad bombers as well." The next day the paper reported that Christian missionary Martin Burnham had been killed in the Philippine jungle as Philippine soldiers attempted to free him from the Islamic terrorist group Abu Sayyaf.[31]

The Society of Professional Journalists, meanwhile warned America's newspeople not to refer to the September 11 terrorists without also referring to "white supremacists, radical antiabortionists, and other groups with a history of such activity."[32] Similarly, we hear that the Democratic Party plots to "steal the war issue from the Republicans by scapegoating the 'religious right,' presenting conservative Christians as the moral equivalent of the Taliban."[33]

Such statements and intentions betray an appalling ignorance both of Islam and of our own culture and heritage. Beyond that is outright cultural self-hatred, as manifested by Karen Armstrong in her tendency to blame Christianity for all the misdeeds of Islam, and by Bill Clinton when he blamed the Crusades and American slavery for the September 11 terrorist attacks.[34] The most disgraceful example of this self-hatred comes from English journalist Robert Fisk, who was beaten by a mob of refugees in Afghanistan soon after the beginning of the war on terrorism. "If I were the Afghan refugees," wrote Fisk, "I would have done just the same to Robert Fisk. Or any other Westerner I could find."[35]

The culture of tolerance threatens to render the West incapable of drawing reasonable distinctions. The general reluctance to criticize any non-Christian religion and the almost universal public ignorance about Islam make for a lethal mix.

These days it's considered in bad taste to point out that the Qur'an and the Bible do not teach identical moral precepts, or that the Muhammad of Islam and the Jesus of Christianity are not interchangeable. Actor Gabriel Byrne expressed a commonplace for many, if not most, modern Westerners when he said that he wanted his children to learn "moral precepts, knowing right from wrong. If they get that from the Koran or the Bible or the Kaballah I don't care."[36]

Were Byrne's children really taught the Qur'an, they would likely become quite different people from what they would be as Bible readers. Gabriel Byrne and millions of others in the West either don't know it or won't admit it, but Christianity, the spiritual foundation of secular Western society, and Islam shape different kinds of personalities.

Human nature is multifaceted. Every individual is subject to an uncountable number of influences during his lifetime. It is usually impossible to isolate with any certainty the real causes that moved anyone to make a particular choice. The terrible imperfection of people who have followed the Jesus of the New Testament is a clear indication that good ideals do not translate smoothly and easily into good actions. Nonetheless, flawed ideals are certainly less likely to do so. That's why it matters what one believes, and why the differences in belief systems are so important.

Consider the difference we saw in chapter four between how Muslims and Christians have reacted to the case of Sufiyatu Huseini, the Nigerian woman sentenced to death for adultery under the Sharia, although she says she was raped. Bello Sanyinnawal, the presiding judge in the case, was intent on carrying out the letter of the law in his concern for the purity of the Muslim community. But at least one Christian had a different response: if expiation had to be made, Anthony Olubunmi Okogie, the Catholic archbishop of Lagos, was ready to make it, offering his own life in exchange for that of Sufiyatu Huseini.

Indeed, the Palestinian Muslim Eyad Sarraj noted the same contrast:

> Christianity's message of nonviolence is very important, and it is not there in Islam, and I believe it is not there in Judaism. I would honestly say that if I could choose a religion, I would choose Christianity and its ideal of

universal acceptance, love, and forgiveness. It is all so beautiful. It is just
so unfortunate that the history of Christianity has nothing to do with
these ideas.[37]

Perhaps Sarraj would enjoy meeting Archbishop Okogie.

We have seen that elements of Islam fiercely resist secularism, as
well as relativism and indifferentism. Some Muslims are suspicious of
non-Muslim cultures and will not assimilate into them, just as they begin
to overwhelm them numerically. If anything is certain in the future, it
is that these elements will cause more conflicts, and that the West should
be prepared for them.

Sheikh ʿAbd al-Hamid al-Ansari, dean of the Faculty of Sharia at
Qatar University, recently called upon the West to reappraise Islam:

> The West must reexamine the foundations of its view towards us and the
> ideas it has formulated about us since the period of Orientalism [i.e. Ori-
> entalist research] which were based on the [perceptions] of the Middle
> Ages—according to which Islam is a religion of violence spread by the
> sword, and the Muslims are wreaking vengeance on modern civilization
> and do not respect human rights, do not guarantee minority rights, do
> not believe in the values of democracy and tolerance, and do not behave
> properly towards women. Similarly, the West needs to refrain from gen-
> eralizing about Islam and Muslims because of the behavior of a small
> minority among them.[38]

It is one thing, however, to ask for a change in the Western perception of Islam, and quite another to provide evidence to make such a
change possible. I would love to take Sheikh al-Ansari at his word and
see Islam as entirely benign and enlightened, but it isn't really me that
he has to convince; it is his fellow Muslims. Yet the children of Osama
and his ilk are not likely to be easily swayed.

Whether or not Islam ever becomes dominant in Western Europe
or elsewhere in the former lands of Christendom, the wars will not end.
Militant Islam will not go away with the death of bin Laden, or Arafat,
or Saddam Hussein, or anyone else. It will clash increasingly with the
weary secular powers that it blames for all the ills of the *umma*. No one
can predict the features of the world that will emerge from these conflicts, except that it will be new, and that it will be difficult—unless there
is some wondrous intervention from the Merciful One.

ACKNOWLEDGMENTS

THIS PROJECT WOULD HAVE NEVER BEEN completed or even begun were it not for Jeff Rubin, whose indefatigable courage, breadth of intellect, and keenness of insight are rare and refreshing.

Thanks also to Paul Weyrich, Lisa Dean, Clay Rossi, and all at the Free Congress Foundation, as well as to H. W. Crocker III, the Rev. Thomas Steinmetz, and the Rev. Eugene Mitchell, BSO, for their kindness and support. I am also grateful for the help of all those who reviewed the manuscript at its various stages of development: Daniel Ali, Dr. Anis Shorrosh, the Rt. Rev. Gerasimos Murphy, BSO, the Rev. Richard John Neuhaus, and others too numerous to name. The conceptual direction of Peter Collier and the editorial assistance of Carol Staswick at Encounter Books have been enormously helpful in trimming excesses, correcting emphases, and bringing clarity to the entire presentation. I am grateful to all these people for what is true and accurate in this book; only I am responsible for its errors.

I postponed a good many games and trips to finish this book, and thank my children for their mature understanding, as well as for their ever-delightful support and love. Above all, I owe a tremendous debt of gratitude to my lovely wife. Her acuity, wit, patience, resourcefulness and love leave me in awe, and fill my life with pure joy.

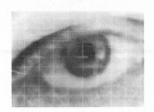

NOTES

Introduction: What Does Islam Really Stand For?

1. Quoted in David Rohde and C. J. Chivers, "Al Qaeda's Grocery Lists and Manuals of Killing," *New York Times,* 17 March 2002, p. A1.
2. "EU Deplores 'Dangerous' Islam Jibe," BBC News, 27 September 2001.
3. Ibid.
4. "Mr. Robertson's Incitement," *Washington Post,* 23 February 2002, p. A20.
5. Alexander Stille, "Scholars Are Quietly Offering New Theories of the Koran," *New York Times,* 2 March 2002, p. A1.
6. Ibid.

Chapter 1: Is Islam a Religion of Peace?

1. George W. Bush, Address to a Joint Session of Congress and the American People, White House Press Release, 20 September 2001.
2. Bill Clinton, Remarks by the President to the Opening Session of the 53rd United Nations General Assembly, White House Press Release, 21 September 1998.
3. Islam has also inspired a few adherents of the "all religions are one" dogma, most notably the Sufi pantheist Ibn al-ʿArabi (1165–1240).
4. Karen Armstrong, *Islam: A Short History* (Modern Library, 2000), p. 8.
5. Ibid., pp. 179–80.
6. www.cnn.com, 14 December 2001.
7. Because of its association in the West with the notorious bounty that the Ayatollah Khomeini put on Salman Rushdie's head, the word *fatwa* is often used as a synonym for a Mafia "contract"—a death sentence. But in fact it means simply a ruling by an imam on a disputed question. In Shia Islam, the dominant sect in Iran, religious teachers (*mullahs*) generally command even greater authority and respect than they do in Sunnism: they're not just interpreters of the law, but guides and exemplars in living it.

8. "Shaykh Saalih al-Lehaydaan Says Deadly Attacks in USA Are a 'Terrible Crime,'" www.fatwa-online.com, 14 September 2001. As for law in Saudi Arabia: traffic laws and other minor statutes are not, of course, dictated by Islamic law, but all major law is based on Islamic religious tenets.

9. "Shaykh Saalih as-Suhaymee Speaks about Current Affairs . . ." www.fatwa-online.com, 18 October 2001.

10. "A Muslim Activist Questioning Sheikh Omar Regarding the Recent Attack on USA," www.almuhajiroun.com, 15 December 2001.

11. *Allah* is the proper name of God in the Qur'an; it can be precisely rendered in English as something akin to "the God" or "the one God." Some translators—notably N. J. Dawood in his Penguin edition of the Qur'an—render it simply as "God." Many Muslims, however, use the Arabic word when speaking and writing English, and I have followed their lead.

12. Osama bin Laden videotape, U.S. government transcript, trans. George Michael, Associated Press, 14 December 2001.

13. "The Salafi Cult: The Modern Day Khawarij," www.wahhabi.info/.

14. Stephen Schwartz, "Seeking Moderation," *National Review Online,* 25 October 2001. Schwartz is author of *Kosovo: Background to a War.*

15. William J. Bennett, *Why We Fight: Moral Clarity and the War on Terrorism* (Doubleday, 2002), p. 85.

16. Capitalization as in the original.

17. Sheikh Omar Bakri Muhammad, "Saudism END Wahhabism," 14 March 1997, www.kavkaz.com/enews4.html.

18. "Declaration of Press Conference Held by Members of Al-Muhajiroun in Lahore Press Club, Pakistan," 21 September 2001, www.al-muhajiroun.com.

19. Thomas Wagner, "British Islamist Issues Warning," Associated Press, 7 January 2002.

20. Quoted in Jeff Jacoby, "Outspoken, Muslim—and Moderate," *Boston Globe,* 16 May 2002.

21. Ibid.

22. Jake Tapper, "Islam's Flawed Spokesmen," www.salon.com, 26 September 2001.

23. "Some Muslim Leaders Seen with Bush Expressed Support for Terrorist Groups," www.foxnews.com, 1 October 2001.

24. Hanna Rosin and John Mintz, "Muslim Leaders Struggle with Mixed Messages," *Washington Post,* 2 October 2001, p. A16. Yusuf had been outspoken before. His friend Jamil al-Amin, an imam and convert to Islam who became notorious in the sixties as black militant H. Rap Brown, was recently convicted of murdering a sheriff's deputy who was trying to serve him with an arrest warrant. A few years ago Yusuf said of him: "He's a man who by necessity must speak the truth. That is a dangerous man. . . . Within this

government are elements who will do anything to silence the truth. They'll assassinate either the person or the character." See "'60s Radical Gets Life in Prison for Murdering Deputy," www.cnn.com, 14 March 2002.

25. Quoted in Bennett, *Why We Fight*, p. 90.

26. Tapper, "Islam's Flawed Spokesmen."

27. V. S. Naipaul, *Among the Believers: An Islamic Journey* (Vintage Books, 1982), p. 103.

28. Seyyed Hossein Nasr, *A Young Muslim's Guide to the Modern World* (Kazi Publications, 1994), p. 15.

29. Badr ad Din az-Zurkashi: *al-Burhan fi ʿulum al-qu'ran,* quoted in Tilman Nagel, *The History of Islamic Theology from Muhammad to the Present,* trans. Thomas Thornton (Markus Wiener Publishers, 2000), p. 1.

30. Caesar E. Farah, *Islam,* 6th ed. (Barrons, 2000), p. 77.

31. Mohammed Marmaduke Pickthall, *The Meaning of the Glorious Koran* (New American Library, 1991).

32. Islam put a stop to the pre-Islamic practice in Arabia of killing infant girls, who were regarded as a financial liability.

33. John L. Esposito, *Islam: The Straight Path,* 3rd ed. (Oxford University Press, 1998), p. 20.

34. All Qur'anic quotations in this book, except where noted, are taken from the translation by N. J. Dawood, *The Koran* (Penguin Books, 1990). One popular English translation of the Qur'an renders this verse "strive hard against The Unbelievers": *The Meaning of the Holy Qur'an,* trans. and with commentary by ʿAbdullah Yusuf ʿAli, 10th ed. (Amana Publications, 1999).

35. Amatul Rahman Omar and Abdul Mannan Omar, "Introduction to the Study of the Holy Qur'an," in *The Holy Qur'an: Arabic Text—English Translation* (Noor Foundation International, 1990), p. 37A.

36. Ahmed ibn Naqib al-Misri, *Reliance of the Traveller: A Classic Manual of Islamic Sacred Law,* trans. Nuh Ha Mim Keller (Amana Publications, 1999), 09.0.

37. Quoted in Aid to the Church in Need, "Religious Freedom in the Majority Islamic Countries 1998 Report: Afghanistan," www.alleanzacattolica. org/acs/index.htm.

38. Quoted in Naipaul, *Among the Believers,* p. 139.

39. Farid ud-Din Attar, *The Conference of the Birds,* trans. Afkham Darbandi and Dick Davis (Penguin Books, 1984), p. 68.

40. "Yusuf Islam Calls for Journalist's Release," www.cnn.com, 3 February 2002.

41. "Boxing Legend Ali Asks for Reporter's Release," www.cnn.com, 31 January 2002.

42. Could Yusuf Islam and Muhammad Ali have imported their ideas of a merciful God from their former religion?

43. "U.S. Evangelist Warns of Violence in Islam," Reuters, 24 February 2002.

44. Kenneth L. Woodward, "In the Beginning, There Were the Holy Books," *Newsweek,* 11 February 2002, pp. 52–53.

45. Ibid., p. 53.

46. Ahmad Von Denffer, *ʿUlum al-Qurʾan: An Introduction to the Sciences of the Qurʾan* (The Islamic Foundation, 1994), p. 17.

47. That is, except those that are qualified in the text itself. For example, the Qurʾan acknowledges that alcohol and gambling "have some benefit for men," although "their harm is far greater than their benefit" (Sura 2:219). But elsewhere it says that "wine and games of chance . . . are abominations devised by Satan" (Sura 5:90). If Satan devised them, they can have no benefits. Most Muslims consider the gentle warning of Sura 2:219 to be, in effect, superseded by the absolute prohibition of Sura 5:90.

48. Farah, *Islam,* p. 79.

49. Irshad Manji, "A Muslim Plea for Introspection," *Jewish World Review,* 2 April 2002.

50. The caliph was considered the successor of Muhammad as the political and spiritual leader of the entire Muslim community. Caliphs reigned in Islam most recently as sultans of the Ottoman Empire. That empire fell in the early twenties, and the caliphate was soon abolished by the new secular state of Turkey. Osama bin Laden has referred to this as a great outrage that must be redressed: the caliphate must be restored. Then, presumably, Islam will unite under the caliph and recover its former glory.

51. Harun Yahya, "Islam Is Not the Source of Terrorism, but Its Solution," www.islamdenouncesterrorism.com.

52. Quoted in Bennett, *Why We Fight,* p. 122.

53. "The Islamic Ruling on the Permissibility of Martyrdom Operations," www.al-muhajiroun.com, 1 November 2001.

54. Quoted in Yotam Feldner, "72 Black-Eyed Virgins?" *Claremont Review of Books,* Fall 2001, p. 17. The "son of pigs and monkeys" epithet may be derived from the Qurʾan. Speaking of the Jews, Allah says, "You have heard of those of you that broke the Sabbath. We said to them: 'You shall be changed into detested apes.'" (Sura 2:65; cf. Sura 7:166).

55. Harun Yahya, "Islam Is Not the Source of Terrorism."

56. John Walker Lindh (doodoo@hooked.net), "Re: Are Shiʾa Muslims?" soc.religion.islam, 6 June 1997.

57. Mohamed Azad and Bibi Amina, *Islam Will Conquer All Other Religions and American Power Will Diminish* (Bell Six Publishing, 2001), p. 33.

58. *Reliance of the Traveller,* o8.7 (10).

59. Ibid., p. vii.

60. Ibid., p. xx.

61. Woodward, "In the Beginning, There Were the Holy Books," p. 53.

62. In this he anticipated the English King Henry II's notorious question about the archbishop of Canterbury, Thomas à Becket: "Will no one rid me of this meddlesome priest?" But Henry was merely a king, not a prophet of God.

63. Maxime Rodinson, *Muhammad,* trans. Anne Carter (Pantheon Books, 1980), pp. 157, 171–72.

64. The payment of the tax on infidels, the *jizya,* was accompanied by a ritual blow on the back of the head, administered by a Muslim magistrate.

65. This practice dates chiefly from the fifteenth and sixteenth centuries.

66. Bat Ye'or, *The Decline of Eastern Christianity under Islam: From Jihad to Dhimmitude* (Fairleigh Dickinson University Press, 1996), p. 81.

67. *Reliance of the Traveller,* 024.2(e).

68. World Evangelical Alliance, "Religious Liberty Prayer List—No. 130—Tue. 21 Aug. 2001," www.worldevangelical.org.

69. Cartoon by Tony Auth, *National Catholic Reporter,* 8 March 2002, p. 28.

70. Samuel D. Bradley, "September 11 and God," *Common Sense Online: The Intercollegiate Journal of Humanism and Freethought,* www.cs-journal.org.

71. Kenneth L. Woodward, "In the Beginning, There Were the Holy Books."

72. Bennett, *Why We Fight.*

73. Quoted in Amir Taheri, *Holy Terror: Inside the World of Islamic Terrorism* (Adler & Adler, 1987), pp. 241–43. The Ayatollah's statement, "Whatever good there is exists thanks to the sword and in the shadow of the sword!" is an intriguing echo of Jesus' words in Matthew 26:42: "He who lives by the sword will die by the sword."

74. "The *Al Qaeda* Manual," U.S. Department of Justice translation, www.usdoj.gov/ag/trainingmanual.htm.

75. Taheri, *Holy Terror,* p. 11.

76. Daniel Pipes, "Who Is the Enemy?" *Commentary,* January 2002. Reprinted at www.danielpipes.org.

77. Quoted in David Pryce-Jones, *The Closed Circle: An Interpretation of the Arabs* (Ivan R. Dee, 2002), pp. 31–32.

78. Farrukh Dhondy, "An Islamic Fifth Column: Muslim Americans and Englishmen Join the Jihad," *Opinion Journal,* 26 December 2001, www.opinionjournal.com.

79. Amir Taheri, "Islam Can't Escape Blame for Sept. 11," *Wall Street Journal,* 24 October 2001.

Chapter 2: Does Islam Promote and Safeguard Sound Moral Values?

1. Seyyed Hossein Nasr, *Ideals and Realities of Islam* (ABC International Group, 2000), p. 82.

2. Quoted in Annemarie Schimmel, *And Muhammad Is His Messenger: The Veneration of the Prophet in Islamic Piety* (University of North Carolina Press, 1985), p. 5.
3. Akbar S. Ahmed, *Islam Today: A Short Introduction to the Muslim World* (I. B. Tauris Publishers, 2001), p. 28.
4. Nasr, *Ideals and Realities of Islam,* p. 58.
5. Ibid., p. 59.
6. Maxime Rodinson, *Muhammad,* trans. Anne Carter (Pantheon Books, 1980), p. 205.
7. Caesar E. Farah, *Islam,* 6th ed. (Barrons, 2000), p. 67.
8. Rodinson, *Muhammad,* p. 207.
9. Muhammed ibn Ismaiel al-Bukhari, *Sahih al-Bukhari: The Translation of the Meanings,* trans. Muhammad M. Khan (Darussalam, 1997), vol. 3, bk. 52, no. 2661.
10. This al-Kindi is not to be confused with the early Muslim philosopher and theologian of the same name, though it is likely he was from the same large clan. He may have been at the court of Caliph al-Mamun, who favored the rationalistic and latitudinarian views of the Mu'tazilites; see chapter seven.
11. Nasr, *Ideals and Realities of Islam,* p. 61.
12. Rodinson, *Muhammad,* pp. 279–83.
13. Other early Muslim traditions give the revelation of the passage a different cause, but one which also revolves around the mutual jealousy of Muhammad's wives. See *Sahih al-Bukhari,* vol. 7, bk. 68, nos. 5267 and 5268.
14. Mohammed Nasir-ul-Deen al-Albani, "The Status of Sunnah in Islam," trans. A. R. M. Zerruque, www.orst.edu/groups/msa/books/sunnah1.html. Evidence of this article's accuracy in reflecting accepted Muslim views is its presence at many Muslim websites, including www.sultan.org, a Muslim apologetics and information site that calls readers to "Correct your information about Islam, The Misunderstood Religion."
15. Wael B. Hallaq, *A History of Islamic Legal Theories* (Cambridge University Press, 1997), p. 60. Hallaq refers to Muhammad ibn Idris al-Shafi'i (767–819), founder of the school that bears his name and an enormously important figure in Islamic jurisprudence as a whole.
16. Abu Abdir Rahmaan, "The Sunnah: The Second Form of Revelation," *Al-Haramain Online Newsletter,* July 2000, http://alharamain.org/english/newsletter/issue38/sunnah.htm.
17. Ahmad Von Denffer, *ʿUlum al-Qurʾan: An Introduction to the Sciences of the Qurʾan* (The Islamic Foundation, 1994), pp. 18–19.
18. Ignaz Goldhizer, *Muslim Studies,* vol. 2 (George Allen & Unwin Ltd., 1971), p. 55, quoted in William Van Doodewaard, "Hadith Authenticity: A

Survey of Perspectives," unpublished article, University of Western Ontario (London, Ontario, 1996).

19. The Arabic plural of *hadith* is *ahadith,* and this is found in much English-language Muslim literature. However, to avoid confusing English-speaking readers I have used the English plural form.

20. John L. Esposito, *Islam: The Straight Path,* 3rd ed. (Oxford University Press, 1998), p. 81.

21. Abdul Hamid Siddiqi, "Introduction to Imam Muslim," *Sahih Muslim,* trans. Abdul Hamid Siddiqi, rev. ed. (Kitab Bhavan, 2000), p. v.

22. Dr. Muhammad Muhsin Khan, introduction to *Sahih Bukhari,* pp. 18–19.

23. *Sahih Bukhari,* vol. 5, bk. 63, no. 3894.

24. Rodinson, *Muhammad,* pp. 150–51.

25. *Sahih Bukhari,* vol. 7, bk. 67, no. 5158.

26. Amir Taheri, *The Spirit of Allah: Khomeini and the Islamic Revolution* (Adler & Adler, 1986), pp. 90–91.

27. Ibid., p. 35.

28. "Questions eligibility of daughter in marriage of woman he touched with lust," Fatwa No. 12552, Fatwa Center, www.islamweb.net/english/fatwa.

29. "Child Marriage 'Violates Rights,'" BBC News, 7 March 2001. United Nations Children's Fund, "UNICEF: Child Marriages Must Stop," 7 March 2001, www.unicef.org/newsline/01pr21.htm.

30. Andrew Bushell, "Child Marriage in Afghanistan and Pakistan," *America,* 11 March 2002, p. 12.

31. Lisa Beyer, "The Women of Islam," *Time,* 25 November 2001. Reprinted at www.time.com/time/world/article/0,8599,185647,00.html.

32. Bushell, "Child Marriage in Afghanistan and Pakistan."

33. *Sahih Bukhari,* vol. 7, bk. 67, nos. 5117–5118.

34. *Sahih Bukhari,* vol. 7, bk. 67, no. 5119.

35. *Sahih Bukhari,* vol. 7, bk. 67, footnote 1, p. 46.

36. Sayyid Mujtaba Busavi Lari, "Temporary Marriages," *Light of Islam,* http://home.swipnet.se/islam/english.htm. See also "Temporary Marriage in Islam," Al Zahra Muslim Association, http://members.ozemail.com.au/~azma/.

37. Ibid.

38. In Shia Islam, the word *Imam* refers to the twelve (in the dominant Shi'ite sect) great leaders of the community following the Prophet Muhammad.

39. See chapter ten.

40. Quoted in Baqer Moin, *Khomeini: Life of the Ayatollah* (St. Martin's Press, 1999), p. 30.

41. Taheri, *Spirit of Allah,* pp. 86–87.

42. Lari, "Temporary Marriages."

43. *Sahih Bukhari,* vol. 1, bk. 8, no. 371.

44. *Sahih Bukhari,* vol. 5, bk. 64, no. 4213.

45. *Sahih Bukhari,* vol. 9, bk. 97, no. 7409.

46. Ibid.

47. *Sahih Bukhari,* vol. 4, bk. 57, no. 3141.

48. *Sahih Bukhari,* vol. 4, bk. 61, no. 3632.

49. *Sahih Bukhari,* vol. 6, bk. 65, no. 4770.

50. *Sahih Muslim,* vol. 1, bk. 1, no. 406.

51. *Sahih Muslim,* vol. 3, bk. 17, no. 4436.

52. *Sahih Bukhari,* vol. 5, bk. 64, no. 4037.

53. *Sahih Bukhari,* vol. 4, bk. 56, no. 3030.

54. *Sahih Bukhari,* vol. 4, bk. 58, no. 3185. This incident is recounted in many other hadiths as well.

55. *Sahih Bukhari,* vol. 5, bk. 64, no. 3960.

56. Martin Lings, *Muhammad: His Life Based on the Earliest Sources* (Inner Traditions International, 1983), p. 232.

Chapter 3: Does Islam Respect Human Rights?

1. Amir Taheri, *The Spirit of Allah: Khomeini and the Islamic Revolution* (Adler & Adler, 1986), pp. 20, 45.

2. Ibid., p. 44.

3. Allah in the Qur'an often speaks with the royal plural, although He is an absolute Unity in the firmly anti-Trinitarian Muslim scriptures.

4. "Mullah Omar Warns AI against Criticizing Shariah," News Network International, 25 May 1998.

5. Ahmed Rashid, *Taliban: Militant Islam, Oil and Fundamentalism in Central Asia* (Yale University Press, 2000), p. 118.

6. Quoted in Aid to the Church in Need, "Religious Freedom in the Majority Islamic Countries 1998 Report: Afghanistan," www.alleanzacattolica.org/acs/index.htm.

7. V. S. Naipaul, *Among the Believers: An Islamic Journey* (Vintage Books, 1982), p. 270.

8. *Reliance of the Traveller,* o8.4.

9. Amnesty International, "Egypt Report 2001," www.amnesty.org.

10. Mullah Manon Niazi, "Fatwa on the Hazaras," 10 August 1998, www.hazara.net.

11. Human Rights Watch, "Massacres of the Hazaras in Afghanistan," vol. 13, no. 1C, February 2001, www.hrw.org.

12. Amnesty International, "Defying World Trends—Saudi Arabia's Extensive Use of Capital Punishment," 11 January 2001, www.amnesty.org.

13. Quoted in James M. Dorsey, "Ismaili Shiite Group Seeks an End to Saudi Religious Discrimination," *Wall Street Journal,* 9 January 2002.

14. Stephen Schwartz, "Despotism in Saudi Arabia," *Weekly Standard,* 18 February 2002, p. 20.

15. Dorsey, "Ismaili Shiite Group Seeks an End to Saudi Religious Discrimination."

16. Shehzad Saleem, "The Condemnation of Slavery in Islam," in *Renaissance: A Monthly Islamic Journal,* www.renaissance.com.

17. Quoted in Bernard Lewis, *Race and Slavery in the Middle East* (Oxford University Press, 1994). Reprinted at www.fordham.edu/halsall/med/lewis1.html.

18. Bat Ye'or, *The Decline of Eastern Christianity under Islam: From Jihad to Dhimmitude* (Fairleigh Dickinson University Press, 1996), p. 108.

19. Coalition Against Slavery in Mauritania and Sudan, "Sudan Q & A," compiled by the American Friends Service Committee, http://members.aol.com/casmasalc/mauritan.htm, 1998.

20. American Anti-Slavery Group, "The Baltimore Sun Story," www.anti-slavery.org/misc/usart2.htm.

21. American Anti-Slavery Group, "Sudan: Women and Children As the Spoils of 'Holy War,'" www.iabolish.com/today/background/sudan.htm.

22. Aid to the Church in Need, "Religious Freedom in the Majority Islamic Countries 1998 Report: Sudan," www.alleanzacattolica.org/acs/index.htm.

23. Brian Saint-Paul, "The Crescent and the Gun," *Crisis,* January 2002, pp. 13–14.

24. Lewis, *Race and Slavery in the Middle East.*

25. Coalition Against Slavery in Mauritania and Sudan, "Mauritania Q & A," compiled by the American Friends Service Committee, http://members.aol.com/casmasalc/mauritan.htm, 1998.

26. David Hecht, " 'Slavery' African Style," unpublished letter to the *Washington Post,* 14 February 1998, The Wisdom Fund, www.twf.org/News/Y1998/SlaveryAfrica.html.

27. Messaoud Ould Boulkheir, "A Response by Messaoud Ould Boulkheir: Slavery in Mauritania," Coalition Against Slavery in Mauritania and Sudan, http://members.aol.com/casmasalc/boulkhei.htm#Rebuttal.

28. *Reliance of the Traveller,* 014.1.

29. Ibid., e12.8.

30. But only if the requisite four male witnesses to the act could be found; see chapter four.

31. Naipaul, *Among the Believers,* p. 164.

32. Schwartz, "Despotism in Saudi Arabia."

33. William J. Bennett, *Why We Fight: Moral Clarity and the War on Terrorism* (Doubleday, 2002), p. 79. For information on these groups in the United States, see Steven Emerson, *American Jihad: The Terrorists Living Among Us* (Simon & Schuster, 2002).

34. Naipaul, *Among the Believers,* p. 81.

35. Ibid., p. 67.

36. Sura 24:2 from *The Holy Qur'an: Arabic Text—English Translation,* as explained by Allamah Nooruddin, trans. Amatul Rahman Omar and Abdul Mannan Omar (Noor Foundation International, 2000).

37. Amnesty International, "Saudi Arabia Report 2001," www.amnesty.org.

38. Naipaul, *Among the Believers,* p. 92.

39. *Reliance of the Traveller,* o11.5(1).

40. Ibid., o14.1. This opinion is held by the Shafi'i, Hanbali and Maliki schools of Islamic jurisprudence. The Hanafi school disagrees.

41. Quoted in Amir Taheri, *Holy Terror: Inside the World of Islamic Terrorism* (Adler & Adler, 1987), p. 242.

42. Felix Onuah, "Nigeria Fears Reprisals after Minister Shot Dead," Reuters, 24 December 2001.

43. "Analysis: Nigeria's Sharia Split," BBC News, 15 October 2001.

Chapter 4: Does Islam Respect Women?
1. *Sahih Bukhari,* vol. 7, bk. 67, no. 5096.

2. *Sahih Bukhari,* vol. 4, bk. 56, no. 2858.

3. Amatul Rathman Omar and Abdul Mannan Omar, "Introduction to the Study of the Holy Qur'an," in *The Holy Qur'an: Arabic Text—English Translation,* p. 43-A.

4. Karen Armstrong, *Islam: A Short History* (Modern Library, 2000), p. 16.

5. Ibid.

6. "Saudi Police 'Stopped' Fire Rescue," BBC News, 15 March 2002. http://news.bbc.co.uk.

7. *The Meaning of the Holy Qur'an,* trans. and with commentary by ᶜAbdullah Yusuf ᶜAli, 10th ed. (Amana Publications, 1999).

8. From Sura 4:34 in *The Holy Qur'an: Arabic Text—English Translation.*

9. Mohammed Marmaduke Pickthall, *The Meaning of the Glorious Koran* (New American Library, 1991).

10. Abu-Dawud Sulaiman bin Al-Aash'ath Al-Azdi as-Sijistani, *Sunan abu-Dawud,* trans. Ahmad Hasan, bk. 11, no. 2138. See also no. 2139. www.usc.edu/dept/MSA/reference/searchhadith.html.

11. *Sunan abu-Dawud,* bk. 11, no. 2141.

12. Ibid., bk. 11, no. 2142.

13. There are several passages of the Qur'an that have been abrogated and replaced by other passages. This is the origin of the "Satanic verses" made infamous by Salman Rushdie: in Muslim tradition there is a story saying that Muhammad, trying to appeal to the polytheists around him, proclaimed a revelation naming some of their gods as "daughters of Allah." Not long afterward, however, he had a change of heart and corrected the verse, attributing the original to Satan's influence. The Qur'an itself refers to its changeable nature: "If We abrogate a verse or cause it to be forgotten, We will replace it by a better one or one similar" (Sura 2:106). The abrogation of verses in the Qur'an is a fascinating study with important implications for Muhammad's status as a prophet, but in any case the "wife-beating verse" is not among those abrogated.

14. *Reliance of the Traveller,* m10.12.

15. "Row over Turkey's Wife-Beating Book," BBC News, 10 August 2000.

16. Flora Botsford, "Spanish Women's Fury at Islamic Advice," BBC News, 24 July 2000.

17. Jamal Badawi, Ph.D., *Gender Equity in Islam: Basic Principles* (American Trust Publications, 1995), endnote 14. Reprinted at www.jannah.org/genderequity/.

18. *Sahih Bukhari,* vol. 7, bk. 67, ch. 94.

19. *The Catechism of the Catholic Church,* 2nd ed. (Libreria Editrice Vaticana, 1997), no. 1604. Although the source quoted is Catholic, it expresses a sentiment to which Protestants and Orthodox would readily subscribe, and which even secular Westerners should appreciate for its articulation of love and mutuality.

20. *Sahih Bukhari,* vol. 7, bk. 67, no. 5193.

21. *Reliance of the Traveller,* m11.9.

22. Amir Taheri, *The Spirit of Allah: Khomeini and the Islamic Revolution* (Adler & Adler, 1986), p. 90.

23. *Sahih Bukhari,* vol. 1, bk. 6, no. 304. Those who point out similar statements by medieval Church Fathers should remember that no one follows any of those Fathers the way Muslims follow Muhammad.

24. *Sahih Bukhari,* vol. 7, bk. 67, no. 5196.

25. *Reliance of the Traveller,* p42.2(4).

26. Jamal Badawi, Ph.D., *Polygamy in Islamic Law,* 1998, www.users.globalnet.co.uk/~iidc/qalam/html/poly.html.

27. Seyyed Hossein Nasr, *Ideals and Realities of Islam* (ABC International Group, 2000), p. 105.

28. "Dhaka Sex Workers Celebration," BBC News, 30 March 2000.

29. Philip Mansel, *Constantinople: City of the World's Desire, 1453–1924* (St. Martin's Griffin, 1998), p. 105.

30. *Sahih Bukhari,* vol. 5, bk. 62, no. 3662.

31. *Sahih Bukhari,* vol. 3, bk. 52, no. 2661.

32. *Sahih Bukhari,* vol. 5, bk. 63, no. 3816.

33. Mansel, *Constantinople.*

34. Kevin Peraino and Evan Thomas, "Odyssey into Jihad," *Newsweek,* 14 January 2002, p. 45.

35. Michael Slackman, "The TV Polygamist Legions of Arab Women Love to Hate," *Los Angeles Times,* 16 December 2001.

36. Akbar S. Ahmed, *Islam Today: A Short Introduction to the Muslim World* (I. B. Tauris Publishers, 2001), p. 74.

37. Nasr, *Ideals and Realities of Islam,* p. 105.

38. Some Muslim sources render this as "I divorce you, I divorce you, I divorce you."

39. Naasira bint Ellison, "Distorted Image of Muslim Women," republished from *Hudaa* magazine at www.islamzine.com/women/distort.htm.

40. *Sahih Bukhari,* vol. 7, bk. 67, no. 5206.

41. David Pryce-Jones, *The Closed Circle: An Interpretation of the Arabs* (1989; Ivan R. Dee, 2002), p. 127.

42. "Pope Urges Judges, Lawyers to Shun Divorce Cases," Reuters, 28 January 2002.

43. Pruce-Jones, *The Closed Circle,* p. 127.

44. *Encyclopedia of Islamic Law: A Compendium of the Major Schools,* adapted by Laleh Bakhtiar (ABC International Group, 1996), p. 415.

45. Taheri, *Spirit of Allah,* p. 51.

46. "Life after Early Marriage," UNICEF Web feature, www.unicef.org/noteworthy/earlymarriage/3.htm, 12 January 2002.

47. Pryce-Jones, *The Closed Circle,* p. 124.

48. Jamal Badawi, Ph.D., "Is Female Circumcision Required?" in *Gender Equity in Islam: Basic Principles.*

49. Ahmad ibn Hanbal 5:75, quoted in Hamdun Dagher, *The Position of Women in Islam* (Light of Life, 1997). Reprinted at www.light-of-life.com/eng/reveal/r5405efc.htm.

50. *Sunan abu-Dawud,* bk. 41, no. 5251.

51. *Reliance of the Traveller,* e4.3.

52. Tantawi's quasi-papal status is bestowed upon him by Frank Gardner, "Grand Sheikh Condemns Suicide Bombings," BBC News, 4 December 2001, www.bbc.co.uk. Tantawi's view of female circumcision is quoted in Geneive Abdo, *No God but God: Egypt and the Triumph of Islam* (Oxford University Press, 2000), p. 59.

53. Quoted in Pryce-Jones, *The Closed Circle,* p. 131.

54. *Reliance of the Traveller,* 024.9.

55. Lisa Beyer, "The Women of Islam," *Time,* 25 November 2001. Reprinted at www.time.com/time/world/article/0,8599,185647,00.html.

56. Naipaul, *Among the Believers,* p. 165.

57. The whole story is told in *Sahih Bukhari,* vol. 3, bk. 52, no. 2661. As Muhammad loved Aisha above all his other wives, the accusation no doubt grieved him, and he was reluctant to side with her accusers. This is not the only time that Muhammad was favored with a revelation from Allah that granted him the desires of his heart.

58. Sisters in Islam, "Rape, Zina and Incest," 6 April 2000, www.muslimtents.com/sistersinislam/resources/sdefini.htm.

59. Sisters in Islam, "Rape and Incest As Penal Code Offences," 30 November 2000, www.muslimtents.com/sistersinislam/resources/spenal.htm.

60. Mark Goldblatt, "Why the West Is Better," *New York Post,* 30 January 2002.

61. "Nigerian Woman Still in Danger of Stoning," *Feminist Daily News Wire,* 10 January 2002, www.feminist.org.

62. Goldblatt, "Why the West Is Better."

63. Obed Minchakpu, "Kill Me Instead of Muslim Mother, Nigerian Archbishop Says," *National Catholic Register,* 10–16 March 2002, p. 6.

64. Sisters in Islam, "Rape, Zina and Incest."

65. *Chicago Tribune,* 3 May 1998, quoted in Yotam Feldner, "'Honor' Murders—Why the Perps Get off Easy," The Middle East Media Research Institute, 16 April 2001, www.memri.org.

66. Andrew Bushell, "Child Marriage in Afghanistan and Pakistan," *America,* 11 March 2002.

67. "Two Saudis Beheaded for Rape," Arab News, 9 May 2002, www.arabnews.com.

Chapter 5: Is Islam Compatible with Liberal Democracy?

1. "'Islam Is Peace' Says President," White House Press Release, 17 September 2001.

2. Dilip Hiro, *Holy Wars: The Rise of Islamic Fundamentalism* (Routledge, 1989), p. 54.

3. Thomas Jefferson, Letter to the Danbury Baptist Association, 1 January 1802. http://w3.trib.com/FACT/1st.jeffers.2.html.

4. Hiro, *Holy Wars,* p. 56.

5. Mohamed Elhachmi Hamdi, "Islam and Liberal Democracy: The Limits of the Western Model," *Journal of Democracy* 7.2 (1996), pp. 81–85.

6. V. S. Naipaul, *Among the Believers: An Islamic Journey* (Vintage Books, 1982), p. 178.

7. Ibid., pp. 85, 101.

8. Hamdi, "Islam and Liberal Democracy."

9. Dinesh D'Souza, *What's So Great about America* (Regnery Publishing, 2002), p. 97.

10. Quoted in David Pryce-Jones, *The Closed Circle: An Interpretation of the Arabs* (1989; Ivan R. Dee, 2002), p. 362.

11. Tore Kjeilen, "Sharia," *Encyclopedia of the Orient,* http://lexicorient.com/cgi-bin/eo-direct-frame.pl?http://i-cias.com/e.o/sharia.htm.

12. Quoted in Amir Taheri, *The Spirit of Allah: Khomeini and the Islamic Revolution* (Adler & Adler, 1986), p. 163.

13. Quoted in Naipaul, *Among the Believers,* p. 113.

14. Quoted in Bassam Tibi, *The Challenge of Fundamentalism: Political Islam and the New World Disorder* (University of California Press, 1998), p. 169.

15. Abdul Qader Abdul Aziz, "Perfection of the Shari'ah," *al-Jumu'ah Magazine,* reprinted at www.islamtoday.com.

16. Hamdi, "Islam and Liberal Democracy."

17. Bernard Lewis, "Islam and Liberal Democracy: A Historical Overview," *Journal of Democracy* 7.2 (1996), pp. 52–63.

18. Hiro, *Holy Wars,* p. 39.

19. Lewis, "Islam and Liberal Democracy."

20. Pryce-Jones, *The Closed Circle,* p. xi.

Chapter 6: Can Islam Be Secularized?

1. Caesar E. Farah, *Islam,* 6th ed. (Barrons, 2000), p. 236.

2. Bill Clinton, Remarks by the President to the Opening Session of the 53rd United Nations General Assembly, White House Press Release, 21 September 1998.

3. Charles Glass, *Tribes with Flags: A Dangerous Passage through the Chaos of the Middle East* (Atlantic Monthly Press, 1990), p. 468.

4. *Music of a Distant Drum: Classical Arabic, Persian, Turkish, and Hebrew Poems,* trans. Bernard Lewis (Princeton University Press, 2001), p. 105.

5. Dinesh D'Souza, *What's So Great about America* (Regnery Publishing, 2002), p. 83.

6. V. S. Naipaul, *Among the Believers: An Islamic Journey* (Vintage Books, 1982), p. 13.

7. David Pryce-Jones, "An Arab Moment of Truth: Which Way the Islamist Fantasy?" *National Review,* 15 October 2001. Reprinted at www.nationalreview.com.

8. "Kabul Residents Relish New Freedoms," 14 November 2001, www.cnn.com.

9. Lewis, *What Went Wrong?* (Oxford University Press, 2002), pp. 115–16.

10. Mohamed Elhachmi Hamdi, "Islam and Liberal Democracy: The Limits of the Western Model," *Journal of Democracy* 7.2 (1996), pp. 81–85.

11. Naipaul, *Among the Believers,* p. 117.

12. Quoted in Amir Taheri, *The Spirit of Allah: Khomeini and the Islamic Revolution* (Adler & Adler, 1986), p. 20.

13. Institute for the Secularization of Islamic Society, "Our Mission," www.secularislam.org.

14. Daniel Pipes, "Roll over, Rushdie," *Weekly Standard,* 22 January 1996. Reprinted at www.secularislam.org/reviews/pipes2.htm.

15. Osama bin Laden videotape, U.S. government transcript, trans. George Michael, Associated Press, 14 December 2001.

16. Andrew Mango, *Atatürk: The Biography of the Founder of Modern Turkey* (Overlook Press, 2000), p. 438.

17. Farah, *Islam,* p. 355.

18. Paul Dumont, "The Power of Islam in Turkey," in *Islam and the State of the World Today,* ed. O. Carre, p. 77; quoted in Farah, *Islam,* p. 355.

19. Mango, *Atatürk,* p. 471.

20. Philip Mansel, *Constantinople: City of the World's Desire, 1453–1924* (St. Martin's Griffin, 1998), p. 27.

21. Ibid., p. 140.

22. Ibid.

23. *Reliance of the Traveller* contains a note from the modern Muslim scholar Muhammad Hamid, declaring that "the fact that it is widespread among people" does not justify the taking of photographs, which is tantamount to image-making and hence idolatry. "It is no different than interest (riba), adultery, drinking, gambling, or other blameworthy acts whose night has overspread the people and darkness enveloped them" (*Reliance of the Traveller,* w50.9).

24. Mansel, *Constantinople,* p. 350.

25. Farah, *Islam,* p. 356.

26. Ibid., p. 357.

27. "Albright Says U.S. Not Happy about Turkey's Islamic Drift," CNN, 12 February 1997.

28. "'Black Voice' Kaplan Dead," *Turkish Press Review,* 17 May 1995.

29. Daniel Pipes, "Islam's Intramural Struggle," *National Interest,* Spring 1994, reprinted at www.danielpipes.org.

30. Taheri, *Spirit of Allah,* p. 287.

31. Sadeq el Mahdi, "Iran: the Message of Revolution," in *Arabia: The Islamic World Review,* February 1981, p. 29. Quoted in Farah, *Islam,* p. 373.

32. Taheri, *Spirit of Allah,* p. 45.

33. Ibid., p. 46.

34. Farah, *Islam,* p. 354.

35. Ibid., pp. 339–40.

36. Ibid., pp. 365–66.

37. Sayyid Qutb, *Social Justice in Islam,* trans. John B. Hardie and Hamid Algar, rev. ed. (Islamic Publications International, 2000), p. 19.

38. Lewis, *What Went Wrong?* p. 23.

39. Naipaul, *Among the Believers,* p. 88.

40. Ibid., p. 204.

41. D'Souza, *What's So Great about America,* p. 194.

Chapter 7: Can Science and Culture Flourish under Islam?

1. Philip K. Hitti, *The Arabs: A Short History* (Regnery Publishing, 1996), p. 120.

2. Ibid., p. 1.

3. Ibid., p. 110.

4. Ibid., p. 5.

5. Ibid., p. 145.

6. Ibid., p. 104.

7. Ibid., p. 93.

8. Robert Byron, *The Road to Oxiana* (Oxford University Press, 1982), p. 176.

9. Ibid., p. 180.

10. Ibid., p. 256.

11. Hitti, *The Arabs,* pp. 141–42.

12. Ibid., pp. 142–44.

13. Ibid., pp. 146–47.

14. *Music of a Distant Drum: Classical Arabic, Persian, Turkish, and Hebrew Poems,* trans. Bernard Lewis (Princeton University Press, 2001), p. 208.

15. Nesimi's verses, while exquisite, strayed from Islamic orthodoxy to such an extent that he was ultimately executed. While announcing his fatwa on Nesimi, the Mufti of Aleppo cried, "He is unclean! His death is unclean! If any one drop of his blood touches any limb, that limb must be cut off!" But when the execution began, some of Nesimi's blood stained the Mufti's finger; he escaped mutilation by explaining that the blood "fell while I was citing an example, so no legal consequence follows." Nesimi, flayed alive and on the point of death, said: "If you want to cut one finger of the zealot he turns and flees from the truth / See this poor devotee who when they flay him head to foot does not cry out." Ibid., pp. 208–9.

16. Bernard Lewis, *The Arabs in History* (Oxford University Press, 1993), p. 147. A. Zahoor, "Abu ʿUthman ʿAmr ibn Bahr al-Basri al-Jahiz," http://users.erols.com/gmqm/jahiz.html.

17. Hitti, *The Arabs,* p. 181.

18. Lewis, *The Arabs in History.*

19. Hitti, *The Arabs,* p. 146.

20. Ibid., p. 158.

21. *Reliance of the Traveller,* r4o.1.

22. Dilip Hiro, *Holy Wars: The Rise of Islamic Fundamentalism* (Routledge, 1989), p. 38.

23. Andrew Marshall, "The Threat of Jaffar," *New York Times Magazine,* 10 March 2002.

24. Aid to the Church in Need, "Religious Freedom in the Majority Islamic Countries 1998 Report: Malaysia," www.alleanzacattolica.org/acs/index.htm.

25. Quoted in Amir Taheri, *The Spirit of Allah: Khomeini and the Islamic Revolution* (Adler & Adler, 1986), p. 259.

26. Ibid.

27. Quoted in Baqer Moin, *Khomeini: Life of the Ayatollah* (St. Martin's Press, 1999), p. 272.

28. Lewis, *The Arabs in History,* p. 151.

29. Bat Ye'or, *The Decline of Eastern Christianity under Islam: From Jihad to Dhimmitude* (Fairleigh Dickinson University Press, 1996), p. 233.

30. Caesar E. Farah, *Islam,* 6th ed. (Barrons, 2000), p. 198.

31. Hitti, *The Arabs,* p. 118.

32. Elias B. Skaff, *The Place of the Patriarchs of Antioch in Church History* (Sophia Press, 1993), p. 169.

33. Bat Ye'or, *The Decline of Eastern Christianity under Islam.* Nestorians were a heretical Christian sect that held that Christ was of two Persons and two natures, in contrast to the orthodox view that He is one Divine Person with two natures, divine and human. Nestorians broke from the Roman church after being condemned at the Council of Ephesus in 431. The Jacobites were another heretical Christian sect, which held that Christ was of one Person and one nature. Jacobites and other Monophysites, as they were called, were condemned at the Council of Chalcedon in 451.

34. Seyyed Hossein Nasr, *Ideals and Realities of Islam* (ABC International Group, 2000), p. 25.

35. Hitti, *The Arabs,* p. 145.

36. Ibid., p. 186.

37. Ibid., p. 46.

38. Ibid.

39. Ibid., p. 49.

40. Wilhelm Windelband, *A History of Philosophy,* Volume 1, *Greek, Roman, and Medieval,* trans. James H. Tufts (Harper & Row, 1958), p. 317.

41. Abu Hamid al-Ghazali, *The Incoherence of the Philosophers,* trans. Michael E. Marmura (Brigham Young University Press, 2000), p. 2.

42. Ibid., p. 8.

43. Ibid., p. 220. Bracketed words are as in the original.

44. Tilman Nagel, *The History of Islamic Theology from Muhammad to the Present,* trans. Thomas Thornton (Markus Wiener Publishers, 2000), p. 211.

45. Al-Ghazali, *The Incoherence of the Philosophers,* p. 226. Emphasis added.

46. *Reliance of the Traveller,* o8.1.

47. Mohamed Azad and Bibi Amina, *Islam Will Conquer All Other Religions and American Power Will Diminish* (Bell Six Publishing, 2001), p. 54.

48. Nagel, *The History of Islamic Theology,* p. 191.

49. Ibid., p. 195.

50. Quoted in Dinesh D'Souza, *What's So Great about America* (Regnery Publishing, 2002), p. 62. Cf. Lewis, *The Arabs in History,* p. 53.

51. Lewis, *What Went Wrong?* p. 3.

52. That is, around the thirteenth century at the latest.

53. Hitti, *The Arabs,* pp. 153, 244.

54. Yossef Bodansky, *Bin Laden: The Man Who Declared War on America* (Prima Publishing, 2001), pp. x–xi.

55. Quoted in Milton Viorst, *In the Shadow of the Prophet* (Westview Press, 2001).

56. Ibid., p. 25.

57. Bodansky, *Bin Laden,* p. xi.

58. Taheri, *Spirit of Allah,* p. 75.

59. V. S. Naipaul, *Among the Believers: An Islamic Journey* (Vintage Books, 1982), p. 8.

60. St. Thomas Aquinas, *Summa Contra Gentiles,* Book 2, *Creation,* trans. James F. Anderson (University of Notre Dame Press, 1975), ch. 25, section 14.

61. Quoted in James V. Schall, S.J., *War-Time Clarifications: Who Is Our Enemy?* (2001), from Stanley Jaki, *Chance or Reality,* p. 242.

62. Stanley Jaki, *The Savior of Science* (Regnery Gateway, 1988), p. 43.

63. Ibid., p. 44.

64. David Pryce-Jones, *The Closed Circle: An Interpretation of the Arabs* (1989; Ivan R. Dee, 2002), p. 380.

65. Quoted in Schall, *War-Time Clarifications.*

66. See chapter six.

67. Naipaul, *Among the Believers,* p. 168.

Chapter 8: The Crusades: Christian and Muslim

1. Osama bin Laden, "Statement released to Arabic news network al-Jazeera calling on Pakistanis to resist an American attack on Afghanistan," 24 September 2001. Reprinted at www.guardian.co.uk.

2. Quoted in Thomas F. Madden, "Crusade Propaganda: The Abuse of Christianity's Holy Wars," *National Review Online,* 2 November 2001, www.nationalreview.com.

3. Quoted in Anne Kornblut and Charles Radin, "Crusader Bush Blunders into His Own Holy War," *Sydney Morning Herald,* 19 September 2001. Reprinted at www.smh.com.au.

4. Bill Clinton, "Remarks as delivered by President William Jefferson Clinton, Georgetown University, November 7, 2001," Georgetown University Office of Protocol and Events, www.georgetown.edu.

5. Mark Twain, *Tom Sawyer Abroad* (University of California Press, 1982), p. 7.

6. Bat Ye'or, *The Decline of Eastern Christianity under Islam: From Jihad to Dhimmitude* (Fairleigh Dickinson University Press, 1996), p. 44.

7. Ibid., pp. 271–72.

8. Ibid., p. 275.

9. Ibid., p. 276.

10. Ibid., pp. 276–77.

11. V. S. Naipaul, *Among the Believers: An Islamic Journey* (Vintage Books, 1982), p. 133.

12. Bat Ye'or, *The Decline of Eastern Christianity,* pp. 281–82.

13. Ibid., p. 283.

14. Quoted in ibid., p. 119.

15. Steven Runciman, *The Fall of Constantinople, 1453* (Cambridge University Press, 1965), p. 145.

16. Bat Ye'or, *The Decline of Eastern Christianity,* p. 296.

17. Paul Fregosi, *Jihad in the West: Muslim Conquests from the 7th to the 21st Centuries* (Prometheus Books, 1998), p. 20.

18. *Sahih Muslim,* vol. 3, bk. 17, no. 4364. The Banu Nadir, Banu Quraizi, Banu Qainuqa' and Banu Haritha were Jewish tribes that inhabited Arabia at the time of Muhammad.

19. *Sahih Bukhari,* vol. 4, bk. 56, no. 2941. For forced conversions, see Caesar E. Farah, *Islam,* 6th ed. (Barrons, 2000), p. 54.

20. Kornblut and Radin, "Crusader Bush Blunders into His Own Holy War."

21. Bernard Lewis, *The Arabs in History* (Oxford University Press, 1993), pp. 163–64.

22. Fregosi, *Jihad in the West,* p. 25.

Chapter 9: Is Islam Tolerant of Non-Muslims?

1. Bernard Lewis, *What Went Wrong?* (Oxford University Press, 2002), p. 114.

2. Quoted in Philip Mansel, *Constantinople: City of the World's Desire, 1453–1924* (St. Martin's Griffin, 1998), p. 414.

3. Godfrey Goodwin, *The Janissaries* (Saqi Books, 1997), p. 34.

4. Dr. A. Zahoor and Dr. Z. Haq, "Prophet Muhammad's Charter of Privileges to Christians: Letter to the Monks of St. Catherine Monastery," 1997.

This is found at http://users.erols.com/zenithco/dharter1.html and many other places.

5. A. Zahoor, "Prophet Muhammad's Treaty with Christians of Najran," 1998. This is found at http://salam.muslimsonline.com/~azahoor/treaty631.htm and many other places.

6. *Reliance of the Traveller*, o11.4.

7. Michael the Syrian, quoted in Bat Ye'or, *The Decline of Eastern Christianity under Islam: From Jihad to Dhimmitude* (Fairleigh Dickinson University Press, 1996), p. 78.

8. Ibid.

9. Ibid.

10. Paul Fregosi, *Jihad in the West: Muslim Conquests from the 7th to the 21st Centuries* (Prometheus Books, 1998), p. 258.

11. Quoted in Ibn Warraq, *Why I Am Not a Muslim* (Prometheus Books, 1995), p. 228.

12. Bat Ye'or, *The Decline of Eastern Christianity*.

13. Ibid., pp. 78–79.

14. Ibid., pp. 112–13.

15. Steven Runciman, *The Great Church in Captivity* (Cambridge University Press, 1968), p. 179.

16. *Reliance of the Traveller*, o11.5(2).

17. Bat Ye'or, *The Decline of Eastern Christianity*, p. 96.

18. Philip K. Hitti, *The Arabs: A Short History* (Regnery, 1996), p. 137.

19. Bat Ye'or, *The Decline of Eastern Christianity*.

20. *Reliance of the Traveller*, o11.5(3–4).

21. Quoted in Bat Ye'or, *The Decline of Eastern Christianity*, p. 98.

22. Elias B. Skaff, *The Place of the Patriarchs of Antioch in Church History* (Sophia Press, 1993), p. 240.

23. *Reliance of the Traveller*, o11.5–7.

24. Bat Ye'or, *The Decline of Eastern Christianity*, p. 85.

25. Ibn an-Naqqash, quoted in ibid., p. 329.

26. Ibid., p. 119.

27. Mansel, *Constantinople*, p. 53.

28. Runciman, *The Great Church in Captivity*, p. 205.

29. Skaff, *The Place of the Patriarchs of Antioch*, p. 159.

30. Bat Ye'or, *The Decline of Eastern Christianity*, p. 91.

31. Runciman, *The Great Church in Captivity*, p. 179.

32. Lord Kinross, *The Ottoman Centuries: The Rise and Fall of the Turkish Empire* (Morrow Quill, 1979, p. 559.

33. Ibid., pp. 559–60.

34. Ibid., p. 560.

35. Bat Ye'or, *The Decline of Eastern Christianity*, pp. 113, 115.

36. Thomas Sowell, *Conquests and Cultures: An International History* (Basic Books, 1998), p. 192.

37. Goodwin, *The Janissaries*, pp. 36–37.

38. Quoted in Mansel, *Constantinople*, p. 51.

39. Ibid.

40. Ibid., pp. 51–52.

41. Ibid., p. 437.

42. Paul Johnson, *A History of the Jews* (Harper & Row, 1987), p. 175.

43. Aid to the Church in Need, "Religious Freedom in the Majority Islamic Countries 1998 Report: Algeria," www.alleanzacattolica.org/acs/index.htm.

44. Aid to the Church in Need, "Religious Freedom in the Majority Islamic Countries 1998 Report: Tunisia."

45. V. S. Naipaul, *Among the Believers: An Islamic Journey* (Vintage Books, 1982), p. 18.

46. Amir Taheri, *The Spirit of Allah: Khomeini and the Islamic Revolution* (Adler & Adler, 1986), p. 84.

47. Naipaul, *Among the Believers*, p. 219.

48. *Sahih Bukhari*, vol. 9, bk. 87, no. 6878.

49. *Reliance of the Traveller*, o8.1, o8.4.

50. "Sudanese Prisoner Released from Hospital," *Compass Direct: Global News from the Frontlines*, 1 June 2001, www.compassdirect.org.

51. Jubilee Campaign, "Persecution of Christians in Egypt," 2000, www.jubileecampaign.co.uk.

52. Anh Nga Longva, "The Apostasy Law in the Age of Universal Human Rights and Citizenship: Some Legal and Political Implications," Fourth Nordic Conference on Middle Eastern Studies: The Middle East in a Globalizing World, Oslo, 13–16 August 1998, www.hf.uib.no/smi/pao/longva.html.

53. Aid to the Church in Need, "Religious Freedom in the Majority Islamic Countries 1998 Report: Morocco."

54. Aid to the Church in Need, "Religious Freedom in the Majority Islamic Countries 1998 Report: Jordan."

55. Aid to the Church in Need, "Religious Freedom in the Majority Islamic Countries 1998 Report: Saudi Arabia."

56. Quoted in Martin Edwin Andersen, "For One Diplomat, the High Road Is a Lonely One," *WorldNetDaily*, 11 February 2002, www.wnd.com.

57. "Saudi Arabia—Amnesty International Report 2001," www.web.amnesty.org/web/ar2001.nsf/webmepcountries/SAUDI+ARABIA?Open.

58. *Reliance of the Traveller,* o11.6.

59. *Sahih Bukhari,* vol. 3, bk. 41, no. 2338.

60. "Saudi Arabia: Foreign Christians Still Locked Up," *Compass Direct,* 28 January 2002, www.compassdirect.org.

61. Jubilee Campaign, "Christian Girl Kidnappped and Forced to Marry Muslim," 19 March 1999, www.jubileecampaign.co.uk.

62. Aid to the Church in Need, "Religious Freedom in the Majority Islamic Countries 1998 Report: Pakistan."

63. Sara Pearsaul, "When Hell Broke Loose," www.persecutedchurch.org/know/story/story.htm.

64. Aid to the Church in Need, "Religious Freedom in the Majority Islamic Countries 1998 Report: Algeria."

65. "Malawi: Christian Teachers Threatened," *Compass Direct,* 28 January 2002.

66. Aid to the Church in Need, "Religious Freedom in the Majority Islamic Countries 1998 Report: Bangladesh."

67. "Pakistan: Christmas Season Tense for Christians," *Compass Direct,* 28 January 2002.

68. Brian Saint-Paul, "The Crescent and the Gun," *Crisis,* January 2002, p. 15.

69. Jubilee Campaign, "Muslim Extremists Pressure Egyptian Christians to Convert to Islam," February 23, 1999, www.jubileecampaign.co.uk.

70. Aid to the Church in Need, "Religious Freedom in the Majority Islamic Countries 1998 Report: Iraq."

71. Aid to the Church in Need, "Religious Freedom in the Majority Islamic Countries 1998 Report: Libya."

72. Aid to the Church in Need, "Religious Freedom in the Majority Islamic Countries 1998 Report: Cyprus."

73. Aid to the Church in Need, "Religious Freedom in the Majority Islamic Countries 1998 Report: Turkey."

74. "Nigeria: Death Toll Mounts in Religious Conflict," *Compass Direct,* 28 January 2002.

75. Aid to the Church in Need, "Religious Freedom in the Majority Islamic Countries 1998 Report: Indonesia."

76. Ibid.

77. *Sahih Bukhari,* vol. 7, bk. 68, no. 5285.

Chapter 10: Does the West Really Have Nothing to Fear from Islam?

1. Quoted in Douglas E. Streusand, "What Does Jihad Mean?" *Middle East Quarterly,* September 1997.

2. Ahmed Rashid, *Jihad: The Rise of Militant Islam in Central Asia* (Yale University Press, 2002), pp. 1–2.

3. Muhammad Sa'id R. al-Buti, *Jihad in Islam: How to Understand and Practice It,* trans. Munzer Adel Absi (Dar Al-Fikr Publishing House, 1995), p. 17.

4. Rashid, *Jihad: The Rise of Militant Islam,* p. 2.

5. Al-Buti, *Jihad in Islam,* p. 20.

6. Quoted in Streusand, "What Does Jihad Mean?"

7. *The Meaning of the Holy Qur'an,* trans. and with commentary by ʿAbdullah Yusuf ʿAli, 10th ed. (Amana Publications, 1999), p. 76, n. 204.

8. Ibid., p. 91.

9. *Sahih Bukhari,* vol. 1, bk. 2, no. 25.

10. *Sahih Muslim,* vol. 1, bk. 10, no. 31.

11. World Islamic Front Statement, "Jihad against Jews and Crusaders," 23 February 1998, reprinted at www.fas.org/irp/world/para/docs/980223-fatwa.htm.

12. Al-Buti, *Jihad in Islam,* p. 94.

13. *Reliance of the Traveller,* 09.0, 09.1, 09.8, and 09.9. The Hanafi school disagrees on the final point: instead of calling for jihad against all except Jews, Christians and Zoroastrians until they become Muslims, it would also allow them to live under Islamic rule if they pay the *jizya.*

14. Nadeem Azam, "Conversation with Dr. Mustafa Ceric," Nadeem Azam's Litmania, www.angelfire.com/hi/nazam/Aceric.html.

15. Bat Ye'or, *The Decline of Eastern Christianity under Islam: From Jihad to Dhimmitude* (Fairleigh Dickinson University Press, 1996), p. 40.

16. Karen Armstrong, *Muhammad: A Biography of the Prophet* (Harper San Francisco, 1992), p. 260.

17. Paul Fregosi, *Jihad in the West: Muslim Conquests from the 7th to the 21st Centuries* (Prometheus Books, 1998).

18. Quoted in ibid., p. 337.

19. Central Intelligence Agency (CIA), "Long-Term Global Demographic Trends: Reshaping the Geopolitical Landscape," 2001, ELDIS: The Gateway to Development Information, www.ids.ac.uk/eldis/age/cia.htm.

20. "Muslim Population Statistics," http://muslim-canada.org/muslimstats.html.

21. Fahd al-Hodhaili, "Saudi Man Dies at 133," *Arab News,* 9 May 2002, www.arabnews.com.

22. Quoted in David Pryce-Jones, *The Closed Circle: An Interpretation of the Arabs* (1989; Ivan R. Dee, 2002), p. 127.

23. Bureau of Democracy, Human Rights and Labor, U.S. Department of State, "International Religious Freedom Report: The Netherlands," 26 October 2001, www.state.gov/g/drl/rls/irf/2001/673.htm.

24. Central Intelligence Agency, "Long-Term Global Demographic Trends."

25. Philip K. Hitti, *The Arabs: A Short History* (Regnery Publishing, 1996), p. 25.

26. V. S. Naipaul, *Among the Believers: An Islamic Journey* (Vintage Books, 1982), pp. 141–42.

27. Ibid., p. 65.

28. Z. Iqbal, "Lesson for Christian Women on Marriage to Any Muslim Man," *Pakistan Christian Post,* www.pakistanchristianpost.com/religion.php.

29. See chapter four.

30. Jami Floyd on *20/20,* ABC, 28 November 2001.

31. Nicholas D. Kristof, "All-American Osamas," *New York Times,* 7 June 2002; John W. Fountain, "A Phone Call Brings Sad News but Fails to Dent Faith," *New York Times,* 8 June 2002, www.nytimes.com.

32. Quoted in William J. Bennett, *Why We Fight: Moral Clarity and the War on Terrorism* (Doubleday, 2002), p. 53.

33. Gene Edward Veith, "Christians As Taliban," *World,* 19 January 2002, p. 14.

34. See chapter one.

35. Quoted in Bennett, *Why We Fight,* p. 62.

36. Barry Egan, "The Road to Healing Was Long and Painful for Gabriel Byrne," *Irish Independent,* 13 January 2002.

37. Quoted in Charles M. Sennott, *The Body and the Blood: The Holy Land's Christians at the Turn of a New Millennium—A Reporter's Journey* (Public Affairs Ltd., 2001), p. 422.

38. Sheikh ʿAbd al-Hamid al-Ansari, "Landmarks in Rational and Constructive Dialogue with the 'Other,'" quoted in "Leading Islamic Clerics Come out for Reform in Arab-Islamic Society," Middle East Media Research Institute Special Dispatch #386, 4 June 2002, www.memri.org.

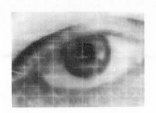

Index